The History

of the

Canterbury Mounted Rifles

1914—1919

By
OFFICERS OF THE REGIMENT

Edited by
COLONEL C. G. POWLES, C.M.G., D.S.O., A.D.C.
New Zealand Staff Corps

[COPYRIGHT]

Printed and Published by
WHITCOMBE AND TOMBS LIMITED
AUCKLAND, CHRISTCHURCH, DUNEDIN AND WELLINGTON

1928

This Book is dedicated to the memory of the Officers, Non-Commissioned Officers and men of the Canterbury Mounted Rifles who were numbered among those, who, at the call of King and Country, left all that was dear to them, endured hardness, faced danger and finally passed out of the sight of men by the path of duty and self sacrifice, giving up their own lives that others might live in freedom.

Contents

Foreword by Major-General Sir A. H. Russell, K.C.B., K.C.M.G. .... vi.

CHAPTER

1.	On the Formation of the Regiment, its Embarkation and Voyage to Egypt	1
II.	Of the Training at Zeitoun	11
III.	Of the Voyage to and Arrival at Anzac and of Life in the Trenches	23
IV.	Of the Desperate Fighting and the Move to New Country	45
V.	Of the Final Days at Anzac and How the Regiment came away	69
VI.	How the Regiment returned to the Horses	79
VII.	Of the Crossing of the Canal and the Advance into the Sinai Desert	92
VIII.	Of the Battle called Romani, but which might have been named the Second Battle of Pelusium	106
IX.	How the Regiment reached the River of Egypt over against the Borders of Palestine	118
X.	Of the Battle of Rafa and the First Crossing of the Boundary into Palestine	130
XI.	Of the Advance into Palestine and the First Battle of Gaza	139
XII.	Of the Second Battle of Gaza and the Holding of the Wadi Ghuzze	151
XIII.	Of the Breaking at Beersheba of the Turkish Line	166
XIV.	How the Regiment Rode Through the Plain of the Philistines	174
XV.	How the Regiment Went Up to Jerusalem and Through the Wilderness of Jericho	192
XVI.	How the Regiment Crossed the Jordan for the First Time	203
XVII.	Down by Jericho	219
XVIII.	How the Regiment Crossed the Jordan for the Last Time	230

APPENDICES

A.	The Thoroughbred, Racing and Remounts: By Major J. Stafford, D.S.O., N.Z. Veterinary Corps	253
B.	Killed in Action, etc.	257
C.	Awards of Decorations and Medals	263
	A Regimental Diary	265

1st (Canterbury Yeomanry Cavalry) M.R.

8th (South Canterbury) M.R.

10th (Nelson) M.R.

Badges of the three Squadrons which formed the Regiment and which were recruited from their parent regiments in New Zealand.

Foreword.

Recruited from the Plains of Canterbury, from Nelson, and Marlborough and the West Coast, the C.M.R. included a squadron from the 1st M.R. (Canterbury Yeomanry Cavalry), the Senior Mounted Corps in the Dominion, and so held pride of place "the right of the line" in the Mounted Brigade. Those who follow their career on the scrub-covered hills and deres of Gallipoli, and in the succeeding years of warfare in the desert and in the Holy Land will realise how fully they lived up to, and justified by their exploits, the distinction conferred by chance.

It was the writer's misfortune to lose sight of the C.M.R. in 1916. After the eventful happenings on Gallipoli, the Mounted Brigade and the Infantry Division parted company with mutual regret, the Mounted Brigade to prepare for, and carry out, the long series of campaigns which led to the final break up of the Turkish Army, ourselves to the rain-sodden fields of Flanders and the victories of 1918.

Science advances—and with each advance methods of warfare change. Allenby's headlong thrust across Palestine may prove one of the last, if not the very last epic in which cavalry take the leading role.

Science advances. Methods Change. But the spirit of chivalry remains,—and possibly the sons of the men who fought in the desert, rode down into the Promised Land and drove the Turks from Beersheba to Dan, will have to exchange their horses for wheel or wing. It is possible that the sound of galloping horses, *quadrupedante pedum sonitu*, no longer shaking the plains, will be exchanged for the whirr of the flying squadron: that the hurried speed of the armoured cars take the place of the swift moving charge. It is hoped not altogether! Be what may, the old cavalry spirit will carry on though all else change.

Foreword

One experience the C.M.R. enjoyed was perhaps unique. They served throughout under one leader. When, as was their good fortune, that leader is at once beloved and respected by his subordinates, wise in his dealings, and a very capable soldier, it is an experience on which they may be congratulated and envied.

[signature]

MAJOR-GENERAL, K.C.B., K.C.M.G.
Commanding
The New Zealand Division in France.

ERRATA.
Under Illustrations.

Page 81.—Major G. F. Hutton, O.C. 8th Squadron, should read:—"O.C. 10th Squadron."

Page 83.—The Canterbury Mounted Rifles on parade, Zeitoun, January, 1926, should read:—"January, 1916."

Lt.-Colonel John Findlay, C.B., D.S.O.
Commanding Canterbury Mounted Rifles.

The Story

OF THE

Canterbury Mounted Rifles.

CHAPTER I.

On the Formation of the Regiment, its Embarkation and Voyage to Egypt.

The history of "The Canterbury Mounted Rifle Regiment" commences on August 12th, 1914, when the first men reported to the Mobilisation Camp at the Addington Showgrounds. This Camp included all branches of the service in the Canterbury Military District. The Regiment when formed consisted of three squadrons, one from each of the three mounted rifle regiments in the Canterbury Military District— the 1st M.R. (Canterbury Yeomanry Cavalry), 8th (South Canterbury) M.R., and 10th (Nelson) M.R. A machine-gun section drawn from these regiments was also included, and sufficient trained signallers to form the Regimental Signal Section.

The squadrons wore their own regimental badges and were known throughout their service as the 1st, 8th and 10th squadrons. In later days reinforcements reaching Egypt were drafted to the squadrons representing the districts from which they came.

The ease and celerity with which the Regiment was formed, and the high standard of training it quickly developed, demonstrated in no uncertain manner the value of the Territorial training. The majority of the officers and men first accepted were Territorials, with a sprinkling of old volunteers and South African War veterans. Lieut.-Colonel J. Findlay (Reserve of Officers), who had a fine record in the South African War, was appointed to the command of the Regiment, with Major P. J. Overton, also a South African veteran, as his second in command.

The squadron leaders were Majors P. M. Acton Adams, P. J. Wain and G. H. Hutton of the 1st, 8th and 10th Squadrons respectively.

During this same period regiments were being mobilised on similar lines in Wellington, Auckland and Dunedin. The Wellington and Auckland Regiments, with the Canterbury Regiment, formed the N.Z. Mounted Brigade, under the command of Colonel A. H. Russell,* who at the outbreak of war was in command of the Territorial Mounted Brigade in the Wellington Military District, and who had served in the British Army.

From the 12th to the 16th August men came pouring into Camp from all parts of the Canterbury Military District, all creeds and walks of life being represented. The medical examination was the cause of many being disappointed in their endeavour to enlist. The one fixed idea of every man was to get away with the force now being mobilised, and by the end of the first week the Regiment was over-strength and had a waiting list that could have formed another regiment.

Equipment was at first a stumbling block, and to equip the force it was necessary to call in all the uniforms and rifles from the Territorial units. Horses were the next item. Many men had ridden in on their own horses; and, if suitable, these were taken over by the Government and re-issued to their former owners. Other horses were given, though many people had a vague idea only of what a troop horse should be. The remount portion of the camp could show anything from a draught horse to an unbroken outlaw. But in a week or ten days it was doubtful if any regiment had ever been better mounted. The C.M.R. horses from the very beginning were good, and the envy of other units.

With the issuing of all necessary equipment, training began in earnest. The Permanent Staff N.C.Os worked us till we dreamt of drill and rifle exercises, and they performed wonders in the short time at their disposal. The keenness and natural ability of the men helped, and they became a fairly efficient machine instead of a disorderly mob. Few

*Afterwards Major-General Sir A. H. Russell, K.C.B., K.C.M.G., commanding the N.Z. Infantry Division in France.

people have given much thought to what these few regular soldiers meant to New Zealand in those days. Most assuredly they trained us and fitted us for the great task that lay overseas. Discipline was strict, but there was no crime nor even minor offences. The warning that "anybody slacking or not playing the game will be left behind" was sufficient. We all knew there were numbers of good fellows waiting and hoping for a chance to join.

Addington proving an unsuitable place for so many men and animals, on September 6th camp was moved to the Plumpton Park Trotting Club Course at Sockburn; the ground here, being of a shingly formation, was more suitable for a camp and did not cut up with the continual traffic.

On September 14th the Regiment was inspected by Sir James Allen, the Minister of Defence, who was evidently impressed by the steadiness and soldier-like bearing of all ranks.

During this period there had been daily expectation of departure, but now, a month after entering camp, it seemed farther off than ever. Day after day the old routine was gone through, and then suddenly the news came that the transports were in Lyttelton Harbour. All was now orderly confusion. Kits were packed and re-packed. It was marvellous the amount that could be crammed into a kit bag. Finally the baggage was got rid of and forwarded by train to the transports.

Early in the morning of September 23rd the Regiment rode out of camp for the last time, taking the road through Sumner to the ships at Lyttelton, and embarked immediately on arrival—Headquarters and the 1st Squadron on H.M.N.Z. Transport No. 4, *Tahiti*; the 8th and 10th Squadrons on H.M.N.Z. Transport No. 11, *Athenic*. Owing to there being insufficient accommodation on the transport *Tahiti*, about forty men and horses were sent to Dunedin to embark with the Otago Mounted Rifles. These forty men were drafted from each squadron and Captain H. H. Hammond of the 8th (South Canterbury M.R.) was placed in charge. The horses took to their confined quarters quietly. Some were on deck, but the majority were down in the holds.

The ships sailed in the evening, and after a quiet trip arrived in Wellington the following afternoon, where it was learnt, to the general disappointment, that all troops were to disembark. No reason was given at the time, for this hitch in the arrangements. Afterwards it was learnt that it was due to the presence of German cruisers in the South Pacific.

The *Tahiti* just before leaving Lyttelton.

On the 25th the *Tahiti* men went into camp at Lyall Bay, and those from the *Athenic* to Trentham, there to await the arrival of an escort capable of protecting the fleet of transports.

The time was fully occupied in looking after the horses, in some tactical training and in speculating on the probable date of departure. On October 14th the escort arrived—H.M.S. *Minotaur* and the Japanese warship *Ibuki*. By 3 p.m. the Regiment was again on board the ships, which immediately pulled out into the stream to await departure the following morning.

The fleet weighed anchor at 6 o'clock, the *Minotaur* leading, closely followed by the *Ibuki*. Some little time elapsed before the first of the transports followed. Then one by one at about five minutes intervals the other boats joined in, following the leader in single file. Not until clearing land, at about 4 p.m. in the afternoon, was this formation altered; then the ships gradually formed up in two lines about half a mile apart and about three hundred and fifty yards between the stern and bow of each vessel. The escort also changed formation, the *Minotaur* being now about six miles ahead, with the *Ibuki* about the same distance on the right. The two small ships *Psyche* and *Philomel* of the New Zealand station of the Royal Navy, also joined the convoy, the former taking up a position on the left and the latter acting as rear guard. All the escorting ships closed in to about three miles at dusk. The first evening at sea showed the transports in the following formation :—

Arawa	*Maunganui*
Athenic	*Hawke's Bay*
Orari	*Star of India*
Ruapehu	*Limerick*
Waimana	*Tahiti.*

Horses on troopship.

A heavy swell was running, and all the vessels rolled considerably. Many men were suffering from sea sickness, but it was wonderful how they stuck to the work of looking after their horses. The latter, poor brutes, had a bad time for a day or two, till they became used to the motion of the vessel.

Hobart was reached on October 21st, and left again on the afternoon of the 22nd. A route march was held through the town. Everybody was glad of this chance of exercise, as the quarters on board ship, to put it mildly, were a bit cramped; and the warm welcome given by the people of Hobart as they flocked in their hundreds to the wharves will long remain a happy memory.

The next Port of call was not known, but the probability pointed to Albany or Fremantle. It proved to be Albany, where the convoy arrived on the 28th. Here were the Australian transports.

Wherever one looked there seemed to be troopships, and all were packed with men in khaki. The New Zealand ships sailed again on November 1st, following immediately after the Australians whose great fleet of 28 transports passed out of the harbour first. The combined fleets now numbered 38 transports, and in addition to the warships which had accompanied the New Zealanders the escort was now increased by the addition of the two Australian cruisers *Melbourne* and *Sydney*.

A foreign tramp left just before the convoy sailed, but was stopped by H.M.A.S. *Melbourne*. A short conversation between the two boats followed, and the tramp returned to port. She was still there when the Regiment left.

All hands soon settled down again and had very little time to think of their troubles, if they had any, for looking after horses on shipboard is a never-ending job, and as the tropics were being entered the horses required even more particular care.

The food was good, and small luxuries could be bought at the canteen on board. There was sufficient fresh water for drinking purposes, but the habit of drinking water was not encouraged. Fresh water is always a serious question on a horse boat, owing to the quantity carried being limited, a ship's daily consumption being roughly 26 tons a day. For all washing and bathing purposes salt water was available, and soap, to lather in salt water, was provided, but it was not very cleansing, and one always had a sticky feeling afterwards. Big canvas baths filled with sea water were erected on deck and full advantage was taken of them.

As all port holes were sealed at night to prevent the appearance of any lights, the atmosphere in the sleeping quarters became so stuffy, that as many men as were able slept on deck. Wind-sails to divert the air below decks were made use of, but in a following wind they were useless. From the time of leaving Albany to the port of disembarkation, the temperature between decks was seldom below 80 degrees, and in the Red Sea reached 98.

On November 9th came word of the battle between the *Sydney* and the *Emden*. As the news had been received the previous day by wireless of the destruction of Admiral Cradock's squadron at Coronel, the *Sydney's* brilliant success was specially acceptable.

It appears that at 6.30 a.m. the operator in charge of the British Wireless Station on the Cocos Islands sent out a message "strange warship approaching"; this message was picked up by the signallers on duty on many of the ships and passed on by the *Arawa* to the *Melbourne*, which was now the senior ship in the escort, as the *Minotaur* had been ordered away the day before. Further messages were jammed by German wireless. But the senior Naval Officer on the *Melbourne* evidently guessed who the strange warship was, and by 7 a.m. the *Sydney* was steaming full speed for the Cocos Islands, which had been passed just before daylight. A period of intense waiting ensued, accentuated by the movements of the Japanese warship *Ibuki*, which came across from the right flank, around the head of the convoy at full speed, ploughing through the long blue swell with white foam leaping from her coal black sides and her great battle flags streaming in the breeze. No sound could be heard and nothing could be seen, for the *Sydney* was soon beyond the horizon. Hour after hour passed by, and then the tension was relaxed when at 11.30 a.m. came the message, "enemy beached herself to prevent sinking." Cheer after cheer went from ship to ship, and as the "*Emden* beached

Orininal Officers Canterbury Mounted Rifles, Addington Camp, August, 1914.
Back row—Lts. L. Chaytor, Taylor, Barker, W. Deans, F. Gorton, Hayter, D. S. Murchison.
Second Row—Lt. Marchant, Capt. Talbot, Lt. Blackett, Capt. Hurst, Capt. Hammond, Lt. Free, Lt. Bruce.
Sitting—Major Wain (O.C. 8th Sqd.), Capt. Cody (Q.M.), Major Overton (2nd in Command), Lt.-Colonel Findlay (C.O.), Capt. Blair (Adjutant), Major Acton-Adams (O.C. 1st Sqd.), Major Hutton (O.C. 10th Sqd.).
Front Row—Lt. Gibbs (Signalling Officer), Lt. Davison (Machine Gun Officer), Lt. G. Dailey.

and done for am chasing merchant collier" came in, it broke out in renewed enthusiasm with the reality of the identity of the "strange warship."

A few days later Colombo was reached, and here, as the ships lay at anchor, the gallant *Sydney*, filled with wounded German sailors, and bearing obvious marks of battle, was received with all ranks standing quietly at attention, out of respect to the enemy's gallant defenders.

No leave was given at Colombo, but a few lucky men got ashore to assist in getting stores for the canteen, and the 8th and 10th Squadrons landed for a route march; but no breaking of ranks was allowed.

Leaving here on the 17th, the Indian Ocean was traversed in beautiful weather advantage being taken to exercise the horses in many of the ships by leading them on the deck on cocoa-nut matting. Several large transports were passed loaded with Territorials from England, who were proceeding to India to complete their training and to replace British troops required elsewhere.

Aden was reached on November 24th, a most uninteresting place to look at from the ships. Nothing could be seen but a huge mass of yellow rock and sand shimmering in the intense heat.

Sailing on the following day the convoy arrived at Suez on December 1st. Here orders were received to disembark at Alexandria, orders which gave general disappointment, for nobody liked the thought of staying in Egypt on garrison duty. First impressions of the country as viewed from the ships were decidedly unfavourable, and later it was agreed that on a closer acquaintance there was no improvement. On arrival at Alexandria on December 3rd the Regiment quickly disembarked, the horses walking down long gangways to the quay. Many were very groggy on their legs, but their relief at finding themselves on land again was plain to all; it was impossible to stop them from rolling in the sand, kicking up their heels, and even breaking loose in their delight at being on land again.

Disembarkation completed, the Regiment entrained for Zeitoun, near Cairo. It was dark when the weary men and horses arrived, but as guides had been asked for, no anxiety

was felt as to quick arrival in camp. But all that could be
found was sand and more sand, and, after much wandering,
an iron fence to which the horses were tied. No baggage
had arrived and it was bitterly cold. Men tried to sleep
huddled up together, or walked about to keep warm. But
everything was soon changed. Next day a few tents
appeared, and in a week it seemed as though a new town had
grown. Mess huts and canteens appeared as though by
magic, and outside the camp area the ubiquitous Greek
erected shops and stores of all descriptions, and the Egyptian
native hawked his wares—"Oringies" and "Eggs-e-cook" to
all and sundry.

CHAPTER II.

Of the Training at Zeitoun.

"How long are we to stay here?" was a question often asked, but nobody attempted to answer it, though there was intense disappointment at not getting to France.

"The powers that be" evidently decided that the Regiment knew nothing of what a soldier ought to know, and drill began again in a manner which demonstrated that training in New Zealand was "child's play" compared with the drill at Zeitoun. The horses were not fit to be ridden for a fortnight, and daily they were led out for exercise, and walking and leading a horse was also beneficial for the man, and hardened him during the four months' training. The work was grumbled at generally, and it was thought that not even men with cast iron constitutions could stand it; but the result was magnificent, for it is doubtful if there has ever been a fitter body of men than the New Zealanders by the middle of April.

Days were long and the usual programme read as follows: Reveille 5 a.m. Stables till 7. Wash, shave, and breakfast. Parade again 8.30. Drill till 11. Stables till 12. Dinner. Parade 2 p.m. till 4 p.m. Stables till 5.30 p.m. Then the time was your own if you were lucky enough to escape guard or horse picquet, which came one's way every third or fourth night.

Four or five hours a day spent grooming, handling and feeding a horse, seems a lot to the uninitiated, but the horses were a credit to the Regiment, who were justly proud of them, and the extraordinary endurance they showed later in the desert proved the wisdom of such treatment.

It may not be out of place to give some idea of the food horses get in the East. Barley, crushed if possible, but more often uncrushed, is mixed with a chaff of barley or wheat straw, known to us as "tibbin." Tibbin is made by dragging a rough wooden frame furnished with three or four knives, not unlike those of a disc harrow, over the straw laid out on an earthen floor. This machine is hauled usually by cows or donkeys. The resulting mess consists of straws from half an inch upwards in length. Besides barley, Indian corn and a small hard grain (millet) fed to camels, was sometimes issued. The total amount of grain allowed was about 12 lbs. per day and as much tibbin as a horse would eat. The hay supplied was of first class quality. A small amount of green food was also issued. This was called "berseem," and is very like lucerne to look at, but is shallow rooted. It stands frequent cutting and requires a lot of water, but makes excellent hay, and later on was put up in small bales for camel transport and sent out to the Regiment in the desert.

Brigade Headquarters at Zeitoun.

The 1st Australian Light Horse Brigade had now been attached to the New Zealanders, forming, with the N.Z.M.R. Brigade, the N.Z. Infantry Brigade and the N.Z. batteries, the Australian and New Zealand Division under the command of Major-General Sir A. J. Godley, K.C.B., K.C.M.G.

Though work was hard there were compensations. Free leave was granted from 6 p.m. to 10 p.m. nightly, and every Sunday from 1 p.m. to 10 p.m. If one had any definite excursion in view it was possible to get away by 9 a.m. on

TRAINING AT ZEITOUN

Sunday. Visits to the many surrounding places of interest filled in spare time. The Citadel with its glorious view of the surrounding city and country, Museum and Gardens, drew the men frequently, while the Pyramids and Sphinx were a never-ending source of interest. Visits to the "Mousky" and native bazaars took all spare money. At first, whilst the money which had accumulated on the voyage lasted, the trip to Cairo was taken in style, in "Gharrys," the native carriage, but it was soon discovered that trains and electric trams were much cheaper, faster and more comfortable. There was an excellent train service from Zeitoun to Cairo, a distance of about six miles, and the fare was one piastre (2½d.).

Ceremonial parades were frequently held. The first, and probably the most important, was the march through Cairo on December 23rd, the salute being taken by Lieut-General Sir John Maxwell, G.C.B., K.C.M.G., C.V.O., D.S.O., commanding the troops in Egypt. This parade was held to impress upon the native population the strength of the British Empire. There is no doubt it succeeded in its object and staved off the revolt that even then was threatening. A similar display of force would probably have squashed the revolt that broke out in later years.

Christmas passed quietly, and on December 30th the Division was inspected by Lieut.-General Sir W. R. Birdwood, K.C.S.I., K.C.M.G., C.I.E., D.S.O., who had taken over command of the Australian and New Zealand forces, now called The Australian and New Zealand Army Corps, or abbreviated A.&N.Z.A.C., from which came the word ANZAC. The Corps consisted of the following:—

(1) Australian Division, commanded by Major-General W. T. Bridges, C.M.G.
    1st (N.S.W.) Infantry Brigade.
    2nd (Victoria) Infantry Brigade.
    3rd (Australian) Infantry Brigade.
    Divisional Troops.
(2) New Zealand and Australian Division, commanded by Major-General Sir A. J. Godley, K.C.B., K.C.M.G.
    N.Z. Infantry Brigade.

Regimental Headquarters on the march through Cairo, December 23rd, 1914.

TRAINING AT ZEITOUN

    4th (Australian) Infantry Brigade.
    N.Z. Mounted Rifle Brigade (Auckland, Wellington, and Canterbury Regiments).
    1st (Australian) Light Horse Brigade.
    Divisional Troops (including Otago M.R. and N.Z. Artillery).
(3) Corps Troops (including 2nd Australian Light Horse Brigade).

On January 9th, 1915, a parade was held, and the men were addressed by the Hon. T. Mackenzie, High Commissioner for New Zealand, who came to Egypt to inspect the troops.

Training went on just the same, usually in the desert, but sometimes through the cultivation that stretched for miles to the north. Everybody grew to hate the sight of Nos. 2 and 3 towers, the watch houses on the ancient Cairo-Suez road. But no matter where one went the dust was there. While on the move one could see perhaps three horse-lengths ahead, and everybody became thickly coated with a grey death-like mask of dust which clung to the skin. There is nothing in New Zealand to equal it. As a part of the training, drinking before mid-day was prohibited, and on long field days, when choked by dust and scorched by the sun, this seemed an unnecessary hardship. But there is no doubt it was a good training. Many would have finished the last drop in their water bottles during the first hour. As it was, the bodies of the men were trained to require a minimum amount of water.

Night work was also engaged in during this period.

A great deal of musketry was carried out, and the Machine Gun Section, under the fine training of Captain P. B. Henderson, grew daily more proficient, enlarging their target practice to include the tactical handling of the gun and night firing. On January 28th the whole Regiment spent some hours in the desert in a tactical exercise with ball cartridge, engaging targets at unknown ranges as the squadrons advanced, culminating in the repulse of an attack by cavalry.

On February 3rd news was received of the attack upon the Suez Canal by the Turks, in the repulse of which the N.Z. Infantry Brigade took part.

After passing from the regimental drill to brigade and divisional manoeuvres the work became uninteresting, so far as the men in the ranks were concerned, but was of course necessary for the training of the officers. It must not be forgotten that many officers were unversed in active service conditions, though most of them had received a sound Territorial training which was invaluable to them and enabled them quickly to assimilate the higher training which these "dismal days" gave them. An average divisional day may be described as follows:—

Move out of camp some time between 4 a.m. and 8 a.m.; proceed leisurely for about two hours; halt when found to be mixed up with other troops; wait here half to three-quarters

The Brigade awaiting Inspection by Sir Ian Hamilton.

of an hour; move on for half an hour; halt one and a half hours (good sleep); move quarter of an hour; halt; told to put nosebags on horses; in five minutes ordered to move at once; move rapidly quarter of an hour; halt one hour; make dismounted attack on sand hill three miles away; move at the double across the sand for two miles; fall down and fire off half a dozen blank cartridges; fix bayonets and charge remainder of distance to hill; find hill occupied by staff who make audible remarks about slowness; horses brought up by horseholders who ask if it was hard-work running in the sand; officers fall out to be lectured by the General; men mount and return to camp by shortest route, the R.S.M. in charge.

Towards the end of February there was a four days "trek" under service conditions to Bilbeis via Nawa. About 25 miles was covered each day, and except for the dust the change from camp life was enjoyed, as the route lay through the rich green Delta. Leaving camp at 9.30 a.m. the Brigade marched through the green lanes of Matarieh, passing by that ancient well called the Virgin's Well, where tradition says Joseph and Mary and the Child rested after their flight into Egypt. Here were great banks of purple Bougainvillea climbing the shady trees arching over the road, which, leading out through the green fields, passes the ruins of On, that ancient seat of learning where Moses was educated. Here, still standing, is a solitary obelisk of red granite, close upon 100 feet in height, with its sides covered with clear sharp-cut hieroglyphics. This obelisk stands straight and tall as it stood when erected nearly 4000 years ago, but looking down now upon a country shorn of the glory of the Temple of the Sun, whose high priest was the father-in-law of Joseph. And looking across the green fields over the city of Cairo, there one saw, even as Joseph and Moses looking towards Memphis had seen, the Pyramids in the distance against the western sky.

The route followed by the Brigade crossed the Ismailia Canal, which forcibly brought to mind the immense importance of England's hold upon Cairo, for a hostile force in possession of the city could with the greatest of ease cut off the fresh water supply of the whole Canal Zone, and so starve out Port Said, Ismailia and Suez.

At the end of the second day's march through the green and smiling Delta the force camped at Belbeis, on the very spot occupied by Lord Wolsley after the battle of Tel el Kebir. Two days were taken on the march back and the Brigade "fought" its way successfully into Zeitoun through a defence put up by the 1st L.H. Brigade.

In March the troops had their first experience of a "Khamsin," that hot dry wind filled with minute particles of dust from the great Arabian desert which is the dread of the people of Egypt. Being fit and well with conveniences in the way of shower baths and tents, the Regiment did not mind it much. The strong hot wind raised an enormous grey pall of

c

Officers Foot ball Team.

sand, through which the sun shone redly. Inside a tent was no better than outside. The very atmosphere consisted of hot sand. But the Regiment was now used to sand, and, beyond an insatiable thirst, suffered little discomfort. In later years, under different conditions, it learned the power of this terror of the desert.

After experiencing the khamsin it was decided to send each squadron in turn to the "Barrage," giving a complete change to men and horses, of green grass everywhere and the most glorious gardens and trees. The mosquitoes were annoying during the evenings, but the men could stand that. The Barrage itself claimed special attention. From it the whole of Lower Egypt is irrigated. The Nile divides here into two the Rosetta and Damietta branches, and both streams have been dammed. Each dam is over 500 yards long. Two main canals run off these streams, and water is turned into them as required.

The whole water supply for the Delta is thus controlled, and lower down the rivers are again dammed, but naturally on a very much smaller scale. The Barrage Gardens are one of the show places of Egypt, and provide a wonderful illustration of what the Nile waters mean to this country. Advantage was taken of camping beside the Nile to practise swimming the horses across the river. A small party of men were rowed across taking with them the end of a long rope. This was then brought back to the starting bank about a chain away from where the rope entered the water. The ends were joined up and a party of men on each bank kept the rope moving, rotating it as it were in a circle. The horses were then brought down one by one, attached quickly to the moving rope and urged into the water. Led by its halter the animal had no option but to swim. A squadron's horses, by this simple means, were crossed safely over in 15 minutes.

On March 22nd the troops were reviewed by Sir Henry McMahon, High Commissioner for Egypt, and Sir John Maxwell, commanding the Army in Egypt. There was a frightful dust, and very few of the men saw the saluting point as they rode past. This day was the first on which locusts were experienced. The sight was an extraordinary one. Flying about two feet above the ground, and reaching to a height that could not be estimated, these insects came from the desert, making towards the cultivations. When they met any obstacles to their flight they appeared confused and lost. Wherever one looked were locusts as far as the eye could see. One was given the impression that a huge dark veil hung over the earth. Once in cultivated ground they ate every growing thing. Crops are eaten to the roots, while trees are stripped bare to the branches. Not a vestige of anything green remains. It is impossible to explain the seriousness of an invasion of locusts and the comparative hopelessness of combating the pest. They come from the desert and pass on, leaving complete destruction in their path.

Buying Oranges in the Desert.

The native vendors of fruit and eggs were always a source of wonder. No matter where one might be, perhaps out in the desert twenty miles from any known habitation, as soon as a halt was called natives came running from all directions. With their "eggs-e-cook, two for a half" and the long drawn out cry of "orangies" they did a brisk trade. But where they came from and the source of their supplies, which seemed unlimited, was unknown and never found out. The newspaper boys were always the butt of the troopers. Unable to speak English, but born mimics, it was quite an easy matter for a trooper to use them to take a rise out of some unpopular member of his Regiment. One would tell the boy to call out "Very good news, Sergeant ——— dead,'' and his papers would sell like hot cakes. The poor unfortunate boy never knew why he was kicked out of the lines by some irate N.C.O. And so life went on. There was growling and grumbling about being kept in Egypt, about the work and about the food. Yet the food was good, the work was necessary and the Regiment's presence in Egypt at this time probably helped to prevent a revolt against British rule, or an invasion by the Turks. It was a very good camp, and by the aid of regimental funds, the food supply was varied. Many of the necessary adjuncts to the camp had been supplied by regimental funds so kindly raised by good friends at home. The New Zealand Government was decidedly parsimonious in money matters, anything asked for was usually met by the cry of "But look what it will cost." In those days there was a mass of red tape to go through, and it was usually quicker and cheaper to do the work and then ask for the money.

On March 29th the troops were reviewed by General Sir Ian Hamilton, G.C.B., D.S.O., A.D.C.

Early in April it became fairly well known that the Infantry were moving to an unknown destination. From the end of the first week troops left daily. One knew nothing of their departure, but every night the camp grew smaller, and by the middle of the month only a few details remained besides the mounted men. Infantry, Artillery, Engineers and Transport had vanished.

With the departure of the infantry much hard drilling ceased, and the heat was too great for strenuous work. Ordinary fatigue duties still continued, but as much as possible was done in the cool of the morning and evening.

The days were now something like this:—Reveille was at 5 a.m., stables 6.30 a.m., breakfast 7.30 a.m. to 9 a.m., route march on foot or dismounted drill. Then came mounted parade, and a leisurely ride out of camp to the cultivation, where musketry or drill was carried out for a short period. Followed a sleep in the shade of the palms, and back to camp about 4 p.m.

Helmets were issued in place of slouch hats. What difficult and uncomfortable things they were for a mounted man! But G.H.Q. at Cairo had passed sentence on the slouch hat in the

Egyptian climate, and there was no appeal, so the helmet was worn until the departure for Gallipoli. In later years G.H.Q. was proved wrong by the wearing of the felt hat in the Sinai Desert and the Jordan Valley, showing that the hat was as good shelter from the sun as the helmet, and far more suitable to mounted work.

May 1st brought the news of the Gallipoli landing, but there was no sign yet of the Regiment moving. The men scanned the casualty lists posted at the orderly room and cursed their luck, but a change was coming. On May 5th orders were given to go to Gallipoli as infantry, the country there being unsuitable for mounted troops. Many were very sad at the thought of leaving their horses, but every man was glad of the chance of proving himself. For had not we all worked hard, and, on the whole, patiently, to fit ourselves? Now we were to be tested. We had been "standing by" long enough.

One cannot leave this period of intensive training without reference to the untiring, unselfish and capable work put in by Captain D. B. Blair*, Adjutant, and Sergeant-Major Norris†, Regimental Sergeant-Major.

Captain Blair had experienced considerable service in the South African War in mounted work, and was always ready at any time of the day or night to give a helping hand to those so eagerly learning the duties of an officer on active service.

And to Sergeant-Major Norris, with his wonderful knack of teaching drill, his fine soldierly presence and unrivalled knowledge of the mounted man's duties in the field, the Regiment owed a smartness and thoroughness that persisted until the end of the campaign.

During the night of the 7th-8th the Regiment entrained for Alexandria, leaving behind the latest reinforcements and such men as were not medically fit. These men, with the assistance of natives, were to look after the horses.

*Major D. B. Blair, New Zealand Staff Corps, Commanded M.G.Bn. N.Z. Div., France.
†Sergt.-Major (W.O.I.) F. H. Norris, Royal Horse Guards (on loan from the British Army). Killed Gallipoli, August 21/15.

CHAPTER III.

Of the Voyage to and Arrival at Anzac and of Life in the Trenches.

The Regiment, consisting of twenty-six officers and four hundred and eighty-two other ranks, arrived at Alexandria about 7 a.m. on the morning of May 9th, and immediately embarked with the remainder of the N.Z.M.R. Brigade on the *Grantully Castle*. One officer, thirty men and seventy one horses embarked

The Embarkation for Gallipoli.
Left to Right—Capt. B. King, Major Wain, Major Overton, Lieut. Free, Capt. Hurst, Capt. Guthrie, Lieut. Gibbs, Lieut. Murchison, Lieut. Deans.

in the *Kingstonian*. The *Grantully Castle* was a fine vessel. Fitted with all conveniences and manned by a crew whose one idea seemed to be to study the comfort of all, it is small wonder that the men looked back with pleasure to the few days spent on her. Though there were three thousand men on board (for in addition to the N.Z.M.R. Brigade there were a number of Light Horsemen), the ship was not unduly crowded, and she sailed in the evening for an "unknown destination," but of course everybody said "Gallipoli."

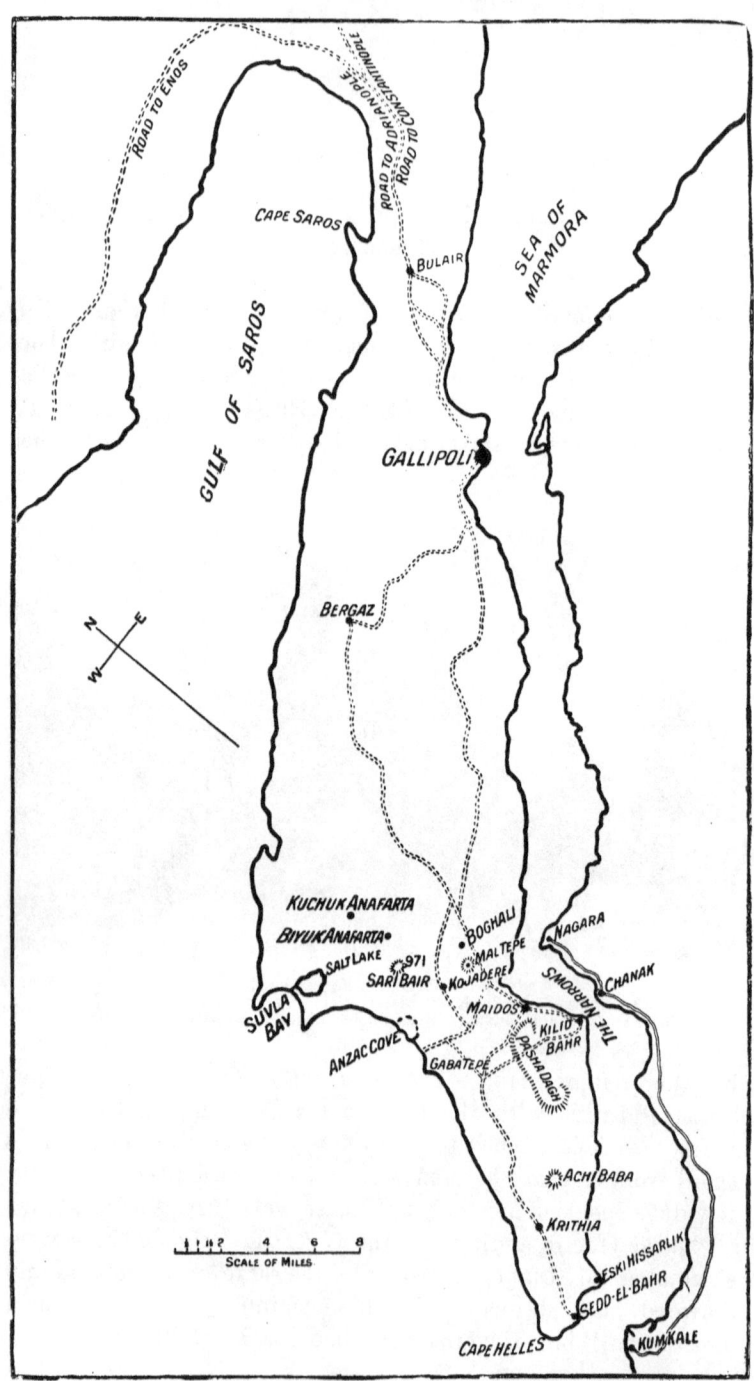

The Gallipoli Peninsular, showing the area occupied at Anzac.

The time was passed in various ways. Some sewed socks on the shoulders of their tunics in an endeavour to ease the weight of their equipment. Others packed and re-packed their kits, and made sundry visits to the canteen, laying in a store of what they considered necessary. After a calm passage Cape Helles was reached on the morning of the 12th. Rain was falling steadily, but gradually cleared off. Boats of all sizes and descriptions were busily moving about the anchorage, but all attention was given to the land from which the mist was slowly lifting.

There came to the eager ears of those young soldiers the sound of artillery fire, and at times the faint indistinct rattle of musketry. Gradually the artillery fire became more intense. Shells could be seen bursting along every ridge and valley. A warship in the Straits at times joined in, her huge shells bursting far inland on the slopes of a rounded hill. Cape Helles did not look an inviting spot, and no one seemed sorry when the ship steamed up the western coast.

The visibility was now good, and though the ship's course lay 4 to 5 miles out, every hill and hollow could be seen, and Achi Baba was recognised—the rounded hill wreathed in the smoke of bursting shells. Several warships were passed, among them the great *Queen Elizabeth*, whose shells were throwing up columns of earth and dust like so many whirlwinds in a desert place.

The ship headed for some high yellow bluffs over which hung more smoke, and at 4 p.m. the anchor was dropped four miles out from what all were to know so well as "Anzac."

A continuous roll and rumble could be heard, and now and again, as the breeze came from the land, the sharp crackling of rifle fire used in earnest, a sound new to the ears of so many of those eager boys.

There was little time to look about, for two destroyers at once came alongside and disembarkation began. In a moment all hands were staggering down the companion way and rope ladders, loaded to the point of endurance. A man with two hundred rounds of ammunition, rifle, pack and haversack stuffed to bursting point, with mess tin, bayonet and entrenching tool hanging from his belt, has quite enough to do to stand upright.

Imagine his feelings on finding himself on a rope ladder, dangling twenty feet above a dancing torpedo boat. But all were soon safely embarked and on the way to the shore, where shells could now be seen and heard bursting on the hills and close to the beach; but whether they were our shells or the Turks there was no means of telling.

Within a mile of the shore the Regiment was transferred to barges towed by picket boats, in which the trip was completed. Bullets were plopping in the water around, and as the shore was approached the sharp crackle of rifle fire grew to be continuous.

Running alongside a heap of stones built out into the water, the barges were unloaded as quickly as possible, helped by a naval officer who caustically commented on the slowness of the new arrivals and the certain chance there was of being shelled if every man did not "get a move on."

Once on shore there was at last time to look about. The Regiment had landed in Anzac Cove, even in those early days a busy crowded place. There was a narrow beach of fine shingle piled with stores, backed by a steep hillside honeycombed with dug-outs, from which here and there a gaunt half naked man looked out to ask who had arrived; and the word being passed that the "Mounteds" had come, men ran up from all directions with welcoming cries and many a jest as to what had become of the horses.

Along the beach many barges were being unloaded, every two or three with an attendant picket-boat ready to remove each one as soon as empty.

The Regiment having landed marched north along the shore, past the Ari Burnu Point and up a steep dry scrub-covered water course. Everywhere grew a thick prickly scrub that caught and tore the clothing. The leading parties climbed to within a few feet of the top of this wild ravine, and the whole Brigade settled down for its first night on Anzac. A few, more energetic than the rest, scooped out narrow beds in the cliffs; but others simply lay down where they were and tried to sleep as best they could, in what came to be called "Reserve Gully."

All night the rifle fire continued, sometimes dying down to a few straggling shots, then increasing again till it became a shrill continuous crackle. To most of those newly landed who had not previously been under fire, it seemed as though violent attacks were being made. Experience soon showed that this was nearly all Turkish fire, and that it went on for every hour of the twenty-four; and so adaptable is human nature that, in the course of a day or so, these men were to become completely unmoved by it. The sharp crack that at first thought seemed to be fire from the Anzac lines was but the noise made by the enemy bullets striking the earth of the parapets or flying harmlessly overhead far out to sea.

Next morning, amid the same indescribable din, a hasty breakfast of biscuits and bully beef, accompanied by a precious drop from the water bottles, was the preparation for what the day might bring forth.

Speculation was rife as to what part of the line the Regiment would take over, and many men had begun to clear away a few of the stones that had marred their rest during the night, when orders came that the Brigade was to relieve the Naval Brigade in the trenches running from the sea up Walker's Ridge, and including the trenches on the plateau on top, which was afterwards called Russell's Top. Beyond this trench line, further up the beach, were two outposts known as No. 1 Outpost and No. 2 Outpost, forming with the trench line, the Northern defences of the Anzac position.

The situation on Gallipoli on May 12th, the day the Regiment landed, was as follows:—The terrible struggle to maintain a footing at Helles and at Anzac had now been going on for a fortnight. At Helles the great attack of 6th-8th May had failed to capture Achi Baba, but the ground held by the Allies had been considerably enlarged and there was room to manoeuvre and space for dumps and hospitals. At Anzac the situation remained as it was immediately after the landing, our troops holding a small semi-circular position with the sea at their backs. Says Waite, in the "New Zealanders at Gallipoli": "the total length of coast line measured on the map, held by the Australians and New Zealanders was 3,600 yards, just two miles, and the distance from the front lines at

Quinn's Post, the centre of the Anzac line, to the sea was about 1,000 yards, a total area of 750 acres. Seven hundred and fifty acres of prickly scrub and yellow clay, stoney water courses, sandy cliffs and rocky hill tops, land that would not support one family in comfort, yet for eight long months men of divers races led a Spartan life there, studding the hill sides so thickly with their rude dug-outs that a Turkish shell seldom failed to find a victim."

The Anzac position was at this time organised in four defence sections, numbered from right to left. General Bridges, with the first Australian Division held sections No. 1 and No. 2 from the sea up to but not including Courtney's Post. General Godley, with the N.Z. and A. Division, was responsible for the remainder of the line to the sea on the north, consisting of Nos. 3 and 4 sections, of which No. 3 comprised Courtney's, Quinn's and Pope's Posts, and No. 4 the table land between Monash Gully (wherein lay the three Posts just mentioned), and Walker's Ridge, thence down this ridge to the sea, with No. 1 and No. 2 Outposts in front on the extreme left flank.

On May 12th these sections were held as follows*:—

No. 1 Section—3rd A.I.F. Brigade.

No. 2 Section—1st A.I.F. Brigade.

No. 3 Section—4th A.I.F. Brigade. Chatham and Portsmouth Bns. (Royal Marine Brigade).

No. 4 Section—Nelson and Deal Bns. (Royal Naval Brigade).

The N.Z.M.R. Brigade took over No. 4 Section from the Nelson and Deal Battalions and the 1st Light Horse Brigade No. 3 Section, thus relieving the four Naval Battalions, who were transferred to Helles.

"Taking over" the trenches on Walker's Ridge, the sector allotted to the Canterbury Regiment, was soon accomplished—the line running from the sea almost straight up Walker's Ridge to the top where was situated General Russell's headquarters. Beyond this on Russell's Top, as the plateau came to be called, was the Auckland Regiment's line, including the famous Nek, and on their right, facing the Turkish position called The Chessboard and overlooking Monash Gully, was the Wellington Regiment.

*Note.—The N.Z. Infantry Brigade did not return from Helles until May 20th.

But the two Outposts which formed part of the Canterburys' section were not taken over until after dark, as it was possible to travel between them and the trenches only during the night. Even then it was not a pleasant job. The Turks had machine guns ranged on the beach, and at odd moments during the night would open fire. It was simply a matter of trusting to luck.

The first work to be done was obviously to deepen the trenches and to improve the bivouac area at the back of the trenches. Shrapnel and stray bullets had to be guarded against. No material was available, and it was simply a case of digging, either into a bank or into the ground on the flat by the sea. Digging with picks and shovels may be hard work, but try a small entrenching tool, a terrace of hard clay with odd stones through it, and dig a hole big enough to contain a man. There was of course the driving power of self-protection. For the benefit of readers who do not know, an entrenching tool is made up of the following: —a short wooden handle, about sixteen inches long, and a piece of steel. The steel is flattened out and forms a scraper about five inches broad. The blunt unflattened end serves as a miniature pick.

Overhead cover was little thought of at first, but a few shells soon showed the necessity. An area being shelled is not amusing to the occupants, though often humorous to an on-looker. A popular N.C.O. once took refuge from shrapnel under a blanket stretched between two poles. At the time the hilarity with which this performance was greeted by those safe in dug-outs was entirely lost upon him. Perhaps it seems cold-blooded to see humour in what is probably costing men their lives, but without humour war would be unbearable, and all concerned would soon be raving lunatics.

Our first casualty occurred on the night of May 14th. The bodies of Australians, killed in their boat at the landing, had drifted ashore between No. 1 and No. 2 Outposts. A party from the Regiment went out to bury them. This was successfully accomplished, but one man was killed.

Just before dawn on May 15th Major Overton set out from No. 1 Outpost on the first of his daring and skilful reconnaissances, which he continued at intervals up to the

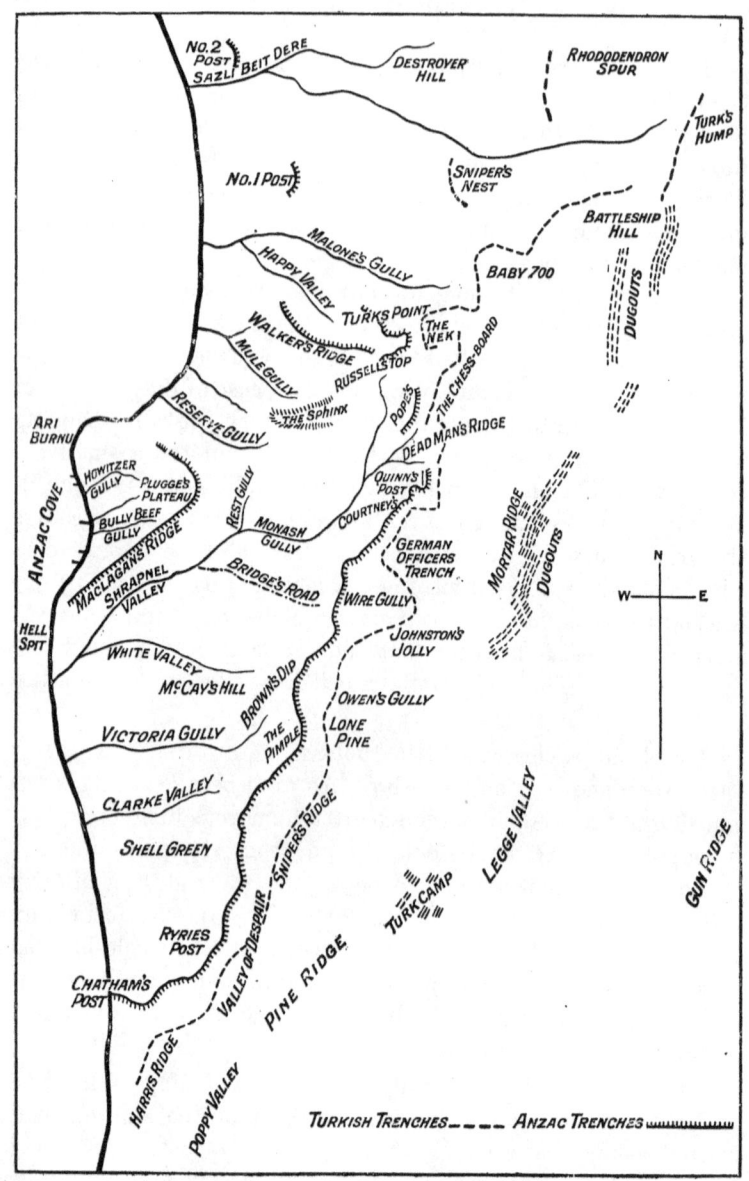

The Position at Anzac.

ARRIVAL AT ANZAC AND LIFE IN TRENCHES

Suvla Bay landing, and which furnished a wealth of accurate information about the topography of the inconceivably rough country that lay to the north of the Anzac position. On this his first enterprise he took with him Corporal Denton, and crossing from No. 1 Outpost to the bed of the Sazli Beit Dere, followed its northern branch to the foot of the long ridge which, falling down from Chunuk Bair, reaches the sea at No. 2 Outpost. This ridge he named Rhododendron Spur, the scrub which grew there much resembling bushes of rhododendron. He followed up the spur until he reached the saddle at the head of the Sazli Beit, and from there made notes of the country to the north as far as the great Abdul Rahman Spur, locating "The Farm" and the several branches of the Aghyl Dere. There were no enemy visible, but on the way back Major Overton and his companion had to lie low several times as they came across parties of Turks. The information gained in this daring reconnaissance, combined with that gained from the later ones carried out by or under the supervision of this enterprising officer, formed the basis for the operations which were carried out against Chunuk Bair in August.

A useful piece of work was done also by Sergt. Fox and Trooper Archer, who went out in front of No. 2 Outpost and "lay low" for Turkish snipers.

On this evening also a small party embarked on a destroyer under Major Hutton, and after dark were landed on the point forming the southern horn of Suvla Bay, on which is a small hill called Lala Baba. The intention was to kill or capture a Turkish observation post, but by the time the party arrived the post had vanished. However, three sheep were captured and made a welcome addition to army rations.

At midnight on May 18th-19th the greatest volume of rifle and machine gun fire yet heard on Anzac broke from the Turkish lines. Warning had already been received by all units of an impending attack and all were prepared. In the No. 4 Sector the main blow fell upon the Nek, and on Pope's and Quinn's in No. 3 Sector, and was completely defeated by the Auckland Regiment and the First Light Horse Brigade. The Aucklanders fought magnificently, and, after stopping the enemy's rushes by rifle and machine gun fire, emerged from their trenches and drove the Turks back with the bayonet. Two troops of the C.Y.C. Squadron, one troop of the 8th and two troops of the 10th were sent by the Regiment to act as a reserve to Auckland. About daylight the Canterbury men on No. 1 Outpost saw the Turks assembling in front of the Nek, and poured such a fusilade of machine gun fire into the rear of this mass that it broke and fled. During the forenoon the attack died away. The Regiment sent out a half squadron between the lines on Walker's Ridge and No. 1 Outpost, the object being to find out if the Turks were watching their flank. They certainly were, as the troops found it impossible to get very far.

This great Turkish attack, in which some forty-two thousand troops were engaged, and which enveloped the whole Anzac line, had been completely shattered mainly by rifle and machine gun fire and by noon some ten thousand turks had been killed or wounded, covering no-man's land with their dead.

In the afternoon occurred a peculiar incident. White flags were suddenly observed, being waved all along the Turkish lines and firing at once stopped. Some time passed, while interpreters vainly tried to find out what was wanted. At length the Turks began to come out in front of their lines in many places in order to remove rifles and ammunition from the dead, and it was observed that fresh troops were filing into the enemy's rear trenches. He was therefore given ten minutes to get back to his line, and the fighting began again.

But on May 24th an armistice was arranged, from 7.30 a.m. to 4.30 p.m., for the purpose of burying the dead that lay thickly between the opposing lines. The absolute silence and stillness, after the rumble and crackle of continuous artillery and rifle fire, was strangely unnatural. Up till a few seconds before the time arranged, there had been the steady cracking of rifle fire, and the bursting of shells; then sudden quiet reigned over the whole scene. White flags were hoisted by both sides, while the men in the opposing trenches, for the first time, had a clear view of the scene between them. The burial parties were all ready, and both sides went about their gruesome task. At 4.25 p.m. the parties separated, and returned to their respective trenches. A minute or two of silence was broken at last by single rifle shot far to the right; then a gradual ripple of musketry along the whole line, increasing till it swelled to a roar, ushered in the old pandemonium again.

The following Articles of an Agreement for the suspension of arms are reproduced, with instructions for giving them effect:—

"Article 1. A suspension of arms for the space of 9 hours beginning at 7.50 o'clock on May 24th and ending at 4.50 o'clock on same day of May 24th, is agreed to for the purpose of burying the dead and removing the wounded between the opposing trenches.

Article 2. Two Staff Officers, two interpreters, two Medical Officers, one hundred men with one hundred white flags, of each force, will meet at a point on the beach two kilometres North of KABA TEPE, at 7.45 a.m.

Dress, Officers—Belts and water bottles; men—water bottles.

On account of the broken ground and the nearness of the trenches to each other, the area to be cleared is to be divided up as may be decided on by the Senior Staff Officers into areas of 1,000 metres long (approximately), in each of which parties of not more than 200 men of either side are to be employed, to avoid a crowd of men working between the trenches. These parties to be without equipment except water bottles, stretchers, and a proportion of picks and shovels.

At 8 a.m. the work of clearing will be commenced and will cease at 4 p.m. or earlier if the work is completed.

If there is a likelihood of another day being required, the Staff Officers will meet at 5 p.m. and refer to their Commanders for orders as to continuing next day.

Article 3. The following procedure will be adopted:—

The delimitation party will move along the position starting from the sea, leaving a man of each nationality with a white flag at suitable intervals as nearly as possible half-way between the opposing trenches.

As the Staff Officers send orders to advance to the stretcher bearer parties allotted to each zone, these parties will move out from their own trenches and clear the zone up to the line of white flags, taking all enemy dead or wounded up to the central line for removal by the other side, with the exception of corpses which cannot be moved, which will be interred where found.

Article 4. Arms and equipment will be disposed of as follows:—

After the dead and wounded have been removed, the Turkish bearer squads can take away all arms and equipment found in the area on their side as far as the dividing line; all arms and equipment found on the British side will be collected and taken

D

to this line where they will be handed over to the Turkish officers after removing the bolts of rifles in their presence.

Similarly, all the British rifles which are found on the Turkish side of the dividing line, will be brought and handed over without bolts to the Officers who are superintending the evacuation on the British side of the zone. The bolts thus removed will be taken away. Arms and equipment of dead or wounded officers will be returned to their own side without restriction.

Article 5. During the suspension of arms, all movements of troops except the bearer and delimitation parties between the lines of trenches is forbidden, and hostile massing of troops behind those trenches will be a sufficient reason for breaking off the suspension of arms.

Article 6. It is understood that no embarkation or disembarkation of troops will take place during the suspension of arms between KABA TEPE and SUVLA BAY, on the other side the Turkish forces actually engaged in the neighbourhood of KABA TEPE will not be reinforced during the suspension of arms.

Article 7. No works on the trenches, saps, communication trenches, or gun emplacements is to be carried out during the duration of the suspension of arms.

Article 8. Should any incident give rise to the suspicion that the above conditions are not being adhered to, either Senior Staff Officer may break off the suspension, giving a period of half-an-hour in which to warn both sides of the cessation; provided always that the troops of both sides may be kept in a state of readiness for defence, without accusation of breach of the suspension; and in the case of unforeseen attack, either party is free to take action as the situation demands.

Article 9. The Staff Officers will fix on a place to which they will arrange for reports to be sent and for communications to go from to their Commanders. The site will be notified to their own troops when decided on.

Article 10. Except through the Staff Officers, no one can give an order for the cessation of the suspension of arms, except in the case of an unexpected attack.

Article 11. x x x x regarding aeroplane reconnaissance.

Article 12. All delimitation parties, and bearer parties, in case of an unexpected outbreak of hostilities are to be free to withdraw to their own lines, and are as far as possible not to be fired on.

Article 13. x x x x Powers of Staff Officers.

Instructions as to manner of giving above Articles effect.

The hour referred to is "Alla Franca" which is 8 minutes ahead of Army Corps time.

Article 1. Firing is to cease at 7.30 a.m. all along the line, but none of the usual daily precautions or lookout arrangements are to be relaxed, nor is any reduction in the garrison to be made.

All ranks are to be warned not to show themselves and thus disclose the position of the occupied trenches or saps.

Article 2. For the clearing up of the area between the opposing trenches and for the collection and burial of the dead a bearer party 200 strong (or less in front of sections where corpses are not very numerous), with a full allowance of stretchers and 8 picks and 8 shovels for interring much decomposed corpses, is to be held ready at 8 a.m. in each section of the defence.

It is not necessary that all should be ambulance personnel, but a white arm band (cloth or paper) with or without red cross, is to be worn on the left arm. Red cross flags, up to 6 per section, are to be taken.

Attention is drawn to the order of dress.

Dead and wounded are to be cleared from the vicinity of our trenches first, gradually working out towards the dividing line.

The delimitation parties will be as follows:—
Staff Officers—Lt.-Col. Skeen, G.S.O. 1. Army Corps. Major Blamey, G.S.O. 3. Australian Division.
Interpreters—One from Australian Division. One from New Zealand and Australian Division.
Medical Officers—One from Australian Division. One from New Zealand and Australian Division.
50 men, each with a white flag, from Australian Division.
50 men, each with a white flag, from New Zealand and Australian Division.

The flag need only be a small white cloth, or even a sheet of paper, but should be fixed to a stake or branch over 4 feet long, sharpened at the end to plant in the ground.

These parties will meet Lt.-Col. Skeen on the beach by Sapper Post at 6.45 a.m. They should have water bottles filled and food for the day in their pockets. The men will receive instructions there as to their actions in carrying out the procedure laid down in the above paragraphs.

All bodies or wounded taken to the dividing line marked by the white flag bearers will be laid out in rows and not in heaps, and treated with every respect due to the dead.

Article 4. Rifles taken up are to be carried in stretchers—at the particular request of the Turkish representative so as to avoid suspicions that they are to be carried away, which might arise if the men handled them in the usual way.

Mauser bolts are removeable by drawing back the bolt, pushing out the left charger guide and withdrawing the bolt. Bolts should then be collected on the stretcher and removed to our lines along with any L.E. rifles handed back by the Turks, as they are collected.

Care should be taken to send these rifles forward at intervals and not all at once.

Articles 5 and 6. Special instructions are being issued on this point.

Article 7. Care should be taken to repair or complete any defensive works before 7.30 a.m. to-morrow.

Article 8. Any suspected breach of the conditions is to be reported at once to Headquarters of the Section for transmission to Divisions and Army Corps Headquarters.

Any report of enemy's action which appears to be contrary to the conditions of the suspension should be verified before report and a careful record kept of the hour and circumstances.

In case of an obvious intention on the part of the enemy to attack, each Commander of a post or section of the defence is responsible for reporting at once and for taking immediate measures to meet it.

Article 10. Here also, though if possible the notice of cessation of the suspension should be formal, post and Section commanders are responsible for taking immediate measures to meet it.

Article 12. Special care should be taken, if the bearer parties and white flag parties have to retire, not to fire at them, or even in their direction unless the military situation demands it.

Army Headquarters,
   23rd May, 1915.''

So far the fighting of our troops had been greatly handicapped by an entire lack of bombs, possessed by the Turks in abundance. To remedy this, a factory was started, each unit supplying a man or two to assist. There was no modern machinery. Into a bully-beef tin a portion of gun cotton was placed with a fuse attached. The tin was then filled with old cartridge cases and bullets and wound round with a piece of wire. To fire the bomb a match had to be used to light the fuse, and the bomb was then thrown, after being held to the extreme limit of safety; otherwise if thrown with a long fuse the Turk might throw it back, as was done so often by our men when bombed by the Turks. Later small Japanese stick bombs were issued. These burst on concussion, but as they were liable to explode if they accidentally touched the side of the trench, no regret was felt when the supply ran out.

Following upon his signal defeat on May 19th, the Turk was observed to be greatly improving his trenches at the Nek and on Baby 700 (the rounded end to the hill overlooking the Nek). New trenches also appeared on Battleship Hill, further north along the main Sari Bair range towards Chunuk Bair. A further disquieting thing happened during the night of May 26th. Soon after daylight on the 27th a new Turkish post was observed on the ridge leading down to No. 2 Outpost, and some 450 yards only from it. It was decided that the enemy must be ejected from his close proximity to this isolated post. So after dark on May 28th Major Acton-Adams led the C.Y.C. Squadron from No. 2 and rushed the trench. The garrison fled.

The C.Y.C. were followed by a squadron of the Wellington Regiment who carried picks and shovels. Major Acton-Adams then withdrew his men and the Wellington squadron was left to improve and garrison the trench. The captured position was named No. 3 Outpost. At dawn the Wellingtons found it impossible to continue digging, being fired upon from the surrounding hills, all of which completely overlooked the position. The squadron held on all day, and after dark was relieved by the 9th Squadron, Wellington Regiment, under Major Chambers. He had no sooner taken over then the post was heavily attacked by a large body of Turks armed with bombs. His garrison was also subject to artillery fire and a

Searching the Right Flank.
Left to right—Colonel Findlay, Major G. A. King, Major Overton.

continuous fire from rifle and machine guns from the main Turkish position on Baby 700, Battleship Hill and Table Top. This attack continued all night and the next day. Attempts were made by the remainder of the Wellington Regiment to reinforce Major Chambers, but the enemy opposition was too strong, every attempted movement up the gullies being dominated by fire from the hills. After nightfall Major Hutton, with the 10th Squadron and two troops of the 8th, guided by Major Overton, worked up a ravine to the post and brought away the much-tried garrison, who had been fighting under terrible odds with no machine guns or bombs, and with no water for nearly two days, in an impossible position dominated at close range on three sides by the enemy.

The retirement was carried out in excellent order, though counter-attacks by the enemy had to be driven off several times. This action cost the Wellington Regiment many casualties.

On May 27th Major Overton led out three parties to explore the country to the north-east. The first, under Lieutenant A. C. M. Finlayson, of the Auckland Regiment, turned up the Sazli Beit Dere, but found their way blocked by the enemy, who appeared to have a well-manned trench across the narrow valley. The second party, under Captain N. F. Hastings, of the Wellington Regiment, worked up the bottom of the Chailak Dere, and, slipping between Turkish posts, reached the point where that valley begins to ascend steeply to the head of Rhododendron Spur. Daylight showed him a strong party of Turks ahead, so he had to return. The third party, under Major Overton, followed along the flat and turned up the Aghyl Dere. His notes showed that the entrance to the dere appeared to be entrenched, but to be occupied by sentries during the day only. He watched a party of 150 Turks come down the dere to occupy these positions and thence, slipping by them along the hillside, he followed the southern branch until he came to a sheepfold, around which there was a bivouac of Turks. After remaining out two nights, and making invaluable notes of the Aghyl Dere country, he returned at daylight on the 29th.

As things went at Anzac, the Regiment's main trenches from the sea to the top of Walker's ridge was a fairly quiet sector. But the holding of the two isolated outposts and the patrolling of the flat and the hills to the north and east gave the restless spirits of the Regiment there their fill of fighting.

Rations and water had to be carried from the beach to the trenches, where there was always work to do in improvements and additions, during every hour of the twenty-four. Periods of duty were 24 hours as garrison to Nos. 1 and 2 Outposts, 24 hours in the main line trenches and 24 hours in support, and so back to the Outposts again. The supporting troops did the work in the communication trenches, on the track up the hill and on the beach, those in the trenches and on outpost deepened and extended their own positions. The heat was terrific, and the narrow trenches by day were like a furnace. Water was scarce, the allowance at this time being two pints a day per man. Hard biscuits, salt bacon and bully beef all tended to increase our thirst. One shaved on order but grudged the water used for that purpose. Sea bathing by day, one of the few pleasures, was greatly interfered with by Turkish shell fire. But as soon as the shelling stopped, even if only for a few moments, the water would be alive again with swimmers, though there were many who bathed only after dark. Indeed this bathing was the men's salvation, for a daily ration of two pints of water for a man exposed to the sun's full heat throughout the day's length was scarcely enough to keep body and soul together, let alone the cleansing of the former.

The day after the armistice H.M.S. *Triumph*, one of the battleships best known to the Regiment, was torpedoed. She was anchored about a mile off shore with torpedo nets down, and many men were watching her firing at the enemy guns at the Olive Grove, a position on the right flank of Anzac from

The Barricade on the Beach at the foot of Walker's Ridge.
A favourite bathing place.

which the Turks fired upon the beach at Anzac Cove. Suddenly there appeared to be a miniature water spout alongside her; then she commenced to heel over. Destroyers came from all quarters, and began circling round looking for the submarine. One, a destroyer well known to the Regiment, the *Chelmer*, whose usual station was on our flank, went right alongside the sinking vessel and began to take off the crew. Men could be seen standing on the deck, then slowly filing off and boarding the destroyer. More and more the *Triumph* turned, till at last, giving a sudden lurch that threw the remaining members of her crew into the water, she turned right over. The keel showed clear above the water, and men could be seen scrambling on to it. Soon she sank, and there remained only the destroyers and trawlers cruising around to pick up the men left struggling in the water, while other destroyers working in ever increasing circles kept up the hunt for the submarine.

On May 28 Otago Mounted Rifles took over the outpost, and the Regiment went into reserve, which meant not rest but digging trenches and saps and making roads. Work on these was never finished. Day and night it went on. No sooner was one task finished than another, equally necessary, was found waiting to be done. Sweltering in the heat, parched with thirst and dead tired from lack of sleep as they were, the men toiled on even with happiness, preparing for that day as yet unknown, when they would take part in the oft-discussed advance.

A note in the Regimental war diary of this date says, "the men are all in good heart and good fighting trim."

The Regiment moved back to its old line on June 4th and held 800 yards of trenches from the 6in. Howitzer, "the glass case gun," near the top of Walker's Ridge, to the sea, and on the 11th took over No. 1 Outpost from Otago M.R. This was now a strong point, garrisoned by 50 men and two machine guns.

At the end of June the Turks again attacked the Walker's Ridge section. The Regiment's only interest in this arose from the fact of our having a working party in the trenches at the time. The 3rd Australian Light Horse Brigade were holding this line, and promptly ordered us all away. As one Australian laughingly put it, "'this is our show, you New Zealanders just leave it to us." Later the Regiment relieved this brigade, and for the month of July did turn about in these trenches with the Australians. Keen on their job and always smiling, what good fellows they were! Here was born that great friendship between the N.Z.M.R. and the Light Horse men which was brought to such a happy maturity in later days at Hill 60, on the desert sands of Sinai and among the mountains of Judea.

About the middle of May the enemy had begun to shell the lines and the gullies in rear of the Regiment, and also the beach. The gun position was in what were called the "W" hills, away across the flat to the north near Anafarta, and came to be called the Anafarta gun. By the end of June it had inflicted some seven hundred and fifty casualties on the Anzac force. The gun's exact position could not be observed, and though our artillery, especially the N.Z. Battery of 18-pounders, on Russell Top, tried to silence it, no harm seemed to be done, for it fired again day after day. On June 20th Lieutenant G. R. Blackett, of the 10th Squadron, with a guide and an interpreter, was taken on a trawler and landed by night at a quiet point on the coast immediately to the north of Suvla Bay. The party made its way inland and lay up all day in the scrub, watching for the gun to fire. However, it probably had several prepared positions, for it was never silenced but for a few hours immediately after being shelled by our guns.

On July 2nd, Major P. J. Wain, O.C. 8th Squadron, and Lieut. T. L. Gibbs, the Regiment's popular signalling officer, were wounded by a shell from this gun.

At the end of June the first reinforcements to reach the Regiment on Gallipoli arrived. These were the 4th Reinforcements, consisting of 3 officers and 44 other ranks. They were received joyfully.

At the beginning of July the Regiment took over the Russell Top trenches, and gave up its comfortable bivouac on the flat near the beach. The men were not sorry to be back in the trenches again. Rest Camp on Anzac was "one of those things no man can understand." A unit goes into rest camp. Then the messages begin to come for working parties. Every officer

Sergeants Harrison and Walker, who were both promoted to commissioned rank.

and man is soon employed with pick and shovel. More messages still come for more men, and the Adjutant gets "strafed" for not being able to supply them. And so it goes on till everybody is glad to get back to the front line.

The first day on Russell Top seemed to be the signal for a fairly heavy bombardment. The Turks possessed plenty of artillery and ammunition. Retaliation was a farce. With all the will in the world, how could the Anzac artillery "retaliate" with two rounds a day per gun, which was the limit imposed? But we had at last a fairly liberal supply of bombs, and the men took part in the new game of "two for one" with great zest, and as the trenches at the Nek were only some twenty yards apart good practice was made.

There was an Indian battery of mountain guns in these

trenches and the Turk's artillery was continually after them. One enemy gun in particular fired high explosive. In position on the Chunuk Bair ridge, this gun, a high velocity 18-pounder, was very annoying. Usually when it started there was a sudden lack of interest in anything but the nearest dug-outs.

Gas helmets were issued with many warnings. No man was allowed to move about without his helmet, but the general feeling was that gas helmets were just so much extra to carry.

Flies had now become a perfect pest, and one could hardly eat anything that was not contaminated by them. Since the attack in June the dead Turks had been lying between the trenches. Such as could be safely got at were dragged into the trenches and buried, but many remained. Round No. 2 Sap, known to many, was a sight one wishes to forget. Fourteen dead Turks were lying in a space of probably six square yards. The sap was crawling with maggots, and the stench was abominable. Yet this sap had to be held day and night. In addition the front line trench had been extended and had now reached the grave-yard of those buried during the armistice. Some men wore inhalers made of lint soaked in lysol, but they were not effective. Is it any wonder that sickness increased rapidly? The regimental roll about the middle of July showed three hundred and twenty of all ranks; and of these one-fourth were unfit for duty. A note by Major Overton in the official diary says, "men very weak," while a Medical officer reports, "men are debilitated and weak, unfit for any sustained effort." And the Regiment was no worse than any other unit. As a matter of fact it was fitter than most, as shown by the record of evacuations to hospital. The food was unsuitable for men suffering from stomach troubles, and such surplus stores as were begged, borrowed or stolen did not go far. Many men exchanged sugar and jam with the Indian gunners, receiving flour or chupattis in return, and a small supply of fresh stores had been procured by Major Overton, who had made a special trip to Alexandria for them on June 22nd; but these did not go far among so many.

The turn in the trenches over, the Regiment went into bivouac near the top of Walker's Ridge, to a place known as Wellington Terrace, after the Wellington M.R. As a trooper pithily put it, "it was a rotten spot." All the shells fired at Brigade Headquarters seemed to burst over this place. Every night about half the Regiment went up the trenches in support." The remainder carried water and rations to a dump half way up the hill.

It was now realised that something was brewing. Reserves of water and rations were being stored up. New bivouac areas were being dug in every hillside and terrace, with nobody to occupy them, and officers commanding regiments were being taken out on destroyers to view the country beyond our left flank. An attack was pending by the Turks according to deserters, so the beach yarn said, and everybody knew of our counter-attack that was to clear the enemy off the hills before us. Indian mule transport and mountain carts had arrived, and by day were concealed in a gully below us. By night they carted stores and ammunition from the landing stage to the various dumps scattered along the foot of the cliffs.

Towards the end of the month the Regiment again handed over the Outposts to Otago. The Maoris, who had just arrived, were digging a sunken road from the beach trenches to both Nos. 1 and 2 Outposts, so that traffic could be carried on by day as well as by night. Within the lines all communication, no matter where, was now below the surface of the ground.

On relieving the Australians again on Russell Top, on what proved to be the Regiment's last spell there, a platoon of Maoris came each night to the trenches, for the purpose of getting used to trench work. They thoroughly enjoyed it, and celebrated the first night by firing all the reserve ammunition into the opposing trenches.

Sergt.-Major Sloan in his Dugout on Walker's Ridge.

The work of the destroyers, the only ships of the British Navy to be seen on the seas since the sinking of the *Triumph* was always of interest. At intervals they would run in close to shore, fire a few rounds, and dash out again; while the Turks tried in vain to shell them. But it was at night that their worth was fully realised. They would creep close in and throw their searchlights over the ground in front of the trenches. One cannot describe the relief of a sentry looking anxiously out to his front, on a pitch dark night, his imagination making every scrubby bush a moving enemy, suddenly finding everything flooded by an intense white light. Good little *Chelmer, Colne* and *Rattlesnake,* you will never be forgotten!

Every night or two during this period constant demonstrations were made by throwing bombs, bursts of rapid fire, coloured lights and the showing on our parapets of dummy figures, in order to draw the enemy's fire and make him waste his ammunition, and to keep him in a constant state of uncertainty as to whether we were going to attack or not. These demonstrations also served to prevent the Turk from sending to Helles reinforcements which would interfere with the attacks now being made in that sector by the British and French.

This last tour of duty in the trenches was uneventful. On relief the Regiment went into bivouac. Spare time was filled in by practising cliff climbing. This had been imagined to

Looking towards Suvla and the Salt Lake, with Walker's Ridge in the foreground.

be the Regiment's main occupation for the last three months! Something was in the air for it was felt that General Russell, with all his wonderful activity, would not have ordered such a violent exercise for nothing. Digging had ceased. Strange troops occupied all the odd gullies within the lines. Batteries of guns appeared in every corner. Colonel Findlay went out in the destroyer *Colne* to view the country to the north. Evidently the time for the advance that had been talked of since the landing was at last drawing near.

CHAPTER IV.

Of the Desperate August Fighting and the Move to New Country.

Before continuing the story of the Regiment's part in the great August offensive, which was to take place in conjunction with the Suvla Bay landing, it will be well to give a summary of the proposed operations. General Birdwood's plan was to seize the Sari Bair range about the high point called Chunuk Bair. This range dominated the Peninsula, and from it could be seen the Narrows, and from it would be commanded the Turkish positions and all his lines of communication. The highest point of the range, Hill 971, was at its northern end; and Chunuk Bair, a somewhat lesser point, was about a mile nearer Anzac, and about 1½ miles from the Nek. From the Nek and over Baby 700 was the natural line of approach, along which attempts were made to advance on the day of the landing. But this route was now closed by the formidable entrenchments of the Nek, Baby 700 and Battleship Hill, and there remained two lines of approach to the crest at Chunuk Bair, one up Rhododendron Spur and the other up the Abdul Rahman Spur. General Birdwood decided to use both.

The force at his disposal consisted of the Anzac garrison—1st Australian Division and N.Z. and A. Division. The former was to hold its ground, and in addition to capture the important position of Lone Pine. The N.Z. and A. Division was to be used to break out from the lines held so long and to attack the Sari Bair range, and would be reinforced by the troops for whom shelter had been dug and stores, water and ammunition provided. These troops were the 13th Division, 29th Infantry Brigade, and one brigade of the 10th Division.

The plan and the allotment of General Godley's command, to which had been added these reinforcements, were as follows:—

The first step during the early hours of the night on which

the grand attack was to be made, was to clear the Turks from the foothills. Upon this attack the whole movement hinged, and the task was allotted to the N.Z.M.R. Brigade, to which was attached the Maori Battalion.

The advance up Rhododendron Spur was given to the N.Z. Infantry Brigade, which was called the Right Assaulting Column. It was to follow through the N.Z.M.R. Brigade and to go up the Sazli Beit and Chailak deres. The task of attacking the Sari Bair range beyond Chunuk Bair was given to a force under General Cox, of the Indian Brigade. This force was called the Left Assaulting Column and consisted of the Indian Brigade and the 4th Australian Infantry Brigade. It would require some protection on the north as it turned eastward to the main range, so a portion of the 13th Division was allotted the task of following through after the N.Z.M.R. and seizing and holding the small cluster of foot hills known as the Damak Jelik Bair.

The remainder of General Godley's force, the 1st and 3rd Light Horse Brigades, were to attack the Turks in front of Quinn's and the Nek respectively. The latter attack was to take place as soon as Chunuk Bair had been captured and held by the N.Z. Infantry Brigade, which would then be in a position to come down the main ridge and attack the Turks on Battleship Hill and Baby 700, which commanded the Nek.

The task of the N.Z.M.R. consisted of the capture and holding of three definite objectives; the first, Old No. 3; the second, Table Top (just below and joining Rhododendron Spur); and the third, Beauchop Hill, which lay between the Chailak and Aghyl deres. Canterbury's task in this most interesting and intricate operation was perhaps the most difficult of the three. In conjunction with the O.M.R. the Regiment was to clear the entrance to the Chailak Dere, advance north as far as the Aghyl Dere, clearing and capturing Taylor's Hollow and Walden's Point, and then to swing to the east and to capture Beauchop Hill. The attack was to be swift and silent, rifles and magazines empty and the bayonet only used. Tunics were discarded, and white patches, 8in. x 8in. were sewn on the back of the shirt and a white armlet on each arm, so that identification in the dark would be easy.

DESPERATE FIGHTING AND MOVE TO NEW COUNTRY 47

As usual, a destroyer was to shell Old No. 3 under the beam of the searchlight until 9 p.m. The shutting out of this light was to be the signal for the attack.

At 8 p.m. on August 5th the Regiment moved out to No. 2 Outpost, a total strength of sixteen officers and two hundred and eighty other ranks.

This last day passed quietly. The men were keen but unfit. Sickness had played havoc with their physique, but their confidence in their ability to carry out the task given them was amazing. As usual when there was "something doing" sick parades fell off; men simply would not go near the M.O. for fear of being kept back. Right through the whole of Anzac there was the same confident feeling.

Regimental Headquarters on the evening of August 6th, just before the attack.
Sitting—Lieut. Marchant, Capt. Blair, Lt.-Col. Findlay, Capt. Guthrie.
Standing: Lt.-Col. Bauchop, Comdg. O.M.R.
Major Overton had just left to guide the Indian Brigade.

As the manual says, everything went "according to plan" as far as the first step went.

Punctually at 9 p.m. on the 6th the Regiment moved out from the shelter of No. 2 Outpost. After getting clear of the trenches the three squadrons halted in a small depression and waited for the signal. The destroyers ceased fire, the searchlight went out and the attack began.

The Regiment advanced with two squadrons abreast—the 1st and 10th, and the 8th in support with the machine guns and a platoon of Maoris. Slightly ahead of the leading troops went a few scouts. A piquet of four Turks was met, and a fight with the bayonet ensued, four men to four, neither side firing a shot. One of the Canterbury men was wounded in the jaw and another in the chest; but all the Turks were killed. A few stray bullets were flying; then by some mischance a searchlight from one of the ships flashed across the squadrons and was gone. But the damage was done. A machine gun on Walden Point opened fire, and heavy rifle fire came from Wilson's Knob. A silent rush across the two hundred yards of flat, then up the scrubby spur and into the enemy trench charged the 10th squadron. Simultaneously the 1st had pushed through the narrow pass separating Walden Point from the end of Beauchop Hill, and thence charged at the gun from its rear. Magazines and rifles were empty, and it was easy for the Turks to shoot them as they climbed the hill, but every man, keeping to his orders, fired no shot and raised no cheer. The enemy could not tell from what quarter any part of this silent attack was coming, and the machine gun was rushed, the Turks near it being bayoneted. Swinging right handed through a small scrubby gully the Canterburys turned inland and advanced in silence up the northern edge of Beauchop Hill.

During the rush on the gun Colonel Findlay was wounded, but so well had he explained his plans, and such was the keenness of every man in the Regiment, that the most difficult of operations—changing direction in the dark when in contact with the enemy—was successfully carried out, and trench after trench was rushed almost without sound, the enemy's garrisons being utterly confused by these tactics. Those in the trenches were bayoneted, but some found in the rear of the positions were captured. The machine gunners had kept up with the advance, but it was here on the northern slopes of Beauchop Hill that they lost their beloved young leader, Lieut. Frank (Mickey) Davison. Owing to casualties in officers and N.C.O's. a certain amount of confusion existed. Squadrons had become mixed up, but always the idea to get forward and up the

DESPERATE FIGHTING AND MOVE TO NEW COUNTRY 49

hill carried the attacking lines on. In the darkness, perplexed by the broken country, fired on from all quarters, small bands of men kept together, dealt with isolated bodies of Turks, and then pushed on to reach the top of the hill. And they got there, such as were not killed or wounded. No detailed story of that wild night is possible. From the moment of the first charge till men found themselves on Bauchop Hill, nobody can say exactly what happened. All they knew was that they struggled and fought with Turk, with scrub and with hill, they fell down gullies, were fired at always, and eventually found themselves at their objective. Here under rifle and machine gun fire they commenced to dig in, tired but confident; and a cheer coming to them across the ridges their confidence was much increased.

This cheer came from the Otagos led by Colonel Bauchop. They too, struggling through all their difficulties, had won to the top of the hill.

While the Canterbury and Otago Regiments were thus accomplishing their tasks, the Aucklanders had rushed Old No. 3, and the Wellington Regiment following them had forced their way up the Sazli Beit Dere and had captured Table Top. So at 1 a.m. General Russell reported that Old No. 3, Table Top and Bauchop Hill were in our hands.

The way was now clear for the Right and Left Assaulting Columns to advance upon their objectives.

Bean, in his "Story of Anzac" (being Vol. 11 Official History of Australia in the War), says:—"By this magnificent feat of arms, the brilliance of which was never surpassed, if indeed equalled, during the campaign, almost the entire Turkish defence north of Anzac was for the moment swept aside, and the way cleared for the Infantry to advance up the valleys to Chunuk Bair. The opening move by the mounted rifles was undoubtedly that upon which the success of the offensive mainly depended. The operation was one which in its conception went flatly in the face of the principles laid down by British Military authorities. "A thorough reconnaissance" said the Field Service Regulations, "is an essential prelude to a night advance or to a night assault... Every commander who orders a night operation which is not preceded by a complete reconnaissance increases

E

the risk of failure and incurs a heavy responsibility....
Reconnaissance from a distance is insufficient." It had been
proved that in such operations there was extreme danger
that various portions of the attacking force would lose touch,
take the wrong direction, and even meet and fire upon other
sections of their own side.

Yet the country through which Birdwood launched these
troops had been explored only by picked scouts in a few
daring expeditions. Its hills and valleys were so rugged and
contorted that even after their capture men at first sometimes
lost their way in them by day. Moreover the enemy's posts
had to be attacked, not by a single advance on a straight
front, but by several detachments moving by various intricate
routes, in some cases to concentrate on the enemy's positions
from widely different directions. For the maintenance of
direction in the dark Birdwood depended almost solely upon
the intelligence and experience of the New Zealand soldiers,
while, to avoid the danger of friend firing upon friend, and
also to conceal their attack from the enemy, they were to
fight through to their respective objectives with rifles
unloaded. It thus fell to them for several hours to bear
down in complete silence, and with their bayonets alone, the
opposition of an enemy who faced them with rifles and
machine guns. What was demanded for such an operation
was not a rigid military discipline but the highest degree of
intelligent self-control, imposed on themselves by men understanding their task and determined to complete it."

Soon after 1 a.m. on August 7th, the enemy attacked several
times, but their attacks lacked force and were easily repulsed
by the combined regiments now under the command of Colonel
Beauchop. This gallant and beloved officer, immediately the
hill was won, set about laying off a trench line for its
defence, and though unknown to most of the men of the
Canterbury Regiment he immediately inspired everybody with
his cheerful confidence. Shortly before daylight he was mortally
wounded while assisting a wounded man.

Many prisoners were captured, together with several old-
fashioned mortars made of bronze mounted on wooden carriages.
These threw a spherical bomb of about 8in. diameter and had

much troubled No. 2 Outpost. The two-barrelled Nordenfeldt, so often used by the Turks to fire upon the destroyers at night, was also taken. Two enemy battalions encamped behind Bauchop Hill in the Aghyl Dere had fled, leaving a large amount of camp equipment behind them.

The Regiment had lost in killed and wounded 40 per cent. of its strength. The Commanding Officer, Colonel Findlay, had been badly wounded in the leg; his second in command, Major Overton, killed. Among all the gallant fellows who died during the bitter August fighting none was missed more than Major Overton. He was one of those rare men to whom the best was not enough. For ever on the look out to do more, to improve the set task, to alleviate the conditions under which the Regiment laboured, he was as an inspiration to all. In addition to the extraordinarily valuable reconnaissances he personally undertook, he summarised the knowledge thus gained in making an excellent raised map, out of clay, of the area to the north of Anzac, showing what was afterwards proved to be a faithful reproduction of that most intricate country. He was killed while leading the Left Assaulting Column through the broken country in the Aghyl Dere, and was buried in Warley Gap, where the Turkish track he had been so ably following winds up towards Abdul Rhaman Bair.

The remainder of the 7th was spent in digging-in; and the Regiment's machine guns were placed in position with those of Otago facing Chunuk Bair, and gave covering fire to the New Zealand Infantry. Throughout the desperate attacks of the 8th, 9th and 10th these guns fired almost ceaselessly.

From the top of Bauchop Hill could be seen the ships in Suvla Bay, but the advance towards Anafarta of the troops landed there was looked for in vain. From here also was seen the great tragedy of the Nek, upon which, on the morning of August 7th in full daylight, the brave 3rd Light Horse Brigade expended itself in vain,—a brilliant, gallant charge and futile slaughter of good men.

The morning of 7th August, which was to have seen the infantry assaulting columns breasting the crest of the Sari

Major Overton.

DESPERATE FIGHTING AND MOVE TO NEW COUNTRY 53

Bair ridge, saw instead these columns still struggling upwards among the lower slopes. Darkness and want of confidence in their guides, who in reality were perfectly trustworthy, had led the infantry commanders to spend precious hours in keeping their battalions together. Turkish reinforcements reached Chunuk Bair in large numbers during the 7th; and the New Zealand Brigade, gallantly led by Colonel Malone

The Graves of Four Members of the C.Y.C. Squadron at Walden Point.

with the Wellington Battalion, reached the crest on the morning of the 8th, and held it during the desperate fighting that day and the 9th, during which they were reinforced by the Auckland and Wellington Mounted Rifles.

By 11 p.m. on the 9th all New Zealand units had been replaced by New Army Battalions and had withdrawn to Chailak Dere and Rhododendron Spur. These New Battalions were heavily attacked at daylight on 10th August, and, giving way, fell back upon the N.Z. Infantry Brigade on Rhododendron Spur, where the Turks' attack spent itself in vain.

With regard to the Left Assaulting Column, consisting of the 4th Australian Infantry Brigade and the Indian Brigade, under the guidance of Major Overton, of the Canterburys, this force during its advance up the Aghyl Dere in the darkness, also wasted much valuable time in endeavouring to clear the hills of small scattered parties of the enemy.

Daylight found General Cox and his two brigades far below their objective, and the Turkish opposition stiffened so rapidly and so strongly that the column was at a standstill by the morning of the 8th August, and hard put to it to hold what ground it had won by the 10th.

The landing at Suvla Bay, begun so well on the morning of the 7th, by the 10th also had come to a standstill. Had this landing been carried out with vigour and had the troops when landed pushed forward to the Kavak and Tekke Tepe and to the "W" Hills, the attack of the Anzac Forces on the Chunuk Bair position must have succeeded.

The position, briefly, on the morning of 10th August was that the Anzac garrison had broken the Turkish lines and had pushed up the slopes of the Great Sari Bair Ridge and were holding on just below the crest, and on the north they had advanced their line two miles and were feeling out on the Anafarta Plain towards the Suvla Bay Force.

This force had landed but had failed to seize the important tactical features surrounding the Anafarta Plain and had not in any way affected the struggle for the Sari Bair Range.

During these days all men who could be spared went to bury the dead and to assist the stretcher bearers with the wounded. Many of these, after being dressed in the field, lay

DESPERATE FIGHTING AND MOVE TO NEW COUNTRY 55

about the clearing stations or on the beach for two or three days waiting to be evacuated. For the Medical officers to cope with all cases was a physical impossibility. And all the time both wounded and doctors were under fire. Whoever was responsible for the evacuation of casualties had sadly underestimated the numbers, and had failed utterly in his provision of means of conveyance.

There fell on 9th August a brilliant troop leader, Lieutenant G. C. Mayne, of the 10th Squadron, who was killed whilst endeavouring to locate an enemy machine gun in country which he considered too exposed for his men and insisted upon going forward by himself.

The 8th Squadron lost a fine young officer in Lieutenant Cyril Hayter. He was in charge of a special patrol sent to gain touch with the Suvla Bay forces on the plain, and met his death in rallying a party of British infantry who were being fiercely attacked by the Turks.

The Regiment, now under the command of Major Hutton of the 10th Squadron, stayed on Bauchop Hill till the 15th, on which day it moved across to trenches at Holly Hill, near the entrance to the Aghyl Dere. Here at first it was in support to a regiment of South Wales Borderers, but the same evening took over their trenches. During the night an old Turkish trench about two hundred yards further forward was occupied and rapidly improved. While this was going on a a covering party lay out in front from twenty to forty yards in the scrub to guard against attack. To be one of a covering party was a trying ordeal. Bullets were plentiful and cover scarce.

This was the Regiment's first meeting with one of the raw units of "Kitchener's Army." Mere boys, and absolutely untrained, they were being expected to behave as Guardsmen.

On the 21st the Regiment was warned of an attack to be made on Hill 60, known as Kaiajik Aghala, a small round hill of considerable tactical importance that lay at the eastern edge of the plain and overlooked the junction of the lines of the Anzac and Suvla Bay forces and also several important wells. The attack was to be made in conjunction with a general advance by the Suvla Bay force on Scimitar Hill and the "W" Hills, by which it was intended to straighten up the line held by the combined forces. The attack was to commence at 3.30 p.m. the same afternoon. General Russell was in command, and was given for the operation the Canterbury and Otago Regiments of his own brigade, amounting to about four hundred men, a detachment of five hundred from the 4th Australian Infantry Brigade and the Connaught Rangers seven hundred strong. Ghurkas, in conjunction with the attack, were to seize the wells on the plain at the foot of the hill. Between the Regiment and its objective lay the ravine of the Kaiajik Aghala. About eight hundred yards had to be covered before

The Beach at No. 2 Outpost looking towards Anzac Cove, after the August fighting.

the enemy's trenches were reached. The direction of the Regiment's attack was straight at the hill, with the Otagos, commanded by Lieut.-Colonel Grigor, on the right, and beyond them further on the right were the Australians, and immediately on the Regiment's left the Connaughts.

An artillery bombardment had been promised, but at the last moment it was decided that the Anzac guns should assist the Suvla Bay attack. Punctually on time, 3.30 p.m., the men jumped from the trenches and raced down the hill. Casualties were numerous till comparative shelter was reached in the bottom of the dere. Then came the climb up the other side, a moment to gather breath, and the rush for the enemy trench 200 yards to the front. It was simply a case of get there, and during the last part of this rush most of the casualities occurred. Major Hutton was wounded, and Major Hurst of the 1st Squadron took command. The Turks in the trench were killed, and a machine gun was captured and immediately turned upon the Turks by the two Harper brothers of the Machine Gun Section. Though the Australians managed to cross the ravine, they could not reach the enemy trenches; and on our left, despite the fact that the New Army troops had seized the Kabak well with a splendid charge and captured the long trench on the eastern side of the hill in their first rush, they failed to hold the ground they had won. The Canterbury Regiment with the Otagos were now holding about 120 yards of enemy trench with both flanks in the air, and with no means of communication across the exposed valley. Both regiments had lost over 60 per cent. of their number in the space of a quarter of an hour. With the depleted numbers it was impossible to go any further, and orders were received from General Russell that the trenches gained were to be consolidated and held. At dusk the enemy fire slackened, and the Regiment was able to get into touch with the Indian Brigade who were holding the captured wells on the flat.

About midnight occurred a peculiar incident. About 200 Turks, fully armed, with fixed bayonets, and carrying bombs slung on their belts, came up to the New Zealand line as though to surrender. Eleven came into the trench and were promptly disarmed. The remainder stood in the open, apparently undecided what to do. Signs were made to them to lay down their arms. Colonel Grigor of the Otagos got out of the trench and endeavoured to find out what they wanted, but a big Turk seizing him by the hand, he jumped back into the trench. Several shots were fired on the flank by those who could not see what was happening, the Turks taking alarm retreated, and fire was immediately opened upon them by the mounted rifles.* It was after this

*Major Hurst, who was now in command of the Canterbury men, says: "There is not a doubt in my mind as to the intentions of the Turkish force. It was purely an attack. We distinctly heard the sound of a bugle about midnight, and as the sound came from the direction of the Turkish lines, our Regiment immediately stood to arms, and about ten minutes later two or three enemy ground scouts appeared creeping through the scrub. I passed the order along not to shoot, but that the Turks should be allowed to come up to the parapet and be pulled in. This was successfully done, and a few minutes later the main body of the enemy appeared, apparently deceived by the fact that no fire was opened on their scouts, who had evidently clambered into our trenches. I think they took this to mean that either our trenches were vacated or that we wished to surrender, and so came close up."

Major P. M. Acton-Adams, D.S.O.,
2nd in Command.

peculiar affair that an incident, so far unrecorded, happened. The fire from our machine guns ignited the clothing of a dead Turk. From here it spread to the scrub and threatened to do what the enemy had failed in—drive us from the trench. Trooper A. Barr of the Machine Gun Section, seized a shovel, jumped out into the open and calmly proceeded to beat out the blaze. Every Turkish rifle in the vicinity opened on him standing there in the light of the fire. Barr coolly worked on, extinguished the flames, and then jumped back into the trench.

The Regiment held on to this position until the evening of the 23rd, when with the Otago Regiment it was relieved by the Auckland and Wellington M.R., and went back to a quieter valley to gather strength for another attack.
6pt. footnote to be set.

Sergt-Major Norris, the gallant and popular R.S.M., was mortally wounded during the afternoon. This warrant officer had been serving in New Zealand when the war broke out, on loan from the British Army as a mounted instructor. He was at all times an unfailing source of help and information to officers and men, and his soldierly qualities did much to raise the standard of efficiency of the Regiment to the high place it held in the N.Z.M.R. Brigade.

C.M.R. getting ready for the Second Assault on Hill 60 August 27th.

The Regiment returned to the trenches at Hill 60 on the 26th. The attack with which it was hoped to complete the operations on Hill 60 was timed to commence at 5 p.m. on the 27th. An endeavour had been made by General Russell to be allowed to carry out the attack in the dark, for which type of fighting the colonial troops had shown themselves peculiarly adapted. But he was over-ruled, and the daylight attack was promised a liberal artillery support. The force, again a mixed one of New Zealanders and Australians, consisted of the N.Z.M.R. Brigade of four weak regiments, totalling three hundred men, with one hundred from the 18th Battalion (5th Australian Infantry Brigade); about three hundred and fifty men of the 4th Australian Brigade; and two hundred and fifty men of the 5th Connaught Rangers. This mixed force was distributed for the attack as follows:—The New Zealanders with the 100 men from the 18th Australian Battalion were in the centre, and on their right were the men from the 4th Australian Brigade, and on their left the Connaught Rangers. General Russell commanded the attacking force, and Major J. H. Whyte, of the W.M.R., the combined New Zealand Mounted Rifles. In the centre the attack was to be made in three successive lines, Canterbury forming the first line under Major Hurst, together with about forty men of the Auckland Mounted Rifles. These latter carried bombs and their duty was to bomb along the east trench which formed the right flank of the attack of the centre party. An intensive artillery bombardment of the hill was to be made for an hour before the assault.

Right on time the men jumped from the trenches. It seemed no distance to go, probably sixty yards, but every yard of ground was swept by enemy shrapnel and high explosives. Casualties were fearful, but the line reached the first trench and disappeared into it. It seemed minutes, but was probably some seconds only, before they reappeared. A short rush and they were over the second trench and into the third on the top of the hill. But mortal man could go no further. In each trench there had remained many Turks in spite of the heavy bombardment from the Anzac guns. These were now killed and their bodies, together with those who had been slain by the bombardment, literally filled the trenches.

On the right the Australians had failed to get into the enemy trench, and on the left the troops could not hold what they had gained in their first rush. Could the mounted rifles themselves hold on, bombed from all sides, with units mixed up, and practically all officers killed or wounded? Yet there was no thought of going back. All night the incessant bomb duel continued; for the first time in the history of Anzac our force was well supplied with bombs, and it is reported that five thousand three hundred were used on this hill during this night. Early in the evening the Regiment had been much heartened by the arrival of the remnants of the 9th L.H. Regiment from the 3rd Light Horse Brigade. These men, old friends of the Regiment, were used to reinforce each flank.

Capt. Guthrie, the Regiment's M.O., in his Dugout.

By daylight the enemy had expended his strength, and his attacks throughout the day were not so violent. But shelling from the higher ground of the Abdul Rahman Bair went on unmercifully. Communication trenches had been dug during the night by the Connaught Rangers and the dead and wounded were removed. Of the one hundred and nineteen officers and men of the Canterbury Regiment who started the evening before there now remained eighteen men. The other regiments of the brigade were in no better plight. Heavy as the losses were, the Turks suffered more. In the first trench captured their dead lay two and three deep.

It was now decided, as there were no more troops with which to carry the whole hill, that the line passing over the summit of the hill should be consolidated and held. To make this practicable it was evident that the trench along the western side, so gallantly taken by the Connaughts during the first attack on August 21st, but which had been lost by them, and which had since been taken and lost by the 18th Battalion 5th Australian Infantry Brigade, must be captured and held. So during the night of August 29th, one hundred and eighty of the brave 10th L.H. Regiment came into the trenches and by a masterly surprise attack completed the capture of this difficult trench.

The position on the hill was now secure, and on the 29th the Regiment, with the other remnants of the Mounted Rifle Brigade, was relieved.

Major Hurst, who was in command of the Regiment on the 27th, and who so gallantly led the first line, had been evacuated wounded, and the following day the Adjutant, Captain Blair, also went, having suffered a complete loss of voice owing to the bursting of a high explosive shell close to him. The only officer remaining with the Regiment at this time was Captain Gibbs, who had just returned from hospital.

So ended eight continuous days and nights of the hardest and most exhausting fighting the Mounted Brigade was engaged in during the whole war.

Throughout those strenuous nights and days every officer and man on the strength of the Regiment had given of his best, and of the sixteen officers and two hundred and eighty other ranks who broke through the Turkish line on the night of August 6th there remained but one officer and thirty-nine other ranks.

The work of the signallers was beyond praise. For days on end they stuck to their telephones almost without rest, and the repairing of lines entailed many casualties. Among those to lose their lives was Sergeant Hamilton, who had been given a commission as 2nd Lieutenant, but did not live to hear of his promotion.

The Regiment lost another valuable and gallant soldier in Sergt.-Major R. Sloan, of the N.Z. Permanent Staff, who was Squadron Sergt.-Major to the 8th Squadron and who had served for many years in the 16th Lancers.

No mention has been made throughout this fighting of the stretcher bearers or machine gunners. The former were marvellous. They followed every attack, and though it was nearly always impossible to remove the wounded, yet they bandaged them and marked the place where they lay. By night they searched the ground over which the troops had advanced in case any wounded had been missed. The call for "stretcher bearers" never found them wanting. The Regiment's medical officer, Captain Neil Guthrie, was finally evacuated to hospital on August 22nd, after the greatest devotion to duty. On May 30th, whilst attending the wounded under fire, he was hit in the wrist, but carried on. On August 6th at Bauchop Hill he was wounded again, and finally during the first attack on Hill 60, while engaged in binding up the wounded under most trying conditions, he was seriously wounded in the neck and forced to be relieved. Chaplain H. Blamires rejoined the Regiment on August 21st and rendered good service to the wounded. He was helping Chaplain Grant of W.M.R. when this beloved padre was killed while attending to the Turkish wounded.

The machine gunners were always where they were wanted. In every attack or counter-attack they were in the front. How they got there, weighted with their heavy loads and weakened by sickness, it is impossible to say. For it must be remembered that the gun they used was the old Maxim, much heavier than the Vickers of later days, and in itself a load for a strong healthy man. Some unknown power, by which men rise superior to their physical weakness, must have been theirs.

The front line from Anzac across the Suvla plain to the hills overlooking the sea, where rested the left flank of the IX. Corps (the Suvla force), now became stabilised, and a period of trench warfare set in. In order to assist the Suvla Bay troops the Anzac garrison was asked to send selected scouts and sharpshooters to the IX. Corps to help in the instruction of their men.

Regt. Sergt.-Major F. H. Norris.

From the Regiment were selected as scouts Corporal R. G. Cooke, 10th Squadron, and Trooper R. A. Young, 1st Squadron. And the following were sent as sharpshooters:—Sergeants W. S. Wright and J. L. Wilson, Troopers L. E. H. Leaman, M. E. Jenkins, J. J. Connell, G. Davis, H. P. Rasmussen, and G. Faulkner.

On September 1st General Russell came to see the Regiment, and his few plain words of appreciation put heart into the tired men. He added that he was trying to get the brigade away from Anzac for a rest.

On September 2nd the Regiment took over the trenches on Cheshire Ridge. This was a fairly quiet place. The Turks had no inclination to attack, nor had the Regiment the strength, though they annoyed each other with an intermittent rifle fire, but that was all. Although literally crawling with vermin, Cheshire Ridge was a haven of rest after Hill 60. The nights were cold, but with the help of Turkish bivvie sheets taken from the enemy's camps, the Regiment kept itself warm. Day and night shell fire continued, but little notice was taken by the tired out men. On September 13th, the 5th Australian Infantry Brigade relieved the N.Z.M.R. Brigade, which, after handing over the trenches, marched down to the beach and embarked the same night on the S.S. *Osmanieh* and sailed at once for Mudros, leaving behind the machine gun section, now reduced to 12 men in position with their guns on Cheshire Ridge.

The following table, taken from the Regimental Record book, tells its own story:—

	Officers	O/Rs.
Landed on Gallipoli 12/5/15	26	459
Reinforcements various dates	6	186
	32	645
Killed in action	5	108
Died of sickness	2	10
Missing	1	45
Hospital sick and wounded	23	443
	31	606

Regimental strength 13/9/15	1	39
Machine gunners to remain	—	12
Total to Lemnos	1	27

Looking down to the Sea from Russell Top.

Arrived at Mudros the Regiment, now under the command of Lt.-Colonel George Stewart, marched to a camp site about three miles from the harbour, near the village of Sarpi. Good food and plenty of rest worked wonders in the brigade. Some men, now the reaction had set in, collapsed and were sent to hospital, but the majority improved rapidly. Beyond physical exercises in the morning nothing was done but ordinary camp duties. On September 16th the Admiral of the French Station inspected the Brigade. The four regiments were drawn up in two lines in the camp, while he rode through. The total brigade state was 151, including brigade headquarters. The Admiral asked General Russell if this was all that remained of his regiment. He did not realise at first that he was inspecting the remnants of four regiments. When he did so he turned round, looked at the men in wonder, gravely saluted and rode off.

A halt at Mudros on the way to Camp, showing all that was left of the Regiment. Lt.-Colonel G. H. Stewart is sitting in the foreground.

On the 6th October the Brigade was inspected by General Godley, the parade state now being 50 officers and 1,362 others, for on October 5th the looked for reinforcements had arrived. For the first week they were not drafted to the Regiment, as it was thought that the men from Anzac were not yet strong enough to take part in all necessary drill.

For a long time a controversy continued among the men as to whether the men from Anzac were drafted to the new arrivals or vice versa. The argument brought forward by the reinforcements was that they were ten times the number of the old hands, whereas the old hands maintained that they were the C.M.R. and the new arrivals their humble reinforcements.

Towards the end of October Lieut.-Colonel G. H. Stewart was evacuated sick to the Mudros Hospital, and the Regiment was taken over by Major J. Studholme, the senior officer among the reinforcements. The old hands were now worked harder as they became more fit, and drill, route marches and tactical schemes amongst the hills were the order of the day. There were long tiring walks with full equipment on, the older hands with packs stuffed with paper instead of clothing. The new officers were good, and time was soon to show the sterling grit of the reinforcements. Permission was given the men to visit the hot springs at Thermos, about six or seven miles away. The luxury of sitting in hot water, even though the baths were small, more than repaid the walk.

October passed all too quickly. The latest arrivals looked forward with intense eagerness to the day when camp should be struck, but the old hands smiled and shaking their heads expressed their willingness, were it not for the fact that their loved comrades lay buried there, never to see Gallipoli again.

On November 10th the Brigade embarked on its return journey. On arrival at Anzac disembarkation was made at the foot of Walker's Ridge, and the Regiment went straight to a bivouac area in Waterfall Gully in the heart of Bauchop Hill. It was now a different Anzac. Light railways ran round the beach. Roads wound in all directions. When the Regiment left tents did not number half a dozen; now they could be seen everywhere. Hospitals were erected on the very place where the Regiment had first taken over its trenches at Walker's Ridge and No. 2 Outpost. The only likeness of the Anzac as the old hands knew it was the noise of rifle fire and bursting bombs.

CHAPTER V.

Of the Final Days at Anzac and How the Regiment came away.

The new camp was a bad place for stray bullets, especially during the evening "hate," but it was subject to little shell fire. During the Regiment's absence the Turks had brought up some heavy artillery and a great supply of ammunition. The Otago Regiment, over the ridge and below the Canterburys, was kept busy dodging 8in. shells fired at a neighbouring battery, but the Canterbury Regiment luckily had no battery near it. Building winter quarters kept everyone fully employed. Long terraces were dug on the hillsides and roofed over with iron, and inside these shelters short tunnels were bored into the hill, to be used when the bivouac area was shelled. Besides this work, the Regiment being in reserve had to find its quota of working parties to dig tunnels at No. 2 Outpost for Divisional Headquarters. No. 2 Outpost was an unhealthy place. Apparently the Turks had accurate knowledge that it was a headquarters, for whenever they shelled they always remembered it. The weather now became very cold, with heavy winds and frequent rain storms.

On 27th November the Regiment relieved the Suffolk Yeomanry and a portion of the 162nd Brigade of the 54th Infantry Division, in the trenches at "King's Own Avenue," off "Hampshire Lane," which was an off-shoot of the Aghyl Dere on the northern side. It was bitterly cold and raining as the men left the shelter of their bivouac in the darkness, and all were thoroughly wet and caked with mud by the time the trenches were reached. These were found to be in a very bad state. Originally a portion of an old Turkish trench system, they were very badly sited from the Regiment's point of view, the field of fire in places being not more than two or three yards. The bivouac area immediately in rear of the trenches, was a bare hillside. Baggage had not come up, and there was very little chance of improving matters till tools were available. All day the storm continued, and at night it came on to snow. The Regiment passed a miserable night. In the morning the ground was covered by a white mantle to the depth of three or four inches. The work of improving the trenches was begun; being on the hill, draining away the water was an easy matter. The bivouac areas were improved, and in a very few hours some degree of comfort was available.

This blizzard of snow was followed by two days and two nights of bitter cold, intensified by an icy wind. But this was partly a blessing in disguise for all mud and standing water froze hard, making the carriage of rations, stores and baggage into the new trenches an easier matter. Every effort was made to keep the men in the trenches warm. Hot tea and coffee were sent up to them at night and rum when they came off duty in the morning. This care and the fact that owing to the move into new trenches everyone was hard at work improving the fire-trenches, digging dug-outs and making tracks, undoubtedly had much to do with the freedom from frost bite enjoyed by the Brigade. Casualties from frost bite and exposure ran into many thousands in the Suvla Bay force.

The trench line held by the Brigade ran from a strong point called Warwick Castle, where lay the left of the 4th Australian Brigade, across the north branch of the Aghyl Dere, up a spur towards the Abd el Rahman Bair until it almost touched a strong Turkish position known as Sand Bag Ridge. The line then bent abruptly west and continued across several ridges to Hill 60, where the Wellington Regiment joined with the Welsh Horse.

The Regiment's portion consisted of the spur which ran from the north branch of the Aghyl Dere to the Turkish position of Sand Bag Ridge. On its right were the Auckland Mounted Rifles, and on the left across Warley Gap the Otagos. Along the front of the position lay a valley, and across this valley the lower slopes of Chunuk Bair. Here the Turkish trenches were some distance away, though at the extreme left the Regiment's line joined the Turks at Sand Bag Ridge. The gully was patrolled every night, and the left of the line was specially protected by hidden machine guns.

On November 24th began what was known as the "silent battle." All firing was ordered to cease until midnight on November 27th.

These orders caused much speculation and rumours of evacuation even were heard.

C.M.R. Headquarters just before the Evacuation.
Standing: Lieut. Anderson (Quartermaster), Capt. Stout (Medical Officer), Capt. Gibbs (Adjutant). Sitting: Capt. R. Harper (M.G. Officer), Major Powles (C.O.)), Major Studholme (2nd in Command).

On December 9th Major C. G. Powles, the Brigade Major of the N.Z.M.R. Brigade, took over command of the Regiment, and Major J. Studholme became second in command. Trench routine, varied by patrolling in the valley and the digging of deep dug-outs for the winter, occupied the days; and the weather becoming warmer again the troops looked forward with very little misgiving to a winter on Gallipoli. There was much jaundice among the men at this time, and the M.O., who promptly sent the sufferers off to the Hospital ships, was remonstrated with by a senior officer who did not know that every opportunity was being taken to evacuate unfit men. Later on, when he himself became as yellow as the proverbial guinea, he strenuously resisted imperative orders to go, and managed to hang on to the end.

Stories were, however, current of winter quarters at Mudros, at which units were to stay in turn. Then on December 12th came definite news of the evacuation and of the preliminary steps to be taken.

Though the idea of evacuation had been spoken of for some time the decision came as a great shock to most of the Anzac garrison. To give up the attempt, after so great an effort and at such a great cost of lives, seemed unthinkable; and then there was the abandonment of all our brave comrades who had lost their lives. The idea was heartbreaking.

But definite movement soon became apparent. All men with the slightest symptoms of sickness were sent away. Then one regiment or one battalion in each brigade disappeared, the Aucklanders going from the N.Z.M.R., "for a spell in a rest camp on Lemnos." This meant a greatly extended line for the C.M.R. to hold; so long was it that "strong points" only were regularly garrisoned, the intervals being patrolled.

As soon as definite orders giving the scheme of the evacuation were received all ranks devoted their whole energy to make the withdrawal a success. Spare stores were gradually burnt in the incinerators and spare bombs and S.A.A. were buried. Many ruses were resorted to in order to deceive the enemy. Parties of men were sent in the dark to the beach and marched back in daylight in full view of the Turks. Fires were lighted in those gullies used by reinforcements and kept burning daily until the end.

To the Regimental Quartermaster fell the task of destroying the surplus rum. He caused a hole to be dug in the ground and the jars carried there. His intention was to take the jars two by two and, breaking them together, consign the liquor to Mother Earth. It is said that three times did he repair to the hole to begin this pitiful task, and that three times his courage failed before he nerved himself to the dreadful deed.

Many ingenious devices were made for the firing of rifles, so that when the trenches were left these rifles would go off at various intervals up to one hour.

Finally there was the dividing of each unit into parties for the final evacuation, which it had been decided was to take place on the night of December 19th-20th. Orders were received to reduce each regiment in the Brigade to nine officers and one hundred and sixty-three other ranks, so the Regiment sent off five officers and one hundred and seventy-seven other ranks during the night of December 18th.

Those remaining in the Regiment were divided into A, B and C parties, the final or C party to be of "active gallant men," as the orders said—the diehards of the Regiment.

The greatest competition was shown for places in the C party, and the Commanding Officer was besieged with requests from all ranks to be allowed to stay.

At last the personnel required for each party were allotted. It was arranged that "A" party of three officers and ninety others from each of the three regiments, should leave the trenches at 1730 hours, and "B" party of three officers and forty-two others at 2135 hours, all marching down to the pier at North Beach. This would leave for the "C" parties three officers and thirty-one others each, who would leave the trenches each in three detachments to assemble in the Aghyl Dere, and then to march independently to the beach.

To the few remaining, the last day, December 19th, passed slowly, but it was a day of hard work. Up and down the trenches moved the skeleton garrison, carrying on sniping or firing just as in normal times. Final reserves of S.A.A. and bombs were buried, all stores possible to burn without raising undue smoke were destroyed in the incinerator, and the final touches were put to the self-firing rifles and to the trip-bombs

"The Diehards," photographed at Zeitoun immediately after the Evacuation.

Final Days at Anzac

that were to be left as a protection in case the trenches were rushed as the final "C" parties left.

The day was fine and clear, and after dark a full moon shone. The "A" and "B" parties got off to time and the Turk kept firing away in his usual style. "Everything normal," as the War Diary said. From 9 p.m. began the most anxious time. The three officers and thirty-one other ranks, with one machine gun, kept up the deception, firing from the usual places and carrying the maxim gun to the various machine gun emplacements in turn. It was a time of anxiety and suspense, but though every man fully realised that in a serious attack they would be overwhelmed, all were too busy to worry. At 0145 hours on the morning of December 20th the first portion of the Regiment's "C" party left the trenches and walked quietly down King's Own Avenue to the Aghyl Dere, where they waited. They were followed by the second portion at 0155 hours, and at 0205 the final lot of the "C" party filed out of the trenches (Sergeant H. Benson, the regimental signaller, finally cutting the telephone wires that led to Brigade Headquarters), and reached their comrades in the Aghyl at 0220 hours. Carrying their rifles, the machine gun and a few personal belongings, "C" party now set out on their last long journey to the beach. Through the silent deres they marched, and past the silent dead, over whom loving comrades had set up crosses of remembrance in those last days. "I wonder if they hear us" passed through many a mind, and a great regret came welling up—a regret that they were being abandoned and the task not done. Not a soul was seen, for all other "C" parties, having a shorter journey to go, had reached the beach. But away up in the first line the dummy rifles were manfully simulating the normal state of affairs, and the old Turk was as manfully firing back again at the now vacant trenches. Anzac Cove was reached at 0330 hours, and half an hour later the lighter was on its way to the S.S. *Osmanieh,* and Mudros was reached at 9 o'clock. Here the final parties found the rest of the Regiment in camp. On December 22nd the Regiment embarked on H.M.T. *Hororata* and sailed to Egypt. Christmas Day was spent quietly on board, and reaching Alexandria on the 26th, the Regiment disembarked and went by train to its old camp at Zeitoun.

The following Special Order of the Day was issued to all units:—

GENERAL HEADQUARTERS,
21ST DECEMBER, 1915.

The Commander-in-Chief desires to express to all ranks in the Dardanelles Army his unreserved appreciation of the way in which the recent operations, ending in the evacuation of the ANZAC and SUVLA positions, have been carried to an issue successful beyond his hopes. The arrangements made for withdrawal, and for keeping the enemy in ignorance of the operation which was taking place, could not have been improved. The General Officer Commanding Dardanelles Army, and the General Officers Commanding the Australian and New Zealand and 9th Army Corps, may pride themselves on an achievement without parallel in the annals of war. The Army and Corps Staffs, Divisional and subordinate Commanders and their Staffs, and the Naval and Military Beach Staffs, proved themselves more than equal to the most difficult task which could have been thrown upon them. Regimental officers, non-commissioned officers and men carried out, without a hitch, the most trying operation which soldiers can be called upon to undertake—a withdrawal in the face of the enemy—in a manner reflecting the highest credit on the discipline and soldierly qualities of the troops.

It is no exaggeration to call this achievement one without parallel. To disengage and to withdraw from a bold and active enemy is the most difficult of all military operations; and in this case the withdrawal was effected by surprise, with the opposing forces at close grips—in many cases within a few yards of each other. Such an operation, when succeeded by a re-embarkation from an open beach, is one for which military history contains no precedent.

During the past months the troops of Great Britain and Ireland, Australia and New Zealand, Newfoundland and India, fighting side by side, have invariably proved their superiority over the enemy, have contained the best fighting troops in the Ottoman Army in their front, and have prevented the Germans from employing their Turkish allies against us elsewhere.

No soldier relishes undertaking a withdrawal from before the enemy. It is hard to leave behind the graves of good comrades, and to relinquish positions so hardly won and so gallantly maintained as those we have left. But all ranks in the Dardanelles Army will realize that in this matter they were but carrying out the orders of His Majesty's Government, so that they might in due course be more usefully employed in fighting elsewhere for their King, their Country, and the Empire.

There is only one consideration—what is best for the futherance of the common cause. In that spirit the withdrawal was carried out, and in that spirit the Australian and New Zealand and the 9th Army Corps have proved, and will continue to prove, themselves second to none as soldiers of the Empire.

A. LYNDEN BELL, Major-General,
Chief of the General Staff,
Mediterranean Expeditionary Force.

The following telegram was received from His Majesty the king:—

"It gives me the greatest satisfaction to hear of the successful evacuation of SUVLA and ANZAC without loss of troops or guns. Please convey to General Birdwood and those under his command my congratulations upon the able manner in which they have carried out so difficult an operation."

20-12-15. GEORGE, R.I.

John Masefield in his "Gallipoli" says:—

"Still," our enemies say, "you did not win the Peninsula." We did not; and some day, when truth will walk clear-eyed, it will be known why we did not. Until then, let our enemies say this: "They did not win, but they came across three thousand miles of sea, a little army without reserves and short of munitions, a band of brothers, not half of them half-trained, and nearly all of them new to war. They came to what we said was an impregnable fort, on which our veterans of war and massacre had laboured for two months, and by sheer naked manhood they beat us, and drove us out of it. Then rallying, but without reserves, they beat us again, and drove us farther. Then rallying once more, but still without reserves, they beat us again, this time to our knees. Then, had they had reserves, they would have conquered, but by God's pity they had none. Then, after a lapse of time when we were men again, they had reserves. and they hit us a staggering blow, which needed but a push to end us, but God again had pity. After that our God was indeed pitiful, for England made no further thrust, and they went away.''

Major Overton's Grave at Warley Gap.

CHAPTER VI.

How the Regiment Returned to the Horses.

Even from the outbreak of war the protection of the Suez Canal was realised to be of vital importance to the British Empire and her Allies, and early steps were taken to increase the Egyptian Garrison. In February, 1915, notwithstanding the presence of a large force of British troops, Australians, New Zealanders and Indians, a Turkish column actually reached the Canal and launched upon it several pontoons. They were driven back with some loss and retired to Palestine, but the fact remains that they proved that the Turks could reach the Canal. It is not to be wondered at, therefore, if the minds of the Young Turk Party, dominated by their German masters, should not have turned at once to the conquest of Egypt after the great victory they believed that they had won at the Dardanelles. At the very least it was reasonable to expect that every effort would be made by Germany's ally to compel Britain to keep the troops from the Dardanelles in Egypt, and not send them on to France, where reinforcements were urgently required; and grave fears, in the light of the 1915 raid, were felt for the safety of the Suez Canal. The evacuation of Gallipoli had released a great Turkish force from the Peninsular, and it also gave to England a large force of men for whom there was no lack of fresh employment. In February Germany's titanic blow fell on Verdun, and the whole Allied line in France was desperately in need of reinforcements, and British fortunes in Mesopotamia had reached their darkest hour. Additional troops were imperatively needed, both for East and West.

In accordance with this situation orders reached Egypt that the great force was to be reduced as quickly as the reorganisation of the shattered divisions made their embarkation practicable, and they were to be transported without delay to the posts of danger. The Suez Canal, of course, must be made safe, and enough troops left to deal with the Senussi on the western desert, but beyond that and the care of the Soudan every man must be made ready to embark.

Such was the situation when the N.Z.M.R. Brigade returned to its old camp at Zeitoun. Orders were received for all mounted troops to be re-equipped as soon as possible, for they were urgently required for the defence of the Delta against the Senussi on the west and for the Suez Canal on the east.

Capt. T. L. Gibbs, the Regiment's popular Signalling Officer and Adjutant.

Shortly after the Brigade's arrival in Zeitoun, Major J. H. Whyte was transferred from the Wellington Mounted Rifles to the command of the Regiment. Major Powles, who had been in command during the evacuation, returned to Brigade Headquarters to his old appointment of Brigade Major, and Lieutenant Gibbs, who had acted as Adjutant for some months, now had his appointment confirmed.

And now began the work of reorganising. It was nearly nine months since officers and men had left their horses, and there was much discussion on nearing Egypt as to whether the horses would be still at Zeitoun, and if there, whether they would be fit to be ridden. The first glance at the well-kept horse-lines, with their overhead cover for protection from the sun, gave assurance, and great was the delight of the old hands when they found their horses in the pink of condition, the result of the devoted care and attention of a band of transport drivers and reinforcements, assisted by native labour, and good indeed it was to see the shining happy face of many an "old hand" as he wandered down the lines and recognised his own beloved horse.

Major G. F. Hutton, O.C. 8th Squadron.

The Regiment had always been proud of its horses and its horsemastership, and a rigorous overhaul of the reinforcements began, each man being individually tested before being posted to a squadron. Many of the old hands, returned from Hospital, were waiting at the camp to rejoin, but with the large influx of newcomers, officers and men were, to a certain extent, strangers to each other, and it was necessary, if the old mounted efficiency of the Regiment were to be regained that both should be allowed time to discover each others peculiarities and to learn to work together. Instinctively the old hours of training in the desert, that had been in force for so many weary months before Gallipoli, were again resumed. Horses and all necessary equipment, also much that seemed unnecessary, were issued, and the old work was entered into with a new spirit—the old hands keen to display the knowledge that had been taught them before the great adventure of Gallipoli, the reinforcements keen to learn and to prove themselves worthy of the Regiment. No man in the Regiment who had fought on Gallipoli ever forgot that he had enlisted as a mounted soldier, and during the darkest days while fighting and taking his full share as infantry soldiers, in his heart he looked upon the campaign there as something aside from his proper role, almost a sporting digression. The trenches had seen many an interesting discussion as to when and how the campaign would be finished if only the horses could be sent over from Egypt. Though for the time being they became superb infantrymen they never forgot their horses.

Weary and worn and sad at heart at leaving behind so many beloved comrades, and with the added depression of a feeling of bitter disappointment at having been given a job which they had failed to do, the Regiment was inspired by the presence of fresh, fit and enthusiastic reinforcements, and the unbounded pleasure of the "old hands" can well be imagined when for the first time each troop "led" off the lines and "prepared to mount."

So the task of reorganisation became an easy one. These were not the untried squadrons which had camped here in 1914. They were a "band of brothers." On the Peninsular they had engaged in every form of infantry fighting, and had lived for months in trenches only a few yards from the enemy. They had engaged in some of the fiercest fighting known anywhere in the War, and their discipline had been tested in desperate night operations and in the evacuation. They were all masters of the craft of fighting on foot, and the old mounted rifle training came back instinctively.

It was now that the services of the permanent staff N.C.O.s were sadly missed, for with one exception they had all fallen on Gallipoli. Horsemanship being an essential accomplishment for a mounted man, daily riding tests were held, and much care, judgment and patience were exercised in the selection of suitable men from the reinforcements to complete to full establishment the squadrons and machine gun sections.

Indifferent horsemen were sent to the regimental "Detail Squadron" for further instruction. This Detail Squadron and those from the other regiments were formed into a Training Regiment which was drawn upon as required by the units in the field. All training units were later on moved to Moascar, which became for the rest of the War the training depot for the New Zealanders and the Australian Light Horsemen.

The Canterbury Mounted Rifles on parade, Zeitoun, January, 1926—with Brigade Headquarters in front.

At Zeitoun there had been built up during 1915 most excellent Instructional Schools, carried on by selected officers from the British Army. These schools were to the troops in Sinai and Palestine what the training camps on Salisbury Plain and the cadet battalions at Oxford and Cambridge were to the troops in France.

On January 18th, 1916, the usual routine was changed, the whole Brigade being inspected by Colonel R. H. Rhodes, who had come from New Zealand on a special mission for the Government. His visit was particularly welcome to the Canterbury Regiment, for he had been for many years in the C.M.R. (Canterbury Yeomanry Cavalry), and at the outbreak of war held command of this one of the parent regiments of the regiment in the field. By this time rumour had it that the Brigade was to move to the Canal, and on the 22nd orders were received to march the following day.

The route lay through the ancient land of Goshen, past the towns of Nawa and Belbeis, Abou Hamad, Kassassin, Abou Sueir and Moascar, and so through Ismailia, to Serapeum on the Suez Canal, close to the Great Bitter Lake. The trek was not completed till the 29th, on which day as the Brigade rode through Ismailia it was inspected by General Sir Archibald Murray, Commander-in-Chief in Egypt, who was accompanied by General Godley and the Brigade's old commander, General Russell. Throughout the journey the weather had been most unsettled, with heavy rain storms and wind and very cold nights. One cheerful evening was experienced, for at Abou Sueir, the ancient Pithom—the treasure city which the Israelites of old made for Pharoah— a large dump of creosoted railway sleepers was found; fires were quickly going in all directions, clothing was dried and all hands had a hot meal.

However, once in camp the Regiment quickly settled down, and the discomforts of the trek were forgotten in the work of training now recommenced. Rifle shooting, machine gun training, tactical exercises, boxing matches, swimming in the Canal, filled up the day, and the hardships and strain of Gallipoli faded away into the dim past.

Lieut.-Colonel J. Findlay, the Regiment's Commanding Officer, re-joined on February 19th from hospital. He had been seriously wounded at Anzac on the night of August 6th, when leading the Regiment against the Turkish machine guns at Walden Point. He was beloved by all ranks, and his arrival on the lines was heralded by much cheering. "Old John," as he was affectionately known, was to carry the Regiment right through to the end of the War, and to achieve the reputation among the Australians and New Zealanders of being the finest regimental commander in the

Anzac Mounted Division, a reputation second to none, for it must be remembered that the Anzac Mounted Division was the original cavalry formation in the Sinai campaign, and the parent of all cavalry formations that came after, among whom it gained for itself the name of being the finest cavalry division in the E.E.F. To much valuable experience gained in the South African War Colonel Findlay brought an alert mind extraordinarily "quick in the uptake," as the Scotch would say, enabling him with ease and surety to keep abreast of the changing vicissitudes of a modern war. No task was too hard nor day too long for this keen soldier, nor was any matter concerning the good of the Regiment or the comfort of the men too small or too unimportant to be given his full and closest attention.

The Suez Canal at Kantara.

Captain Blair also rejoined from hospital in February, and Major Whyte returned to the Wellington Regiment. Captain Blair took over the duties of Adjutant and Lieutenant Gibbs again became Signalling Officer. Lieutenant Robin Harper, of the machine gun section, was appointed Brigade Machine Gun officer and his brother, Lieutenant Gordon Harper, took over the regimental section.

It was during this period that the New Zealand Division was being formed at Moascar in preparation for its move to France, and to complete the Division it was necessary to form a new infantry brigade and some batteries. To fill these new establishments many officers, N.C.Os and men were taken from the Mounted Brigade and from the Brigade's surplus reinforcements, and the Regiment lost many tried soldiers who had worthily upheld its honour in the desperate fighting on Gallipoli. The officers taken from the Regiment were Majors Blair and Studholme, Captains Free and Wray, Lieutenants Louden, Bishop and Williams. From those on the roll at Zeitoun there were taken Captains Harris, Orr and Talbot, and Lieutenants Hayter, Hayhurst, Jones, Stallard, Dailey, Morrison, Garland, Riley and Harley.

On March 5th we received orders to relieve the 22nd Brigade, A.I.F., in the trenches at Railhead, Ferrypost, and the move was completed by the 7th, the Regiment going into squadron camps. The 8th Squadron, under Major Hammond, and Headquarters were in the centre, calling their camp "Hagley Park"; the 10th Squadron, under Major Hurst, were about 1½ miles north-west, the camp being known as "Nelson Camp"; while the 1st Squadron, under Major Acton Adams, were about two miles south-east of Headquarters in a camp called "Sphinx Post."

There was no doubt about being in the desert now. As far as the eye could see not a tree was to be seen, nothing but miles of sand extending in broken ridges to the horizon. In some places, sharp bold ridges and small hills of sand appeared, but these changed in appearance and height with every wind that blew.

The Brigade was now close to that "Oldest Road in the World"—the Darb El Sultani or the King's Road, along which from time immemorial had marched invaders from east and west, Egyptians and Babylonians, Assyrians and Persians, Greeks and Romans, Crusaders and Saracens, and Napoleon in his attempted conquest of Syria. The Child Christ, fleeing with His parents from the wrath of Herod, came down this road to Egypt.

Sinai, across which this great highway runs, lies as a bridge between Asia and Africa. It is a great waterless tract of burning sand and arid mountains. The Darb el Sultani begins at Kantara (or in Arabic "the crossing"), just where the Nile inundations fail to reach the line of the Bitter Lakes, and, leading across the sands, follows the coast to Southern Palestine. The only other road between Asia and Africa across the Sinai Peninsula strikes south-east and crosses the mountains.

Along the former there are wells in the sand formed by the winter rains, scanty though they be; and along the latter those who passed by in ancient days cut great cisterns in the rock which, filled occasionally by passing thunderstorms, gave sufficient water for small caravans.

The ancient Greek historian Herodotus, who lived some 400 B.C., remarks that "the only entrance into Egypt from Phoenicia is by the desert. Now the whole tract between Jenysus (El Arish) on the one side, and Lake Serbonis and Mount Cassius on the other—and this is no small space, being as much as three days' journey—is a dry desert without a drop of water.

"I shall now mention a thing of which few of those who sailed to Egypt are aware. Twice a year wine is brought into Egypt from every part of Greece in earthen jars, and yet in the whole country you will nowhere see, as I may say, a single jar. What then, everyone will ask, becomes of the jars? This too I will clear up. The burgomaster of each town has to collect the wine jars within his district and to carry them to Memphis, where they are all filled with water by the Memphians, who then convey them to this desert tract. This way of keeping the passage into Egypt fit for use by storing water there was begun by the Persians as soon as they became masters of the country."

General Sir Archibald Murray, the Commander-in-Chief in Egypt, decided that to protect Egypt the oasis area along the Darb el Sultani, the same route the Persians used, should be held, and, to prevent the Turks from advancing through the mountains, the rock cisterns should be emptied. How he provided his own armies with water in this dry region we were soon to see.

The 5th Mounted Brigade (Yeomanry) were sent to the Katia oasis area in conformity with this plan, and the Australian Light Horse completed the destruction of the cisterns.

There were rumours of the enemy being about, and patrols daily scoured the desert in front of the Brigade's position. There was little variation in the work. Patrolling by day far out into the desert and providing standing patrols by night were only varied by cleaning out and improving the trenches of our main line. The weather was hot and work in the trenches during the day was very trying. Sand storms were frequent, continually filling the trenches with sand. As often as this occurred they were dug out again. Any spare time was used in putting up wire entanglements. Yet probably this was one of the happiest times the Regiment had experienced since leaving New Zealand. Officers and men who had been on Gallipoli were rapidly recovering from that strenuous time, and the heat was not as yet too great for health and comfort.

Loading up Camels.

Each squadron had its own allotted task and camp, and the rivalry between them to gain the approval of the C.O. tended to keep everyone in a high state of efficiency. Horses were in the hardest condition, well groomed and well fed. It was here that men began to realise the necessity of keeping the horses perfectly fit, and, although regular stable hours were kept and horses groomed for $2\frac{1}{2}$ to 3 hours daily, yet many men were to be seen at odd times giving their mounts an extra polish. And here it was that the

Regiment learned how to load and how not to load the "Ship of the Desert." For the desert on the east of the Canal is so soft that all wheels were left at Serapeum, and everything that everybody owned had either to be piled somehow on to a camel or be left behind.

Rations were plentiful but monotonous, consisting of tinned beef and hard biscuits. Water was very scarce, and all that was required for drinking and washing and for the horses came to the camps on camels, each carrying two fantasies, as the large tin vessels were called, holding fourteen gallons apiece.

H.R.H. the Prince of Wales, riding round the Regiment's Lines, March 21st., 1916.

On March 21st we were visited by H.R.H. Prince of Wales, who inspected the trenches and camps. Accompanied by Colonel Findlay, he rode round the front line to Sphinx Post, where he had lunch, and then returned through the camps. As many men as could be spared from patrol were in the camps to meet the Prince, who charmed all ranks by his genuine interest in all he saw.

Visits of inspection were made by Generals Godley, Russell and Chaytor towards the end of the month.

About this time rumours of another move passed through the camps, and the appearance of a brigade of the Australian

Imperial Forces lent colour to this. On the last day of March orders were received to move back to Serapeum the following day. Accordingly the Regiment handed over its lines to the Australians and rode to Railhead, where it joined the rest of the Brigade. A hot and dusty ride followed, back to the old camp at Serapeum. But the stay here was short, for on the 6th the Brigade was again on the march; this time to Salhia, which was reached on the 7th after camping one night at Moascar.

This move to Salhia, the place from which Napoleon set forth upon his attempt to conquer Palestine, and where he organised the army that reached Acre, was made for the purpose of concentrating the newly formed Australian and New Zealand Mounted Division (afterwards commonly called Anzac Mounted Division). It consisted of the following:—

New Zealand Mounted Rifle Brigade.
1st Australian Light Horse Brigade.
2nd Australian Light Horse Brigade.
3rd Australian Light Horse Brigade.
4 Territorial R.H.A. Batteries—2 Scottish and 2 English (The Ayrs and Inverness and the Somersets and Leicesters), equipped with the 18-pdr. guns.

The old training recommenced, varied by compass and map work for officers and N.C.O.s. A football match between the officers of W.M.R. and the Canterbury Regiment caused great excitement, though probably not much first-class football. The game resulted in a draw, no score; but it was freely asserted by both sides that the referee, a veterinary officer, always blew his whistle if either team seemed likely to score.

Here was experienced a heavy sandstorm that lasted the whole of one day. Tents were blown down and everything smothered in sand. Towards evening the storm subsided, but it seemed days before one felt clean again. The sand seemed to penetrate the very pores of the skin.

At 3 p.m. on April 23rd, Easter Sunday, orders were received to be ready to move at 8 p.m. to Kantara, on the Suez Canal. The Brigade was to travel as light as possible, and any surplus baggage was to follow when transport could be arranged. Gift stores from New Zealand had been issued that day, but there was little hope of carrying them. No reason was given for this hurried move, but it subsequently became known that a Turkish force, under cover of a dense fog, had attacked and inflicted heavy losses upon the Yeomanry advanced posts in the desert at the wells of Katia and Oghratina.

CHAPTER VII.

Of the Crossing of the Canal and the Advance into the Sinai Desert.

After a long and weary march across the sand in the darkness the Canal was reached at daylight. There was some excitement at the sweet water canal near Kantara. The only means of crossing this was a railway bridge with planks laid between the rails. There were no sides to the bridge, and it was a matter of crossing in single file. The majority of the horses took it quietly, but some, whose owners had evidently been visiting the feed bin in unauthorised hours, were feeling above themselves. One long sergeant of the 1st Squadron let his horse go, thereby saving himself a ducking, to the audible regret of those watching. In the end all were safely across with the loss of one horse killed.

Kantara East was reached at 7 a.m., and after halting for an hour the Brigade rode on to Hill 70, about five miles east of Kantara, and bivouacked, thus completing a forced march of 37 miles. All sorts of rumours were flying about, some that the Turks were advancing on Kantara, after having smashed the Yeomanry at Quatia; others that they had retired again. Reliable news was scarce, and beyond the fact that Duiedar had been successfully defended, nothing could be learnt.

On the 25th the Regiment moved to the head of the military railway that Sir Archibald Murray was beginning to push across the desert, and camped at what was known as the "Loop," later called "Canterbury Post."

The Anzac Mounted Division had taken over the outer line of No. 3 Section Canal Defences, and established posts of Light Horse at Dueidar and Romani, fifteen and twenty miles respectively from the Canal, with the Canterbury Regiment guarding Railhead.

Patrols and escorts were now the order of the day, but there was no sign of the enemy. Daily patrols visited

Advance into Sinai Desert

Duiedar and Romani, connecting there with the Australian Light Horse.

Rations and water were short for men and animals, all supplies of both these necessaries having to come by rail from Kantara. Probably nobody yet realised the difficulty of keeping a large number of men and animals in the desert, and Headquarters at Kantara had not reached the height of efficiency they were to attain in later days. However, there was very little grumbling, everybody still hoping for a chance of a brush with the enemy.

But there was very little to vary the monotony of the patrols till May 10th, when the Regiment was ordered to Romani. Kits had arrived during the stay at the Loop, and everything had to be moved. Fortunately camels were plentiful at this time, and the whole camp, with tents and baggage, were moved in one load. This was the only occasion during the whole campaign when sufficient transport was available to move everything with the Regiment, and it was only possible now because the camel camp was close by at Railhead, and the camels had to go to Romani for water, whether required by the Regiment or not.

One night only was spent at Romani, and on the 11th the Regiment moved across to Bir et Maler. Here there were no wells, but plenty of water could be obtained two or three feet from the surface. Fatigue parties soon got to work, some digging wells, and others fixing the horse troughs. These consisted of a piece of canvas about twenty yards long stretched by a rope on each end, the sides being held in an upright position by wooden pegs at regular intervals. The pegs were composed of three pieces of wood which fitted into each other, forming three sides of a square, and when dismantled were easily packed. Sometimes when sandbags were plentiful foundations were built for the troughs, but usually the troughs were resting on the sand. The water at Bir et Maler was brackish, and not fit for human consumption. However, it was all there was for the horses, and although some of them at first refused to drink, nothing better being available they soon took to it.

It was a remarkable thing that the water obtained in the desert wells, perhaps only a hundred yards apart, varied very much in quality. Some wells were too salt even to wash in, and others close by were comparatively good for all purposes except drinking. Even the best of the desert wells, such as Katia, would not brew tea; though during some of the long reconnaissances, very little fresh water being available, the men did use it by making strong cocoa, but it was necessity that made it palatable, just as it was necessity that made it imperative for the troops to drink the well-water when the camel-borne supply was insufficient. Well-digging in the sand is a difficult and tedious business, necessitating the removal of immense quantities of sand before the water can

Horse Trough and Pump in the Desert.

be reached; and many camel loads of timber had to be carried with the troops to provide the necessary sheathing to keep out the sand. Much satisfaction therefore was felt by the whole Division when the Field Engineers perfected what was called the "Spear Point Pump." A $2\frac{1}{2}$ inch pipe was pointed and perforated. This was driven into the water area by means of a small "monkey," or by a sledge-hammer; and additional lengths added if necessary. The ordinary G.S. "Lift and Force Pump" was then attached.

The old game of looking for the enemy continued, but the patrols were now in new and more interesting country. There were occasional hods with clumps of palms where welcome shade from the sun could be obtained; the battle grounds at Katia, Hamisah and Oghratina, where many of the Yeomanry fought their last fight only a short time before, were full of interest. In these places small mounds of empty cartrige cases marked the Yeomanry positions, and enabled us to form some idea of their fight. As battles measured by the standard of the Great War these had been unquestionably minor affairs only; nevertheless they provided valuable instruction, for this was the first time mounted troops had been engaged on the Sinai front.

Ordinary troop patrols, carried out by an officer and twenty to twenty-five men, were varied by an occasional reconnaissance by the whole Brigade, entailing long tiring days in the hot sun, and heavy responsibilities. On the information they brought in, the safety of the whole force might rest. Small parties of men left camp in the darkness of the early morning bound for Katia, Oghratina or Mageibra. Once clear of the camp they spread out in one line, riding three or four yards apart, with a section of four men in diamond formation in front and two men far out on each flank. As daylight increased the men in front and on the flanks spread out and kept further away from the main body, but never so far that they could not communicate by signals. The distance varied in broken country; sometimes they might be within a couple of hundred yards of the troop, on open plains eight hundred to one thousand yards away. The section in front took their direction from the troop; as the latter turned, so did they. Out in the desert where the different landmarks constantly changed, the compass and map carried by the troop leader were the only guide. Riding on, halting only to spell their horses for a few short minutes, they would probably reach the particular spot they were bound for about 11 a.m. Posting a lookout with a pair of field glasses on the most prominent ridge, the rest of the party would make a thorough search through the palms for any trace of the enemy, such as camel tracks, footmarks, or signs of fires. Nothing being discovered, sections would then go out a couple of miles south and east on further reconnaissance. Stray Bedouins, of whom there were a few in the larger hods, were brought in to be interrogated, and then sent to concentration camps in Egypt. About 2 o'clock the troop would start to return to camp. The formation was still the same, except for a rear section who now watched behind them. At dusk they

1st (C.Y.C.) Squadron Officers.

would still be some distance from camp, and then the stars were used as a guide. Riding on, the deep silence of the desert broken only by the swish of the horses' feet in the sand, or the howl of a desert dog, the patrol would listen with anxious ears for the challenge from the night post in front of the camp. The answer given, the patrol passes through. Half an hour's ride brings it to its own lines, where a welcome and hot tea awaits the tired men. The troop leader goes to make his report, and the day is ended. Very few of these patrols covered less than thirty miles a day, and sometimes considerably more. Map distances show an air line of probably twelve miles, but dodging steep terraces of sand, riding in and out and about sand dunes, would increase that to twenty.

So the Regiment learned to live in the desert, even as the Bedouin lived, and to realise, in this waste of sands, man's dependence on his horse. And here it was that the horsemastership so earnestly impressed on all ranks by that capable veterinarian, Major Stafford, came to that high pitch of excellence which stood the New Zealand Mounted Brigade in such good stead in the years to come, a standard that eventually impressed itself upon the whole Anzac Mounted Division.

May 7th and 8th were occupied in cutting a canal from the sea to the western end of the Sabkat el Bardawil, the great salt marsh which stretches for some 50 miles along the coast between Port Said and El Arish. The Arab name means Baldwin's Marsh, after the Crusader King Baldwin, of Jerusalem, who died nearby in 1118 A.D., and it is the Lake Serbonis of Herodotus, and was the Pelusiac arm of the Nile through which all the Mediterranean trade reached Egypt in those ancient days. Upon its banks stood the city of Pelusium, whose site is now known as Tel el Farama, and whose glory faded away after the earthquake which closed this branch of the mighty river for ever. The object of this canal was to flood the Bardawil so as to furnish an additional protection to the Suez Canal, but as fast as the cutting through the sand was made the waves filled it up again and the project was abandoned.

On May 15th and 16th a regimental reconnaissance was carried out to Oghratina, and patrols were pushed forward as far as Bir el Abd. An enemy camel patrol was sighted, but refused to stay to be interviewed. The 1st Squadron carried out a separate patrol to Mageibra, but did not sight anything. On the 16th a khamsin was blowing, and the heat was almost unbearable. By midday, in the shade of the palms at Oghratina, the thermometer registered 129 degrees, and the 1st Squadron reported 124 degrees at Mageibra. Men and animals suffered severely. No drinking water, other than the water bottles carried by each man, was available, and the flow of brackish water in the shallow wells was insufficient for the horses. The sand carts of the Ambulance were soon full of men, suffering from the extreme heat, and at 6.30 p.m. the Colonel decided to return to Bir el Maler, which was eventually reached in the early hours of the morning of the 17th. As a result of the heat, four officers and nineteen men were evacuated to hospital, and many more were unfit for duty for some days.

This, the first experience of a khamsin in the desert, was an eye-opener to all. There were no shower-baths or cool drinks available now. There was a job to do, and khamsin or no khamsin, the work had to be done. Riding on, dripping with perspiration, dazzled by the glaring soft yellow sand, praying for a cool breeze and meeting instead a continuous blast from a glassy furnace that seemed to burn the skin, racked by an insatiable thirst, and with the water in the water-bottles too hot to drink, is it to be wondered at that men, unaided by a compass, lost all sense of direction. One could well understand the stories hitherto laughed at, of men who went mad in the desert. This was a typical reconnaissance, though the heat was abnormal, and the report sent in by Colonel Findlay will show how the thorough knowledge of the country to be fought over was built up. The total distance was thirty-six miles as the crow flies, probably about fifty miles in actual riding.

CANTERBURY MOUNTED RIFLES REGIMENT.
BIR ETMALER.   17th MAY, 1916.
         Report on Reconnaissance to Hod ed Dababis.
REFERENCE MAP, KATIA, 1/100,000.

    The Regiment, less one squadron (1st), moved out of camp at Bir Etmaler at 1400 on Monday, 15th May, 1916, and marched via Hod Umm Ugba to Oghratina, arriving there at 1830.

Advance into Sinai Desert

Signal communication was maintained throughout. At Hod Umm Ugba there is one good well (built) and good water, but barely sufficient to water one troop. At Oghratina good shelter for one regiment in palm trees. Camped half a mile west of Hod, near position of Yeomanry camp. Position not good for regiment—too many men required for outpost duties, but the position best available. Camped here for the night, and moved out at 0430, reaching Hod ed Dababis at 0600. At Hod en Negiliat good shelter for a regiment. No wells dug. Plenty of water at Hod ed Dababis. No wells made, but easily obtainable. Passed through Hod el Atsham en route. No made wells, but water obtainable although very brackish. Shelter here for one regiment. At 0515 after leaving Oghratina, captured an unarmed Turk two miles N.E. of Oghratina. Lt. Priest examined prisoner through interpreter. Report attached. Advanced guard pushed on to Bir el Afein. Three built wells. Water foul. Cleaned out one well without improvement. At 0700 the advanced outpost sighted three Turks on camels two miles east of Bir el Afein. Patrol pursued them to Bir el Abu, but did not come into touch with them. One built well at Bir el Abu, but very brackish.

Communication was maintained by telephone to Brigade Headquarters, and to W.M.R. Regiment on Hill 102 by heliograph. Failed to get any communication with the Light Horse Regiment. Waited until 1200 and then decided to return, advising Brigade Headquarters our intentions. Weather very hot. Outposts and Signallers suffered severely. Halted at Hod el Atshaw for ten minutes and then moved to Oghratina. At Hod Dababis defence position good for a Brigade or a Regiment.

At Bir el Abu about 20 fresh camel marks were noticed moving to the east. Reached camp 2200. Horses stood journey well.

J. FINDLAY, Lt.-Colonel,
Commanding Canterbury M.R. Regt.

On the 29th, 30th and 31st another reconnaissance was made, this time by the whole Brigade, accompanied by an 18-pounder gun (mounted on wheels with ped-rail attachment) from the Ayrshire battery. The object was to endeavour to find out the strength of the enemy at Salmana, but to avoid a serious engagement. This meant night work, and night marching in the desert is not easy. With a compass, a map and the stars as a guide, there were thirty miles to travel into the desert to find a pinprick on the map, not the simplest matter if one could go straight on a given bearing, but sometimes the route led north, south and east in the space of a few miles. It was just as if one were keeping a sailing ship at sea on her course; due allowances and careful calculations had to be made at every turn, together with a very strict and accurate estimate of the distance marched. It was indeed surprising to find how many men possessed an inborn sense of direction and locality.

The Brigade marched out of Et Maler at 10 p.m. on May 29th, and, travelling all night, reached Dababis, at 7 o'clock the next morning, and rested there all day.

Leaving Dababis at 9 p.m. on the 30th the Brigade advanced. The Canterbury Regiment led, with the 10th Squadron as vanguard. Passing through Bir el Abd, which was found all clear, the 1st Squadron was ordered to attack Salmana from the north, while the 10th Squadron pushed straight on, the 8th Squadron being held in reserve. Auckland Mounted Rifles were on the right. At 4.30 a.m. shots were exchanged with an outpost of the enemy near Salmana, but the post very soon bolted, leaving four dead. The situation was just developing when orders were received to retire. Evidently the staff had learned all they required about the enemy's strength, but the men were disappointed. However, orders were orders, and the return journey was at once commenced. Stopping to feed and water horses at Dababis and at Oghratina, the Regiment eventually arrived at Bir et Maler at 11.30 p.m. on the 31st.

At half past six on the morning of June 1st sounds of loud explosions at the Australian Light Horse camp at Romani were heard. These were caused by enemy aircraft bombing the camps in return for the New Zealand Brigade's visit to Salmana. A number of men and horses were killed and wounded in the 1st Light Horse Brigade camp, and thenceforward for the rest of the campaign the Turk lost no opportunity of dropping bombs upon the horses. Being bombed from the air is probably the worst experience that men undergo in modern warfare. One sees a plane flying at anything from three to eight thousand feet up; then comes the sound, a whirr, gradually rising to a shrill shriek of the descending bomb, then the explosion and a cloud of thick blackish grey smoke slowly rising from the ground. If the bomb falls into horse lines the sight is not a pleasant one. Men and animals are gashed and torn in an indescribable manner. A curious thing about bombs from the air is that one falling even a mile away seems by the sound to be dropping from directly overhead.

On June 4th Major Wain, the second in command, was invalided, and Major Acton-Adams was appointed in his place. This caused a general shuffle of officers. Major Hurst took command of the 1st Squadron, with Captain D. S. Murchison as second in command. Major Hammond remained with the 8th, with Captain Blackett as second; while Major Bruce took over the 10th, with Captain Gorton as his second in command. During this month also Colonel Findlay temporarily commanded the Brigade, handing over for the time the command of the Regiment to Major Acton Adams.

"Ginger" and Haggerty.

On June 5th and 6th a special reconnaissance was carried out to Bir el Abd, but beyond a few fresh camel tracks, no trace of the enemy was seen.

Reconnaissances, in strength, now seemed to be the fashion. One was carried out to Mageibra on the 10th and 11th, in which a night fog had to be contended with, of so great a denseness that members of the 1st Squadron to this day still talk of it! and on the 14th and 15th reconnaissances were carried out to Katia and Hamisah, in conjunction with the Australian Light Horse.

The march to Mageibra on the 10th and 11th was most trying to all concerned. The difficulties of travelling in the desert by night are very great, but with a dense fog added they become well nigh insuperable. All sense of direction is lost, and the problem of keeping in touch between troops and between the advanced guard and the main body is an additional worry. Everything is so black that one cannot distinguish the man riding alongside. All one is able to see is a darker mass in the fog. At last, worried as to your present position, you halt, and, with the aid of an electric torch, if you have one, or a carefully shaded match, consult your map. You work out the different bearings you have been travelling on and the time occupied in marching, and then decide your approximate position, and you go on, trusting to luck and a sight of the stars if the fog should lessen.

Days in camp were full of work; "stand to" in the morning added to the strain, while patrols and fatigues took up all the rest of the day. The hot weather, lack of suitable food and scarcity of drinking water was affecting everybody. Sick parades had largely increased, and many men were suffering from septic sores. Yet very few men were evacuated to hospitals. "Stand to" meant that the camp was aroused an hour and a half to two hours before daylight. All horses were saddled and everything and everybody ready to move out at a moment's notice. The vitality of man is supposed to be at its lowest during these hours, and according to theory, though it was not found so in practice, this is the time selected by an enemy to attack a hostile force. About this time a message from General Headquarters gave great pleasure to all ranks. General Murray, in a letter to the Divisional Commander, said: "Whatever I ask your people to do is done without the slightest hesitation and with promptness and efficiency. I have the greatest admiration for all your Command."

The month of June was memorable for the fact that leave to go to Port Said was granted to ten per cent. of all ranks for two days at a time.

But relief was in sight, and a return was made to Hill 70 for a spell. Leaving camp at 10 p.m. on the 23rd the Regiment

ADVANCE INTO SINAI DESERT

marched all night and arrived at Hill 70 at daylight on the 24th. Here was more comfort. Tents were plentiful and some shelters were provided for the horses. Fresh water was available from a pipe line that had been laid from Kantara. Arrangements were rapidly completed for squadrons to camp for a week at a time at Kantara, so that the men could have the benefit of the bathing in the Suez Canal. The 10th Squadron was the first to go, being relieved by the 8th, who in turn were relieved by the 1st, the place of the absent squadron being taken by a squadron of the Warwickshire Yeomanry.

On July 3rd the 1st and 8th Squadrons went to Dueidar to act as supports to the 5th Australian Light Horse Regiment, who were carrying out a raid on Bir el Jefeir. Nothing exciting occurred, and both squadrons returned the following day.

On the 17th two members of the old main body, Sergts. D. A. Lusk and A. J. Black, left to join the New Zealand section of the Imperial Camel Corps, both receiving commissions as 2nd Lieutenants. Lieutenant J. G. McCallum went to the same unit with the rank of captain to command the New Zealand Company. Sorry as the Regiment was to lose them, yet it was promotion well earned by all three. McCallum led his company with conspicuous success till he fell, mortally wounded, at Rafa six months later.

While at Hill 70, Lewis guns were issued to each troop, and the machine guns were withdrawn from all regiments and formed into a separate unit, consisting of 8 officers and 221 other ranks with 12 Maxim guns, which were replaced by Vickers guns later in the campaign. This doubled the original machine gun power of the Brigade. 2nd Lieut. R. P. Harper was promoted Captain, and took over the command of the New Zealand Machine Gun Squadron, in which Lieutenant Gordon Harper and Sergt. Craven, both of this Regiment, were appointed section commanders, the latter being promoted 2nd Lieutenant.

On the evening of July 18th the country to the east of Romani had been reported clear of the enemy except for small parties, both by British airmen and by the Light Horse

reconnaissances which were made daily from Romani by the
1st and 2nd Light Horse Brigades, to the latter of which
the W.M.R. was at this time attached. On the following day,
an air reconnaissance with General Chaytor, the Brigade Commander, as observer, discovered long lines of Turks approaching
westward in the vicinity of Bir Bayud, Jamiel and Bir Salmana
on a frontage of approximately eight miles.

Capt. R. E. Harper, M.G. Officer.

Immediate steps were taken by the Divisional Commander
to keep in touch with the enemy and to draw him on to
the Romani position, which was now held on a frontage
of about six miles by the 52nd Division, who had their left
resting on the sea at Mahemdiya and their right on the huge
sand-hill Katib Gannit. This position, well dug in and wired,
covered Railhead, but was open on its right or southern end
where it was guarded by the 1st and 2nd Light Horse Brigades.
Further south on the old road was Dueidar, held by the 5th
Light Horse Regiment and backed up by the New Zealand
Mounted Brigade at Hill 70. The 5th Light Horse Regiment
was included in General Chaytor's command, taking the

place of the Wellington Mounted Rifles, still attached to the 2nd Light Horse Brigade. Hostile aircraft flew over the camps, but no bombing occurred, although the horse lines must have provided a splendid target. On the 29th a patrol under Lieuts. Macfarlane and Mathias went to Bir el Nuss to watch the enemy, returning three days later after an interesting trip.

Very little news was available, but what there was served to show that the Turk meant to make a bold bid for Egypt. Daily he pressed forward, from Bir el Abd to Oghratina, thence to Er Rabah and so on to Katia, steadily consolidating his positions as he advanced. By the end of the month it was known that he might attack any day. Every would-be tactician in the Regiment had his own idea of what the Regiment's role should be when this occurred. The idea that found most favour was that General Chaytor's force should make a flank attack from the south, while the infantry defended Romani. The man who put this forward had a friend, who, in turn, had received it from the General's batman. Sick parades were nil, and the few men detailed under the doctor's orders to remain at the camp grumbled and growled. They pointed out how even the Medical Service had deteriorated when a blank fossil like that could not tell the difference between a fit and an unfit man. Even the M.O. grew short tempered during those days of waiting, and woe-be-tide anybody within reach if he discovered even a cigarette butt during his daily inspection of the camp.

CHAPTER VIII.

Of the Battle called Romani, but which might have been named the Second Battle of Pelusium.

"And the Egyptians lay encamped on the banks of the Nile, which runs by Pelusium, awaiting Cambyses. The Persians crossed the desert and, pitching their camp close to the Egyptians, made ready for battle. Stubborn was the fight that followed, and it was not until vast numbers had been slain that the Egyptians turned and fled."—Herodotus.

Now the ruins of ancient Pelusium are to this day to be seen a few miles from the wells of Romani, and it was just outside Pelusium in the year 528 B.C. that the invading Persians conquered the Egyptians. Upon this self same ground, 2,500 years later, the invaders of Egypt were to be defeated in the battle of Romani.

In the early hours of the morning of August 4th orders were received to be ready to move at 8 a.m. With the Regiment as advanced guard the Brigade moved in the direction of Dueidar, and heavy firing could be heard away in the direction of Romani. It looked as though the General's batman was right, but after travelling about three miles towards the east the direction of the march was changed north towards Canterbury Post. Nobody knew why, but later it was learnt that the Turks were making a flank attack on the railway in conjunction with their main attack on Romani, and that the Brigade was to hold them, and, if possible, drive them back.

Skilfully led by guides, who evidently knew every foot of the British position, the enemy had attacked in three columns, one, a holding attack well backed by artillery upon the 52nd Division in their entrenched position, and the two other columns upon the open flank between Katib Gannit and the caravan route. These two columns encountered the outpost line held by the 1st Light Horse Brigade, and they attacked it about midnight on August 4th.

This Brigade gallantly withstood the attack, and, backed up by the 2nd Light Horse Brigade, slowly fell back pivoting on their left, where it joined the 52nd Brigade.

The Turks' attack was well led, and having overwhelming numbers they pressed back the Australians almost to the railway line and established themselves on the big sandhill, Mt. Royston. It was this determined thrust that had caused General Lawrence, who commanded all the troops in this section of the Canal defences, to divert the N.Z. Brigade from its original plan of a wide flanking movement.

Mount Royston.

By 10.30 a.m. touch was obtained with the enemy, who were holding a strong position on Mt. Royston, and the Brigade immediately attacked with the Canterbury Regiment leading. The 1st Squadron was in the centre, with the 8th and 10th Squadrons on its right and left, and the Auckland Mounted Rifles in close support. The 5th Australian Light Horse Regiment, who took the place in the Brigade of the Wellington Regiment fighting with the 2nd Light Horse

Brigade, were to join up on the right of the 8th Squadron, but did not arrive in time. Some Yeomanry came up on the left, and at 3 o'clock in the afternoon a general advance was made by the Canterbury and Auckland Regiments under cover of the fire from the Somerset battery. The enemy resisted stubbornly, but by half-past five they were driven off the hill and the railway was safe, and the turning point in the Battle of Romani had been made. A large number of prisoners were taken, the Brigade alone capturing over one thousand, besides machine guns and a complete mountain battery. Field glasses were very scarce, and those issued being of a poor quality, competition was very keen for the Zeiss glasses of the prisoners, but very few were secured.

The 42nd Infantry Division came up and took over the line as darkness set in, and the Regiment rode to the railway at Canterbury Post to water horses and bivouac for the night, tired out but happy with the thought that the Turk had been hammered in this the Regiment's first fight in the desert. Considering the heavy fire and lack of cover, casualties were light, due to the skilful handling of their squadrons by the Squadron Commanders and the fine initiative of the individual men.

By half-past three on the morning of the 5th the Brigade was off again, this time to Bir el Nuss; thence on to Katia, passing on the way a complete field hospital abandoned by the enemy.

The Turks were reported to be holding Katia in strength. Orders were issued for the N.Z. Brigade to attack from the south, the 3rd Australian Light Horse Brigade to clear Hamisah and come up on the right, while the 1st and 2nd Light Horse Brigades and the Yeomanry attacked from the north-west and west. A great line of galloping horses went right at the Katia oasis. Shell fire was unheeded, bullets buried themselves in the sand-dunes as the horses surged over them, and then, the ground becoming too swampy to hold the horses, the men dismounted and went in on foot.

Heavy machine gun and rifle fire swept the ground, and the enemy artillery searched the sandhills for the horses. The attack on foot was steadily pressed, and if the 3rd

Australian Brigade had come up on the right the enemy would have been caught in large numbers before he could get away from the oasis. Throughout the long afternoon the Regiment hung on waiting for this promised attack, but it did not come, and at 8 p.m. orders were received to break off the action and return to water at Bir et Maler.

Machine Guns in Action.

Considerable difficulty was experienced in getting the wounded away, but by half-past nine the Regiment was again in the saddle. A reaction had now set in, and the men and animals were feeling the strain. During the short halts that night it was no uncommon thing to see the horses, as soon as their riders dismounted, lie down on the sand, thoroughly tired out. The ride to bivouac was made more tiring by a stupid guide who lost himself and made the journey hours longer than necessary. This guide had been specially selected by the Division, but any N.C.O. in the Regiment could have done better.

Two hours' rest only, and the Brigade was again moving out towards Katia. The Infantry had left earlier with the heavy artillery, and if the Turks were still there they would have to contend with a force much superior to that of the previous day. But they did not wait. Lieutenant Bowron, with one troop, who went out to scout for the infantry, found Katia deserted and the enemy retired upon Oghratina. The infantry remained at Katia whilst the mounted men pushed on to watch the movements of the enemy. This day was an easy day compared with the last two, pressure being kept on the enemy, sufficient to keep knowledge of his movements. At dusk the Brigade withdrew to Rabah for the night. Touch was kept with the enemy all night by means of officers' patrols.

The heat since leaving Hill 70 on the morning of the 4th had been steadily increasing, and officers and men suffered severely, several having to be evacuated to hospital. The 7th was a replica of the 6th, the enemy being driven back to Negiliat, whence he made great play with his guns. We were on the move again by 3.30 a.m. on the 8th, but the enemy had again withdrawn, and was now holding a strong position at Bir el Abd. The Regiment remained all day at Debabis and finally bivouaced there for the night. This spell was very welcome to all.

Horse Lines in the Desert.

Next morning, August 9th, all available mounted troops were on the move before daylight. The Turks were reported to be holding Bir el Abd in strength. The attack was to be made from the west and south-west, and the 1st and 2nd Australian Light Horse Brigades combined were to attack the north flank of the enemy. The 3rd Australian Light Horse Brigade was ordered to pass south of the enemy, and then come into action from the direction of Salmana, thereby cutting his line of retreat, and menacing his rear. At 5.30 a.m. our advanced regiment, Auckland Mounted Rifles, was fired on, and the 8th Squadron went up in support of its left. Almost at once they were heavily engaged, and the two remaining squadrons of the Regiment came into action on the left of the 8th Squadron. The Regiment's right flank now rested on the old caravan route, the left feeling round towards the 2nd Light Horse Brigade. The 8th Squadron pushed steadily on, driving the enemy off a low sandy ridge facing east. The 1st and 10th Squadrons advanced at the same time, finally securing the high ground west of Bir el Abd, the Canterbury Regiment being on the left of the "Old Road" and the Aucklanders on the right of it, and later the 5th Light Horse Regiment, still temporarily attached to the Brigade, came up on the right of the Auckland Regiment. The main Turkish defences could now be seen. They consisted of a series of entrenched redoubts with rifle pits in front. Later it was found that all these redoubts were connected by telephone with their artillery—three batteries of 77 m.m. and one 4.2 battery and several 5.9 inch howitzers.

Against these the Anzac Mounted Division had only four batteries of 18 pounders.

The Turks had about 6,000 men in the line against our total of about 3,000 dismounted rifles. They were mostly reinforcements from El Arish who had not been engaged at Romani, while our men were suffering from extreme physical exhaustion.

The task before the British force was therefore formidable and the only chance of success was, as at Katia, that the 3rd Light Horse Brigade should succeed in beating down the enemy's extended left flank and in shaking the Bir el Abd defences by threatening the Turks communications.

Up till now their artillery had been annoying, but did not cause much damage, but once the high ridge facing the Oasis was crossed our men were in full view of their gunners. The 8th Squadron were in the most exposed position and suffered severely. Lieutenant Menzies, signalling officer, was killed, and Major Hammond and Lieutenant Blakeney dangerously wounded.

Early in the fight the Turks began to disclose their strength. Soon after 6 o'clock they advanced with the bayonet in their first counter attack, but were stopped by the

Lieut. Robin Harper, afterwards commanded Divisional M.G. Squadron.

Lieut. Gordon Harper commanded M.G. Troop.

Canterburys and Aucklanders, aided by the splendid shooting of the Somerset Battery, which, as usual, fought with the N.Z.M.R. Brigade.

The line was again advanced until the Canterbury and Auckland Regiments were well down the forward slopes leading to the wells, but by 10.30 a.m. the enemy guns showed increased activity, severely handling the combined 1st and 2nd Light Horse Brigades on the left.

The Warwickshire Yeomanry now came up to reinforce the N.Z.M.R. Brigade, and the increased activity apparent among the Turks indicated that they were making every effort to get away their supplies and transport.

Shortly before noon came the second counter-attack, and the full force was received by the Regiment, but every man held firmly to his ground, and by accurate and deliberate fire, aided most effectively by the fine shooting of the machine guns, the successives waves of enemy infantry were shattered.

By 2 p.m. the enemy's counter-attack was in full progress along the whole of the line, and both the Light Horse Brigades on the left and the 3rd Light Horse Brigade on the right began to give round, the regiments retiring for about a mile under heavy punishment with every available man in the line. As the Turks recognised the possibility of overwhelming the British force, their gun fire gathered intensity until it reached a degree of severity unknown either at Romani or on Gallipoli.

The New Zealand Brigade was now in a very difficult position in being well down the forward slopes with both flanks exposed, and had it not been for the accurate shooting of each individual man, backed up by the machine guns and the Somerset Battery, the entire Brigade would have been overwhelmed.

At 5.30 p.m. General Chauvel ordered a general withdrawal. It was recognised that this would be a difficult task, but, provided the horses could be reached, the heavy ground would save the regiments from a hand to hand encounter with superior forces of the enemy's fresh troops. As soon as the movement was perceived the Turks assaulted strongly, and such was the position of the N.Z.M.R. Brigade that General Chaytor decided that the better course was to hang on until dark.

Just at dusk after a very heavy attack which fell chiefly upon the Aucklanders, the latter withdrew with the 5th Light Horse Regiment and the Yeomanry, leaving the Canterbury Regiment as rear guard.

A great fight had been put up by the machine guns, and under their cover the Regiment slowly withdrew. Lieutenant Gordon Harper, the gallant commander of the section of guns attached to the Regiment, was mortally wounded and brought out with great difficulty by his famous brother Captain Robin Harper, O.C. Machine Gun Squadron, who had all guns available playing on the advancing Turks, breaking up their attack when within 100 yards of the New Zealand position.

M.R. Graves at Bir el Abd.

As has been already told, Captain Hammond of the 8th Squadron had been wounded earlier in the day. Though suffering from illness on the morning of the battle and recommended for evacuation to hospital, he insisted on remaining with and leading his squadron, and fought his men with great brilliancy and determination throughout the long day.

Colonel Findlay, on hearing that Captain Hammond had been severely wounded and could not be moved, worked his way up to the firing line, and, though managing to escape the heavy machine gun and rifle fire, was wounded in the hand by a piece of the shell which mortally wounded Lieutenant Gordon Harper. The care and evacuation of the wounded was an exceedingly difficult task, and much praise was due to the M.O., Captain R. Orbell, and his stretcher bearers, for the excellent work they performed throughout these trying days. Visual signalling was out of the question at Bir el Abd, but the signallers carried out all that was required of them as runners; and for the maintenance of communications throughout the day R.S.M. Denton deserves great praise, and as a runner Trooper Graham Scales did yeoman service.

The Brigade withdrew to Debabis, carrying back the wounded, who were sent to Railhead at Romani by camel cacolets, and suffered extremely from the jolting.

The 10th and 11th were spent quietly at Debabis, and the time was occupied in reorganising. Lieutenant Macfarlane took over the 10th Squadron, vice Major Bruce evacuated to hospital; Lieutenant Wood the 8th, in place of Major Hammond killed in action; and Captain D. S. Murchison the 1st, from Major Hurst, wounded. R.S.M. Denton, S.S.M. Parkinson and Sergeant J. Tennant were promoted 2nd Lieutenants.

The 12th saw the Regiment again on the move. Bir el Abd was found to be evacuated, but the advanced guard came in touch with the enemy posts about two miles west of Hod Salmana. The Regiment sat and watched them all day under an intermittent shell fire, but neither side seemed very keen on forcing a fight. At dusk the Turks withdrew towards El Arish.

And so ended a week that few who went through are likely to forget. During the long hot days the sufferings from lack of water and food were harder to bear than the fire of the enemy, and the nights were taken up by long rides back to Railhead to draw rations and fodder. The few minutes of rest were broken by patrols and fatigues, though the latter were cut down to an absolute minimum. But through all difficulties the men behaved magnificently. In action or out of it they earned the highest praise, worthily maintaining the Regiment's great reputation.

The result of these operations was the complete defeat of an enemy force of 18,000 men, of which he lost 4,000 in prisoners, and with killed, wounded and other casualties a total of 9,000, or half his force.

The original plan of using the mounted forces to cut his communications while the infantry defended Romani was undoubtedly sound, and if followed might well have completely crushed his entire force.

At Bir el Abd. Colonel Findlay meeting wounded coming in.

Throughout the whole week's fighting the Turk displayed the greatest determination, and his systematic falling back from prepared position to prepared position, combined with the lack of water for our horses and the extreme weariness of our men, debarred any serious interference with his flanks. His guns were well served with an unlimited supply of ammunition, and the fact that he had transported guns of 5.9 inches calibre across the yielding sand of the desert speaks volumes for his engineering ability.

The bid to break the Suez Canal and to conquer Egypt was a bold one, and was made by picked troops led by a skilful German staff. Though the attack upon Egypt failed and the attacking force lost half its numbers, the Turkish Government thought so highly of the enterprise that it awarded a special star to the survivors.

That these operations, and the attack upon the Canal in January, 1915, were not merely raids, but were genuine and determined attempts to conquer Egypt, was amply proved to our troops afterwards when they were able to see the great and thorough preparations in Palestine. A new railway had been built, extending the Palestine system to the Wadi el Arish, and alongside it was constructed a fine motor road. Permanent works were constructed for the conservation of water along the route; and at the Wadi el Arish enormous rock cut reservoirs were being made.

CHAPTER IX.

How the Regiment reached the River of Egypt over against the Borders of Palestine.

Another quiet period now ensued. The Turks had no inclination for another advance, and the British Forces had to wait for the railway, which was being pushed rapidly forward. There had been a serious outbreak of cholera in the Turkish army in this area, and there was a fear of it breaking out among our troops. It may be mentioned, to show what a clean fighter the Turk is, that he had marked wells and areas as being cholera infected. These notices were written in both Turkish and English. By camping on clean ground and by a careful system of inoculation, only a slight outbreak occurred.

On August 20th the Regiment took over the duties of advanced regiment from the Auckland Mounted Rifles, and once more was split up into squadron camps, the 1st being at Barda, 10th at Hod Hisha, and the 8th three-quarters of a mile north of Bir el Abd. Constant patrolling was carried out, but nothing occurred. The Regiment in turn was relieved by the 5th Australian Light Horse a week later and returned to Hod el Amara.

Everything was very quiet. No leave was granted owing to the cholera scare. On September 11th a return was made to the old camp at Bir et Maler, where duties were light—a few odd patrols, but otherwise only camp fatigues to attend to. There had been some talk of sending officers and men to the seaside to recuperate, and on September 20th three officers and ninety-five men left for a week at Sidi Bishr, near Alexandria. This was an ideal place for a rest camp, situated on the open beach, and everybody had a turn there. Those remaining in camp did only enough work to keep themselves and animals fit.

By the middle of October a warning was issued for another move. Kit inspections were almost a daily affair.

Quartermasters laboured to make up shortages, and wondered how everyone seemed to be in possession of most unnecessary gear. However, in a week even the Regimental Quatermaster seemed to think the Regiment properly equipped and ready to move out.

On the 23rd October a move was made to Bir el Abd, a long ride which the horses felt severely, and the following day to Willega, to relieve the 10th Australian Light Horse Regiment, and then after two days to Mosefig. A squadron went on to Hill 157, and a detached troop to Bir Geisi.

Enemy planes came over daily, but there was no other sign of the Turks. The Regiment escaped bombing, but, being in a line for the anti-aircraft guns, received more than its share of shellcases and duds.

The Sergeant's Mess on the move.

It may not be out of place to give the various distances travelled, as measured on the map. Broken country, and deviations made for various purposes, of course increased them, sometimes to double the map distance.

Thus Hill 70 to Dueidar .. .. .. 7 miles
„ to Bir et Maler .. .. 15 „
„ to Romani .. .. .. 17 „

Bir et Maler to Katia .. .. 7 miles
„ to Mageibra .. .. .. 14 „
„ to Oghratina .. .. .. 14 „
„ to Bir el Abd .. .. .. 24 „
„ to Salmana .. .. .. 31 „
„ to Mazar .. .. .. 46 „

The railway was progressing steadily, and had now passed Salmana and made necessary a further move, so on November 13th a trek was made to Mazar, with the 8th Squadron on outpost at Malha. But the railway construction soon pushed the Brigade on again, and on the 25th Mustagidda was reached, the 8th Squadron having rejoined from Malha. There was still no sign of the enemy, though he was reported to be holding El Arish and Masaid with a strong force.

Those who had been casualties in the August fighting now began to rejoin, as the following extract from the War Diary will show:—

"Lieut.-Colonel Findlay, C.B., resumes command and Lieut. Gibbs resumes as Adjutant.

Temp. Lieut.-Colonel P. M. Acton-Adams relinquishes temp. rank of Lieut.-Colonel and command of Regiment and resumes 2nd in command of Regiment.

Temp. Captain D. T. Wood relinquishes temporary appointment of Adjutant and is posted to 2nd in command 1st Squadron.

Major H. C. Hurst relinquishes 2nd in command of Regiment and is appointed O.C., 1st Squadron."

On December 3rd the 1st Squadron moved to Zoabatia, and on the 4th the 8th Squadron to Arnussi, relieving squadrons of the 1st Australian Light Horse Regiment.

The weather was much cooler. Football became the rage, and regular matches were played between squadrons and regiments. It was really wonderful how the N.C.O.s managed to have footballers available about a camp, though men for fatigues were always scarce.

The desert here was just the same as that nearer to the Canal. Everywhere stretched the apparently limitless sea of sand, with ridge after ridge, dune after dune, in ceaseless monotony; in places covered with a stunted scrub, but bare of other vegetation. At localities where wells had been sunk centuries ago there might be a small grove of date palms, but these were few and far between.

It was in a small hod near Bir el Abd that the first signs of the Roman occupation of the highway into Egypt came to light, in the shape of a stone watering trough some 50 feet in length and with the plaster still in a perfect state of preservation. As it lay close to the old caravan route, it had apparently been a stopping place for the Roman caravans moving to and from Egypt. This example of the characteristic care of the Romans for water supplies was but the forerunner of many wonderfully preserved examples we were to see as we journeyed into Palestine.

On the Salt-marsh. The Sabkhet el Bardawiz.

The few glories of the desert are the sunset and the dawn. The colouring then requires a Kinglake to describe. Night after night on outpost one watched and marvelled at the wondrous tints. As the sun sinks below the rim of the horizon, the whole sky glows with coloured bands of light, then these gradually fade out, leaving a clear blue sky studded with innumerable stars. During the night in autumn and winter there is much lightning, or rather curious balls of fire which hang and glow on the dark distant hills. At dawn streaks of colour spread over the sky, and begin to brighten the darkness, then quickly comes a full blaze of light across the sky, the colouring is gone, and it is broad daylight. There is no twilight and everything in the desert stands out in sharp contrasts of black and white.

At Mustagidda the Regiment was not far from the sea, but in between lay the Sabkhet el Bardawil, and from here our patrols penetrated as far as Masmi some three miles from El Arish, spying out the country.

It soon became evident that there would be another advance. The railway had now passed Mazar, and was approaching Hill 133, where huge dumps were growing and large water tanks were being erected. Side by side across the desert General Murray, with that wonderful completeness in organisation so characteristic of him, had brought the Nile water in steel pipes. After passing under the Suez Canal the water was held in storage tanks and filtered and chlorinated before being sent across the desert by relays of pumps at approximately twenty-mile intervals. This pipe line Sir Archibald eventually took right into Palestine. Perhaps he was inspired by the old tale of Herodotus, who says, in speaking of the difficulties experienced by Cambyses in crossing the desert, that "there is another tale, an improbable story, but, as it is related, I think I ought not to pass it by. There is a great river in Arabia called the Corys, which empties itself into the Erythraean sea. The Arabian King, they say, made a pipe of the skins of oxen and other beasts, reaching from this river all the way to the desert, and so brought the water to certain cisterns which he had dug in the desert to receive it. It is a twelve day journey from the river to this desert tract. And the water, they say, was brought through three different pipes to three separate places." Surely, though old Herodotus says, "it is an improbable story," it is truly a remarkable fact that it was to become true some 2,000 years later.

On December 20th the Regiment moved out to Ghurfan el Gimal. As it was only five or six miles all baggage, overcoats, etc., were sent by camel transport. A large concentration of infantry, artillery and transport at this place, the present head of the railway, looked as if a big move was imminent. The Regiment settled down to await baggage, but was suddenly ordered off, word having been received that the Turks were evacuating El Arish, and a long night march over heavy sandhills followed. This night is remembered as probably the coldest yet experienced in the desert. At 3 a.m. a halt was made for an hour on a high sandhill called Um Zugla. How everyone regretted that the overcoats were on the camels, but "once bitten twice shy," never again was the Regiment caught without them. At dawn Masmi was reached, after covering about thirty miles since leaving camp. From the top of a high sand ridge the Turkish position covering El Arish could be seen, but the Turks had gone. Along the beach for two

The busiest men in the Regiment—farriers at work.

or three miles stretched great groves of palm trees, while nearer us lay the town. East of the town is the Wadi el Arish, which is the Biblical "River of Egypt." It is usually a dry watercourse, but floods heavily during the rainy season. It was up this Wadi that the garrison of El Arish had retired to Magdhaba.

The weather had now completely changed, and heavy thunderstorms made things uncomfortable for everybody, though the fall in temperature was most grateful.

The day after arrival at Masmi one of the wood-gathering parties took eleven prisoners, who were evidently stragglers from the retreating enemy. At short notice on the evening of the 22nd the Regiment moved to the Wadi el Arish, and the early hours of the morning of the 23rd found the Mounted Division riding steadily towards Magdhaba. The fires of the enemy camp at Magdhaba having been observed at 3.50 a.m. the force continued to advance until 10 minutes to five, and then halted and dismounted in an open plain some four miles from its objective, while the Divisional Commander (General Chauvel), with the brigade commanders, went forward to reconnoitre. The number of bivouac fires indicated a considerable force, and the brightness of the lights was very misleading as to distance.

This careless showing of lights by the enemy clearly indicated how impossible he thought it that tired horses and men, after an all-night march of 30 miles, could possibly set out immediately upon another 30 miles march to the position to which he had retired.

General Chaytor with the New Zealand Brigade and the 3rd Light Horse Brigade was given orders to move on Magdhaba by the north and north-east and to endeavour to cut off all retreat. The Camel Brigade (for these operations taking the place in the Division of the 2nd Light Horse Brigade) was to advance straight up the Wadi, following the telegraph line, and the 1st Light Horse Brigade was for the present to be in reserve. The Division's batteries soon got to work, but the targets were hard to find. The enemy's guns and trenches were exceedingly well concealed, but by 10 o'clock the New Zealand Brigade had closed well in. News then coming in that our aeroplanes could see the Turk withdrawing east, the 1st Light Horse Brigade was sent in direct on Magdhaba. By 12 o'clock all three Brigades and the Camel Brigade were hotly engaged, but on account of mirage and dust clouds good observation was impossible.

General Chaytor sent forward the Canterbury and Wellington Regiments—the Wellington on the right and the Canterburys on the left, and to the left of them the 10th Light Horse Regiment. Steady progress was made over country flat and bare of cover beyond small bushes.

By one o'clock the progress of the two regiments had caused a gap to appear between them, and into this gap General Chaytor sent the 8th and 9th Light Horse. The line now pressed strongly forward, each squadron moving forward by rushes, covered by the fire of the Lewis and machine guns, and by 3 o'clock were within five hundred yards of the enemy trenches.

The beginning of the Advance on foot at Magdhaba.

More ammunition was brought up, and, under cover of the machine guns, ground was gained in short rushes, until, with a final charge with fixed bayonets, the nearest trenches were reached. The Turks immediately began to surrender, and the 1st Light Horse Brigade on the west and the 10th Light Horse Regiment on the east pressing in, the whole system of redoubts enclosing the houses of Magdhaba surrendered.

It had been a race against darkness and water, for if Magdhaba had not fallen there was no water nearer than El Arish, and if darkness had fallen before the trenches were captured most of the Turks would have got away.

One of the decisive events of the afternoon was the capture of a battery of four mountain guns by Lieutenant A. B. Johnstone, with his troop of the 8th Squadron. This battery had given much trouble and was still firing when Johnstone with six men rushed the emplacement, and the garrison consisting of 2 officers and 15 men surrendered. Casualties were light in spite of the prolonged nature of the fighting; among those who fell was Lieutenant H. A. Bowron, of the 10th Squadron, who was hit during the early advance over the bare plain.

The sufferings of the wounded were again accentuated by the long distance they had to be carried to Railhead, a matter of just over 50 miles, and from Magdhaba to El Arish the journey had to be made by cacolet. From El Arish to Railhead the most serious cases were taken in sand carts or carried on improvised sledges, both of which means of conveyance through rough country were infinitely better than the dreaded cacolet.

Magdhaba was a mounted man's action; it would have been impossible for infantry. As Gullett says in his history of the Australians in Sinai and Palestine—"The unqualified success at Magdhaba supplies a classical example of the right use of mounted riflemen. In scarcely more than twenty-four hours the Light Horsemen, New Zealanders, and Camels had ridden upwards of fifty miles, had fought, mounted and dismounted, twenty-three miles from their water supply and fifty miles from Railhead, and had surprised and annihilated a strongly placed enemy. The engagement brought out all the effective qualities of these mounted men: the excellent discipline of the silent night-ride, the rapid approach before dismounting, the dashing leadership of the junior officers, the cleverness of the men, while maintaining their advance, in taking advantage of all cover, the effective use of machine guns and Lewis guns, and the eagerness of the troopers for bayonet work as they got to close quarters."

In an address to the Brigade the following day General Chetwode (who now commanded the forces east of the Canal and called the Desert Column) said that the mounted men at Magdhaba had done what he had never known cavalry,

HOW THE REGIMENT REACHED THE RIVER OF EGYPT

in the history of war, to have done before, i.e., they had not only located and surrounded the enemy's position, but they had got down to it as infantry and had carried fortified positions at the point of the bayonet. But the work was not yet finished. Prisoners had to be collected and horses watered. Time did not permit of much being done, so a regiment was left to clean up the battlefield, and the column started on its long ride home. It was a bitterly cold night and men and horses were tired. It must be remembered that they had been marching and fighting for thirty hours without pause, and for most of them this was the third night without sleep. To pass one night without sleep is trying; two nights is absolutely painful; but the third night without sleep, after heavy fighting with all the added strain and excitement, is

A Camp near El Arish.

almost an impossibility. Men and horses were dropping off at the oddest times and in the oddest positions. The dust was intense, and to the lightly clad men bereft of their overcoats, the cold seemed to penetrate to the bone. Men saw or fancied they saw plantations, towns with large buildings lighted up, precipices or a gradually closing wall. A man would halt, thinking he was on the edge of a cliff, then seeing others riding on he knew it to be imagination only. But all journeys end, and Masmi was reached at 6 o'clock on the morning of Christmas Eve. The result of the raid was one thousand two hundred and eighty-two prisoners, four mountain guns, machine guns, rifles, ammunition and stores of all description.

Christmas Day was wet and cold, but the men were rested as much as possible and rapidly recovered from their fatigue of the previous days, and received with equanimity just when they were preparing their Christmas breakfast, a bombing by an enemy plane in retaliation for the raid upon Magdhaba. Two days after Christmas a new camp on the beach at Masaid was set up. A peculiarity of the beach here was that there was a plentiful supply of fresh water in the sand only a few yards from the sea, obtained by digging into the sand to the depth of a few feet.

In the new camp by the seaside in the palms, with the help of a few tents, the men were very comfortable. The weather continued bleak and cold with a strong north-west wind that blew continuously. Owing to the difficulty of obtaining supplies, it was decided to move back to the Railhead at Kilo 139. Advantage was taken of January 1st, 1917, being a comparatively fine day, to move. The new camp was very uncomfortable and seemed exposed to every wind that blew. The watering arrangements for animals were poor, and did not seem capable of improvement, so after three or four days much relief was felt when the Regiment moved back to Masaid. A fine day was not chosen for this move, and everybody got a thorough soaking. But Masaid was a comfortable camp, and all hands enjoyed to the full the luxury of living in a tent again. The cool clean air and bracing sea breezes improved the standard of health wonderfully, and everyone felt, lying here on the borders of Palestine, that something had been attempted and done. And one earnest wish filled every heart—the continuance of the advance into Palestine.

El Arish was found to be rather different from the villages of Egypt. The houses were of the same type, low and flat topped, but with their light yellowish plaster made from the clay found in flats of the "river of Egypt," they looked much more clean; and the town, to men wearied of many months in the desert, had a bright and cheerful appearance.

The Wadi el Arish is for 10 months of the year a dry water course, with its shingle beds and low alluvial flats, much resembling a New Zealand river. But in December and January heavy rains in the mountains of Sinai cause it to flood heavily, and much joy did it give to both men and horses to splash through quickly running water over a hard shingle bottom.

Crossing the Wadi el Arish.

Long reconnaissances were made daily to get into touch with the Turk, and the men of the 1st Light Horse Brigade on the north side of the town were full of tales of long rolling downs covered with turf which lay stretching north towards Palestine.

And then came reports of an enemy position at Rafa, where stood the customhouse on the border line between Egypt and Palestine. These reports were confirmed by aeroplane observation and photographs, and showed a formidable system of trenches and redoubts.

Rafa lies on the boundary line between Turkey and Egypt so that one might say that the battle of Rafa was fought on the borders of Asia and Africa. Here in ancient days there occurred a great battle between Antiochus and Ptolemy, in which one hundred elephants were used. It is now but a small village containing a Customhouse and Police Barracks, and two stone pillars belonging to the series of boundary pillars that stretches from the Mediterranean Sea to the Gulf of Akaba.

K

CHAPTER X.

Of the Battle of Rafa and the First Crossing of the Boundary into Palestine.

The Division received orders to move on the evening of the 8th January, 1917, to attack the enemy at Rafa at dawn next day. This time the Division was to be accompanied by the Camel Brigade (with its Hong Kong and Singapore Mountain Battery) and by the 5th Brigade (Yeomanry) with a battery of the Honourable Artillery Company (18-pounders). The whole force was to be under the command of Sir P. Chetwode.

It is necessary to lay some stress upon the difficulties of the undertaking, because the famous cavalry raids of history offer no real standard of comparison.

In the European wars of 1866 and of 1870, cavalry actions did not take place at any great distance from their base, and even then there was food and water in plenty in the country. Again in America the great raids of Jeb Stuart and of Morgan were undertaken through country upon which the raiders could live. Our mounted troops (the cavalry of the Great War), on the other hand, made their raids in the desert, where all supplies even so far as water for the horses had to be carried with the column. If a man fell out of the column and wandered alone, he perished miserably; and where, if a water bottle by mischance were overturned or leaked, there was no water for the owner for perhaps another twenty-four hours; all this under a burning sun by day and in bitter cold by night, in which he became soaked to the skin with dew; and man cannot march and fight for more than a very limited time without food and drink.

Then, again, the task set our mounted troops in these raids must be considered. To attack and overcome a stubborn enemy strongly entrenched with both field and machine guns is at all times a difficult task. How much more so is it when

Battle of Rafa and Crossing into Palestine 131

the attacking force has a few paltry 18-pounders behind it, however well served these be. Yet these difficulties were gloriously overcome again and again by these young soldiers from the Southern Seas. Dash and determination, combined with an infinity of painstaking forethought, were the qualities demanded by such tasks. The last round of ammunition, the last pound of "bully" and biscuits, and the last pint of water had to be worked out. When supplies could not be carried by the men, they had to be carried to them, and delivered at the very moment when wanted.

Yet all this was done. Men who had hunted and farmed fought as veteran soldiers, full of dash and determination and cunning; and he who had carried on a business or wielded a pen took his place and supplied and fed men and horses as never had been done before, or could have been done, even by the justly famed A.S.C. in the British Army.

Boundary Pillars between Egypt and Palestine.
These two are on the battlefield close to Rafa.

Aeroplanes had reported the Turks to be holding a strong position at Rafa, about a mile south-east of the police station on a low hill called El Magruntein. Leaving Masaid at midday on January 8th, the Desert Mounted Column concentrated in the Wadi el Arish. Mounted men and camel corps were the only troops participating. Moving out at dusk they followed the old telegraph line to Sheik Zowaiid, which was reached about 10.30

p.m. Leaving here again at 1 a.m. on the morning of the 9th, daylight found the horsemen on the borders of Turkey and Egypt at a small Bedouin camp named Shokh el Sufi. These Bedouins were supposed to be hostile, and were quickly rounded up. The noise they made must have notified any Turks within miles that there was something unusual happening. Such a Bedouin camp had not been seen before, and was examined with much curiosity. Their tents are low shelters, like a verandah, about four feet high, open to the east; men, women and children and animals living in them indiscriminately. In the chill of the early morning the women huddled over their tiny fires set up their weird shrill lament. This lament has the strangest sound, a shrill high-pitched tremolo. It was answered from all directions. Later, as the Regiment rode into action it still continued, and one could almost fancy it came from some evil spirit of the air.

The country had completely changed during our night ride; much of it here was in crop, and everywhere the grass grew luxuriantly. What a relief the green was from the glare of the sand, and how greedily the horses cropped the sweet grass and young corn.

The battle of Rafa followed the same course as that of Magdhaba, the long night approach, the contact at dawn, the closing in during the forenoon, the determined attack in the afternoon, and the surrender at dusk.

But here the task was greater. At Magdhaba the Turk's strength lay in his invisibility, the well sited trenches in the level ground took hours to find. Here his strength lay not in the flatness of the position but in the rising ground with its tiers of fire and splendid observation. The centre redoubt crowned a conical hill some two hundred feet above the surrounding plain, which was bare of cover and as smooth as a lawn. Spread out fanwise from the central redoubt were cleverly sited series of trenches, invisible in the grass.

The N.Z.M.R. were to attack from the north-east, the Australians and Camel Brigade from the south; and the 5th Yeomanry Brigade was held in reserve. By half-past nine each regiment was off, riding swiftly round to its appointed position. The 8th Squadron, under Major Bruce, formed the advanced guard to the Canterbury Regiment. As it rode to the north of Rafa to cut the Turks' communications it came into full view of the enemy, who opened on the squadrons with shrapnel and rifle fire, but, riding in open order, the Regiment escaped with only two or three casualties. Here it was that Lieutenant Mathias, in charge of the advanced troop, did good work by capturing the Police station, taking fifty prisoners, then galloping on and cutting off the retreating Turks, many of whom were endeavouring to escape over the sandhills near the coast.

A portion of the Firing Line at Rafa early in the afternoon.

This gallop, in which the whole Regiment participated, gave the Canterburys possession of a line of half completed works running from Rafa to the east, yielded the surrender of six Germans and two Turkish officers with one hundred and sixty-three other ranks, and gave the Regiment complete command of the enemy's line of retreat.

From the small rise at the Police station a good view of the enemy position was obtained. Two thousand yards to the south-west lay a low round hill, with a well grassed plain sloping gently up towards it from the edge of the sandhills which fringed the beach. This plain was devoid of anything that would give cover. The Turkish trenches could be seen on the forward slope of the hill, and rifle pits were to be distinguished in front of them. The 8th Squadron were already working quietly out over the plain. At 11.30 a.m. the 10th Squadron, under Major Murchison, went into action on the right of the 8th, and half an hour later the 1st Squadron, under Major Hurst, took up a position on the right of the 10th. The 8th Squadron had, in the meantime, linked up with the Auckland Mounted Rifles on the left. Enemy machine gun and rifle fire was at first very heavy, but our troops slowly gained the ascendancy. The Lewis guns were doing excellent work, and the machine guns, from a low ridge in our rear, supported the firing line. The advance was slow but steady, the men advancing on foot as though they were carrying out manoeuvres. Everything worked like clockwork. A troop would rise from the ground and, covered by the fire of their comrades on either flank, dash forward a few yards, the men throwing themselves down, and bringing fire to bear on the trench in front of them till the remaining troops had come into line. During a lull in the advance occurred one of those incidents that help one to bear the strain. A wounded man was being carried to the rear. A few enemy shells were landing just in rear of the firing line, so the stretcher bearers decided to wait a few minutes for the fire to slacken. Putting the stretcher down, they flattened themselves out on the ground beside it. Evidently this did not agree with the views of their patient. Getting off the stretcher, he proceeded to leg it at a pace the stretcher bearers had no chance of improving on, in the direction of the nearest dressing station. The look of disgust on the faces of the two men with the stretcher can be better imagined than described. The Padre also caused some amusement. He was with the Colonel, whose headquarters were about 2,000 yards behind the firing line, and clear of the rifle and machine gun swept zone. Suddenly the enemy's shells began bursting round about, and the order was passed round for everyone to dig in for cover, and the Padre was observed furiously attempting to dig himself in with a spoon.

By 11 a.m. all brigades were closely engaged, and the Yeomanry Brigade was sent in to the west of the enemy position between the Camels and the right of the Canterburys, who formed the right of the New Zealand attack.

A steady rifle and machine gun fire, backed up by the Territorial batteries, was pouring on to the Turks. The attack was a determined one but conducted cautiously; rashness would have availed nothing and perhaps led to disaster, for the force was fighting some twenty-five miles from the source of supply (Railhead), and the Turk was known to possess large reinforcements but a few hours march away, at Gaza, and also on the Beersheba railway. For more than three hours the regiments held their positions, the clear grassy plain preventing any movement. During one of its short rushes the leading company of the Camels, the 15th (New Zealand), led by McCallum of the Canterbury Regiment, came under a withering enfilade fire, and the company's gallant leader was mortally wounded.

At 2 o'clock the Yeomanry effected a junction with the Canterbury Regiment on the edge of the sandhills and the Magruntein position was encricled. About an hour later a shortage of ammunition was felt, the reserves having been left at Sheikh Zowaiid, and the Inverness Battery, covering the attack of the New Zealand Brigade, went out of action.

Shortly before 4 p.m. detachments of the 8th Light Horse and of the Wellingtons, who had been thrown out to the north and east to watch for enemy reinforcements, reported much movement. This information was endorsed by the British airmen, who estimated the Turkish reinforcements at two thousand five hundred. General Chetwode, therefore, after discussing the situation with General Chauvel, decided to break off the fight and withdraw, and the 5th Yeomanry Brigade was pulled out.

But elsewhere his instructions fell on deaf ears, for General Chaytor had just issued an order for the final charge, and the line surged forward in a great rush carrying the centre keep. As the men went forward every available rifle and machine gun was firing, particularly fine work being done by four guns attached to the Canterbury Regiment, and the hill "smoked like a furnace." The Turks would not meet the bayonet and surrendered. This success was the beginning of the end. The Australians and Camels, seeing the New Zealanders on the hilltop, quickly rushed the series of trenches they were attacking.

It was still a race against time, no one knowing what the Turkish reinforcements were doing, so prisoners were mustered and hustled off towards Sheikh Zowaiid, and orders were issued for the whole Division to withdraw.

The Ambulance carts, of which there were sufficient, were still busy, and the work of collecting and attending to the wounded was carried on far into the night, and a regiment of Light Horse was left until morning to cover this work. At Sheikh Zowaiid the Wellington Regiment remained until the morning of the 11th to ensure that no man had been overlooked, and to give Christian burial to those of the British Forces who had lost their lives.

Altogether Rafa was a notable victory, and one of which the Regiment had every reason to be proud. Further, it destroyed the last Turkish force in Egypt, the Sinai desert being a province of Egypt. The Regiment arrived at Sheikh Zowaiid shortly after 10 p.m., but the day's work was not yet finished. Horses had to be watered, and though the Field Troop of Engineers had done very well, it takes a long time to water two thousand animals at three small troughs. Horses once watered, the allotted camp sites were found, where rations and fodder had been dumped. After a few hours very welcome sleep the Regiment saddled up and rode quietly back to camp at Masaid, watering the horses en route at the 52nd Division troughs in the Wadi el Arish.

The infantry gave the Division a splendid reception, each camp turning out and cheering as it rode past. Also, what was appreciated very much, they volunteered to man the pumps till all horses had been watered.

The Column arrived in camp about 2.30 p.m., tired but proud. In just forty-eight hours it had covered over seventy miles, taken 1,450 prisoners, a battery of mountain guns and much other booty.

On the 12th there was a ceremonial parade of the Brigade, when it was thanked by the General Officer commanding the Division for the brilliant work at Rafa.

Three or four days after Rafa another member of the old Main Body, Lieutenant G. L. Stedman, left to join the Royal Flying Corps.

The weather still continued cold and wet, but there was little to do, apart from ordinary camp duties, and more tents having been brought up during our absence at Rafa everybody was much more comfortable. Football was again started, and hard matches were played against the other regiments, Auckland and Wellington, also the Infantry and Australians. The Infantry, 52nd Lowland Division, were fine fellows who played a great game of football. Their boast was that they and the Anzac Division were the only divisions who had not used the railway or wire road since crossing the Suez Canal. The Regiment saw much of this Division till they finally went to France, and the more we saw of them the more we liked them. They suffered heavy casualties at the second battle of Gaza, because they preferred death to surrendering as prisoners.

It will have been gathered from the preceding pages that the Sinai desert was no place for a man on foot. At the battle of Romani, when ordered to attack Katia on the second day of the battle, the 42nd Division marched six miles and lost about 400 men per battalion, who were evacuated to hospital with heat stroke, of which many died. On the advance being resumed towards El Arish it was impossible for the railway to bring forward all infantry units, so where the hardened surface of the Darb el Sultani was not available, many miles of wire netting was laid down to take infantry in fours. Three three-foot strips of ordinary wire netting were laid on the sand side by side and pegged down, not only making a good road for infantry, but capable of bearing light motor traffic.

In between football days the staff tried to work in some field work so that the reinforcements lately arrived should have the benefit of a little desert training; daily classes were also held for officers and men in signalling, map reading and compass work.

During this period the Turk's planes were over daily, and often at night, bombing the various camps.

The infantry had established a strong camp east of the Wadi el Arish, and the railway was pushing forward. El Arish, during the last six weeks, had altered considerably. The town itself remained the same, but between it and the sea, a new town of tents, wooden buildings, railway yards and shore dumps had sprung up, showing a remarkable change for a few short weeks. Later El Arish was to become one of the main depots and station for our advance into Palestine. Hospitals and rest camps were then scattered along the beach, and even a school of instruction was established.

After Rafa.

CHAPTER XI.

Of the Advance into Palestine and the First Battle of Gaza.

It was one of the paradoxes to which history sometimes treats us that the younger nations of the world should begin to make history amid the scenes of the oldest civilisations.

When we disembarked in Egypt we found ourselves in a land whose history stretches back to the most distant times. Three mighty Empires had had their day and passed away. The soldiers of each of these Empires had trodden the road we were to tread, captured the same cities and fought on the same battlefields. Beyond the earliest of these Empires (about 4000 B.C.) we now know that the Nile Valley was occupied for a long period by a population which lived chiefly by pastoral pursuits, but had made some advances in civilisation; and each fresh discovery, although unfolding an earlier page still, leaves the origin of these people in obscurity.

The route across the desert of Sinai was the ancient northern route from Egypt to Palestine, and had been used from time immemorial as the connecting link between the two countries. For it must be remembered that Palestine has, for the greater part of its history, been closely connected with Egypt. This road has been justly called "The oldest road in the world," and the armies of nearly every great Power for the last 5,000 years have passed along it at one time or another. Pepi I. (VI. Dynasty, about 3000 B.C.) appears to have been the first Egyptian king to attempt the conquest of Palestine, and successive invasions are known under the great Kings of the XII. and XVIII. Dynasties (2479-1600 B.C.). The famous Tel el Amarna tablets give a wonderful insight into the state of Palestine during the closing years of the XVIII. Dynasty. The great Empire of the Hittites had arisen in northern Syria, and to meet it Seti and Rameses the Great led their armies along the same road (1370). During the next fifty years there seems to have been a systematic spoliation of Palestine, as we read of no fewer than fourteen expeditions in that time. To supply these armies, great arsenals and bases were built at Rameses and Pithom, west of the Canal. These are the "Treasure Cities" of Exodus I. 11, and excavation of Pithom (Tel Maskuta), close to Ismailia, by Neville, have revealed great barns and warehouses for storing supplies.

After the Israelites had settled in Palestine the power of Egypt began to decline. Soon after the death of Solomon, Southern Palestine was ravaged by Shishak, possibly to place the "son of Pharoah's daughter" on the throne of Judea.

Rows of Pits dug by the Turks to stop our Horsemen.

During the next 300 years the connection between Egypt and Palestine was fairly close; a constant claim seems to have been maintained by Egypt over the south-east border cities in the neighbourhood of Gaza. By the beginning of the seventh century B.C. the tide of invasion had begun to set in the opposite direction. The great powers of the East, Assyria, Babylonia and Persia, were beginning to press westward. Sennacherib, after ravaging Palestine, appears to have attempted to invade Egypt, but his successors were more fortunate, and for ten or fifteen years Egypt was under Assyrian rule. Before the final collapse of Egypt as a world

First Battle of Gaza

power, she made one last rally, and Necho (2 Kings 23, 29) for the last time marched an Egyptian army across the Sinai desert, overthrew the Jewish King Josiah on the plains of Megiddo and met his fate at the hands of Nebuchadnezzah at Karkemish in 605.

In 525 B.C. Persia, which had by now become the greatest power, crossed the desert and defeated Egypt at Pelusium. The Persian rule lasted about 100 years, and after a few troubled years of native rule, the last native king of Egypt was overthrown by Alexander the Great, and all Egypt, Sinai and Palestine passed into the power of the Greeks. From that day to this Egypt has been under foreign rule. A century or two later and the desert road was trodden by the feet of Roman legions, and in due course Arabs, Crusaders and Turks passed to and fro over it. Finally, to complete an historic survey, must be mentioned Napoleon's famous march from Kantara to El Arish in 1799.

Truly our march over the desert may have been watched with interest by the shades of countless thousands of heroes of bygone days, who had seen the same sights and gone through the same experiences as we had. The old road had long been at peace; once again it was to "hear the tramp of thousands and of armed men the hum."

We were now to enter Palestine even as these old Egyptians had done by way of the Sinai desert, to pass up the broad and fertile plains of the Philistines and to look upon that blue wall of the Judean mountains so often beheld by the Crusaders of old; passing by their old castle of Darum and the city of Gaza, we were to encamp at Ascalon and Jaffa, the two cities held by Richard Coeur de Lion, and from there, even as he did, to make an advance upon Jerusalem.

Time passed quickly, and on February 22nd this comfortable camp was left for the last time; the Regiment marched to Sheikh Zowaiid, and, dumping all surplus gear here, moved out on the evening of the 23rd to ascertain the strength of the enemy at Khan Yunus, a small village about six miles east of Rafa. At the break of dawn the main body of our brigade was too close to the advanced guard, who had dismounted to attack and capture an enemy outpost. Their led horses came galloping through Brigade Headquarters. But the enemy were only holding their outlying posts lightly, and these were soon rushed. By 9 a.m. the village was surrounded, but the action was broken off. The instructions had been not to force a serious engagement, and owing to the village and outlying cultivation being bordered by thick cactus hedges, there was a possibility of being seriously involved if the advance had continued.

Left to Right.—Capt. Macfarlane, Capt. Rhodes, Capt. Gibbs, Lt.-Col. Findlay.
Taken at Tel el Fara.

After a short halt at Rafa the return journey was made to Shiekh Zowaiid.

On the 28th Khan Yunus was again visited, but the Turks had retired to their strong positions at Weli Sheik Nuran.

First Battle of Gaza

They were taking no more risks with isolated positions. Magdhaba and Rafa had taught them the folly of that. At Weli Sheik Nuran they held a strong position, well entrenched and wired. The ground in front was open, and here was first seen the series of deep holes in the ground about five feet in diameter by which the Turk hoped to ward off the dreaded horsemen. From the high ground east of the village was obtained the first view of Gaza, which all were soon to know more intimately.

Everything pointed to our attacking Weli Sheik Nuran, but the Turks again retired, this time across the Wadi Ghuzze to the Gaza-Beersheba line. The Brigade also moved forward from Sheik Zowaiid to the beach at Rafa.

The desert was now far behind, and all reconnaissances were into grass covered country or among cultivated fields with green crops showing above the ground.

The country around Rafa and up to the Wadi Ghuzze, which was now the limit of our patrolling, was an open down with no fences and very few trees, but a wealth of wild flowers. Along the coast lay a strip of sand-dunes from two to five miles in width.

In Khan Yunus, most probably the "Darum" of King Richard's times, lay the ruins of a great crusader castle. Here also was the first deep well to be harnessed with a modern pump and engine by our engineers, and which gave an almost unlimited supply of good, sweet water.

While at Rafa the Desert Mounted Column held the first meeting of the Rafa races, open to all horses of the mounted regiments, and a Canterbury horse, running under the name of the popular D.A.D.M.S., won the "Promised Land Stakes."

On March 11th the Regiment carried out a reconnaissance in the direction of Gaza. To a student of history this is always an interesting name. Gaza, whose history goes back 4,000 years or more, standing as it does near the edge of the desert, is the first town reached after crossing the desert; or, from the east, the last before commencing the desert journey. It is said to have sustained more sieges and been sacked and destroyed more often than any other town in the world. Egyptians, Israelites, Assyrians, Persians, Romans, Arabs, Crusaders, Turks and Frenchmen have all taken and retaken this town.

Gaza was one of the few cities that dared to defy Alexander the Great, and held up his advance upon Egypt for two months.

Colonel Findlay.

It is mentioned in the 10th Chapter of Genesis, and again many times in connection with Samson, the strong man of Israel who fought the Philistines. It was at Gaza that, being warned that his enemies were upon him, he rushed away with the city gates, and it was here that, blind and friendless, he performed the last great act of his life by pulling down the Temple of Dagon and destroying some three thousand Philistines.

The Wadi Ghuzze lies about two miles south-west of Gaza. Usually dry, with a few water holes, it nevertheless floods heavily during the rainy season. Throughout most of its course the sides of the Wadi are precipitous cliffs. The principal crossings are near the mouth, opposite Gaza, and at Shellal and Esani. Later our engineers constructed crossings at other points, for which the Regiment duly found its quota of road-making parties. At two places on the southern bank of the Wadi there are enormous mounds of earth, Tel el Jemmi and Tel el Fara. These are probably the sites of ancient fortresses built to defend the crossings. The country on all sides was under crop, beautiful barley just coming into ear, a great temptation to our horses, and grazing in crop was strictly forbidden, though this did not seem to be understood by many of the horses. Our patrols had an

Major Hurst with a captured Arab pony.

interesting, though not an exciting time. Across the Wadi was a small plain, and then the ground slopes gently upwards towards the ridge on which our maps told us the Gaza–Hareira–Beersheba road ran. At the Gaza end of this ridge the high point known as Ali Muntar commands the approaches to Gaza, while from it project several spurs, namely Mansura, Sheik Abbas and Atawineh. All this we could see, and rising far beyond, the main mountain range of Judea, a blue misty wall. The Turks offered no opposition to the patrols crossing the Wadi, though they watched all movements closely.

In the evening the Regiment withdrew and returned to camp.

On March 25th a final reconnaissance of the crossings over the Wadi Ghuzze was made, and the Regiment went into bivouac at Deir el Belah.

The capture of Gaza presented a similar problem, though a more difficult one, to that of Rafa. From our Railhead to Gaza was 20 miles. The town was held by a strong garrison, and reinforcements could be sent from Beersheba, on the east flank of our attacking force, and from Huj, eight miles northeast. Both of these places were on the Turkish railway system, and in addition there was the Gaza–Beersheba line, strongly entrenched, which would have to be pierced.

The British force, now greatly increased in numbers and called Eastforce, consisted of the Australian and New Zealand Mounted Division, the Imperial Mounted Division (Australians and Yeomanry), the 52nd, 53rd and 54th Infantry Divisions, the Imperial Camel Corps Brigade, and two extra Yeomanry Brigades, all under the command of Major-General Sir C. M. Dobell.

His plan was as follows:—The Anzac Mounted Division by a night march was to place itself across the main road and communications on the north of the town, and to be ready to co-operate in the attack upon the town by the infantry who were to operate from the south. The Imperial Mounted Division was set the task of holding off enemy reinforcements from the direction of Huj; and the 54th Division those who might advance from Beersheba or the railway leading to that town. In order to protect the lines of communication back to Rafa the 52nd Division took up a position towards the east of Khan Yunus. The 53rd (Welsh) Division was selected to make the attack on the town from the south.

At 2.30 a.m. on March 26th the New Zealand Brigade left its bivouac at Belah with the Anzac Mounted Division and crossed the Wadi. There was a heavy fog, but skilful leading on the part of the advanced guard (2nd Light Horse Brigade) took the Division through the Gaza–Beersheba line just east of Ali Muntar, the hill overlooking Gaza. A small enemy post was encountered and mopped up, and the Division pushed on and at 9.30 reached Beit Durdas, to the northeast of Gaza. The fog was so dense that this advance was quite unknown to the Gaza defenders, though the column was fired upon by several enemy planes.

At Beit Durdas General Chauvel established his Headquarters, and sent the 2nd Light Horse Brigade to establish a line to the sea; in the process of doing this they captured a Turkish divisional general and a number of prisoners. The New Zealand Brigade took up a position facing Gaza, having the 2nd Light Horse on its right and the 22nd Mounted Brigade (Yeomanry) on its left.

Gaza was now completely encircled, and the mounted troops waited with impatience for the infantry attack to develop.

C.M.R. Headquarters near In Seirat after First Battle of Gaza.

Owing to the 53rd Division being unable to move in the fog great delay had taken place, and it was 2 o'clock before orders were received to close in on Gaza.

Our intelligence reports had put the garrison at about two battalions of infantry, several batteries manned by Austrians, and some 200 cavalry, a total of about 4,000, and this estimate was confirmed by a deserter, who added that the nearest supports were at Huj, eight miles away, and that all the wells except three had been blown in.

Gaza lies in a hollow in the midst of orchards, each of which is surrounded by a tall and thick hedge of prickly pear. On the eastern side the town is shut off from the cultivated plain by a low ridge, which culminates at its southern end in the hill Ali el Muntar, the hill up which Samson carried the gates of the city, and which formed the key to the Turkish defence.

The Brigade advanced at a gallop with the Wellington Regiment on the right and the Canterburys on the left and Auckland in support. This ridge was seized and, dismounting, the men pressed on towards Gaza. Wellington were soon among the prickly pear hedges and after some fine work captured two enemy guns. The Canterbury Regiment meanwhile made ground to the south along the ridge, attacking the garrison in Ali Muntar, who were desperately engaged with the leading battalions of the 53rd Division.

Everyone realised that it was now a fight against time; and the Turk was forced from his trenches, shot out of his hedges and driven back into the town. Such good progress was made that at 6.40 p.m. the 10th Squadron closed in on to the top of Ali Muntar simultaneously with the 53rd Division.

The position now was that Ali Muntar, the "keep" of Gaza, was in our hands, the 2nd Light Horse Brigade was in the outskirts of the town to the north and the Wellington Regiment in the town on its east side. Everywhere the Turk was giving way, and the general opinion was that as soon as it was daylight the remainder of the garrison would surrender.

It can be imagined therefore with what astonishment orders were received for the whole Division to withdraw. General Murray's despatch gives the reason that the horses were in want of water, whereas they had all been watered and we were in possession of ample wells. Apparently the trouble lay with those who were out to the east watching for enemy movement from the railway line. They had imagined they saw overwhelming reinforcements coming towards Gaza, and had reported this to General Dobell, who thought that what had been gained could not be held.*

*Whereas Gaza was practically at our mercy, and our invading troops held all the strong positions and were well placed to hold them.

Intense darkness and a strange country thickly intersected with prickly pear hedges made the withdrawal a difficult one and it was after midnight before the Regiment was on its way back to Belah. Major Stafford distinguished himself during this night by successfully bringing away the two field guns captured in Gaza by the Wellington Regiment.

The Regiment now settled into camp at Belah, but had by no means an easy time. There were outposts along the Wadi to be found and working parties for road-making at the Wadi. Taking over an outpost line at night in strange country is a most difficult and tedious operation.

The Shellal Crossing on the Wadi Ghuzze—The Shellal mosaic was found on the top of the conical hill.

The Regiment would leave camp after dark with instructions to hold a line detailed on a map. Knowing nothing of the general formation of the country, on reaching the appointed place it was very hard to place the posts in the best positions, or where they could do most good in the event of being attacked. Usually two squadrons held the line in a series of detached posts, while the remaining squadron was held in readiness to support. Mounted patrols, each consisting of five or six men, were sent out at intervals during the night, patrolling, in open country, for two or three miles to our front.

The whole East Force was in a difficult position at this time. The right flank was always open to attack. For the next six months precautions had to be taken against the possibility of an attack by a wide turning movement on our right directed against our line of communications. The desert afforded some protection, but an active mobile force could have given a lot of trouble. Considerable reinforcements were being brought up during this period, including several tanks which were concealed among the palm groves at Belah, and our artillery was being strengthened daily. The railway also had been brought right up to Belah; roads and cuttings were constructed into the Wadi, and everything pointed to another attack on Gaza. The Turks could be seen daily preparing fresh lines of trenches along the Gaza-Beersheba line.

On April 16th the Regiment left Belah and moved up the Wadi to Shellal, where the whole Division was concentrated.

CHAPTER XII.

Of the 2nd Battle of Gaza and the Holding of the Wadi Ghuzze.

On April 16th orders were received for the second attack on the Gaza line, which was now practically continuous from the sea, passing just south of Gaza, and approximately along the Gaza-Beersheba road to Tel el Sharia on the Wadi Sheria, the tributary of the Wadi Ghuzze which comes down from the mountains of Judea. Behind this line lay the railway terminus of Huj and the railway to Beersheba. It was a very strong position and commanded all the country to its front down to the Wadi Ghuzze, across which the British troops would have to attack. General Dobell's plan was a simple one. The three infantry divisions were to make a frontal attack on the line from the sea to the Mansura ridge, the main Gaza position, while the mounted divisions pressed back the Turk flank towards Beersheba, prevented the withdrawal of reinforcements from there to Gaza, and held themselves in readiness for the pursuit.

The attack was to be conducted in two stages. In the first stage the infantry were to cross the Wadi and to seize Mansura ridge. As soon as this was done the position was to be wired and strengthened and the heavy guns brought forward ready for the general attack on the following day.

At half past six on the evening of the 16th April the Division moved off, and after a night march, in which the Canterbury Regiment formed the advanced guard with the 10th Squadron leading, reached the crossing at Shellal at half past four on the morning of the 17th. There was a small enemy post here with a machine gun in position on a conical hill, afterwards famous as the site of the "Shellal Mosaic," which was discovered when the machine gun trench was seized. Enemy aircraft were active and bombed the column as it crossed the narrow passage. The country was reconnoitred towards Beersheba, and enemy movement about Sharia noted and reported. At dusk the Division withdrew to Shellal, leaving a Brigade of Yeomanry in observation.

During this day the first phase of the attack on Gaza was successfully carried out by the infantry divisions, which seized the Sheikh Abbas position at Mansura.

The Shellal Mosaic—The gaps show where the Turkish trenches cut through this ancient floor.

The next day, April 18th, the Anzac Mounted Division repeated the movements of the 17th, and the Imperial Mounted Division covered the right of the infantry attack, which, after desperate fighting right along the line, was brought to a standstill by the strength of the Turkish positions and their use of powerful and numerous guns.

The Imperial Mounted Division and the Camel Brigade made some progress, but such was the dread the Turk had of the mounted men that, realising their attack would fall on his left flank, he had massed heavy infantry reinforcements and numerous batteries on this portion of his line.

SECOND BATTLE OF GAZA

At dusk orders were received for the Anzac Mounted Division to march under cover of darkness and to be ready to reinforce the Imperial Mounted Division at dawn. At 2300 hours the Regiment moved off and joined the Brigade across the Wadi. It was a black dark night, and as the War Diary says, "after many turnings connected up with the remainder of the Division." Many who read this history will remember those "many turnings" and how the Brigade caught its own tail.

By 9 o'clock on the third day of the battle all guns of the Division were in action, and the Wellington Regiment was sent in to support the 5th Yeomanry Brigade in its attack on "Sausage Ridge," which contained a very strong work known as the "Hair pin redoubt."

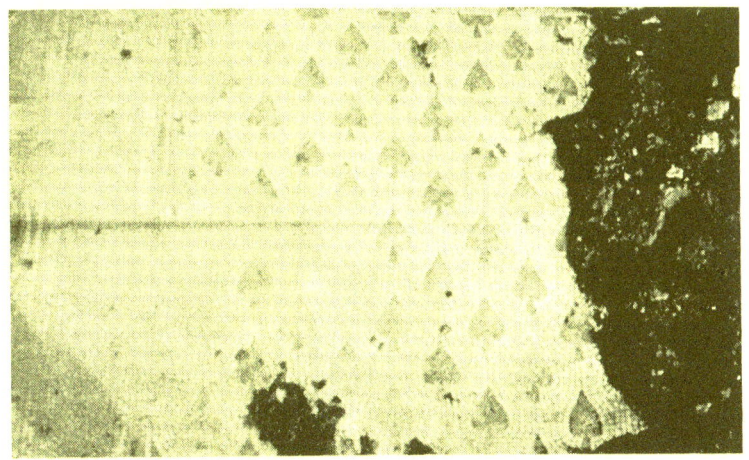

A mosaic floor found at Umm Jerar, close to the Wadi Ghuzze.

The Canterburys for some time waited in reserve and were severely bombed from the air.

At 2.30 p.m. the Regiment went forward, led by Colonel Findlay at the gallop, under heavy shell fire, and went in on the left of the Wellington Regiment, leaving the horses on the plain, where they were shelled and bombed for the rest of the day, but marvellously escaped with few casualties. One section of machine guns suffered much from shell fire while advancing with the first line of troops, but owing to the courage and resource of 2nd Lieutenant L. A. Craven the guns were soon in position, from which they made excellent practice, stopping a big enemy rush at 400 yards. Later in the day this fine young officer was severely wounded, subsequently dying in New Zealand from his wounds. For his splendid work this day he was awarded the M.C. and given accelerated promotion.

The Vickers Gun Section under shell fire.

One of the most striking sights during this strenuous day was the view of the plain covered with the led horses of the Brigade. The holding and control of led horses at all times is a difficult task. Yet owing to the skilful way they were disposed, and to the grit and determination of the horse-holders, though at times quite obscured from view by the mass of shells and bombs which fell in and around them, no horses got away and the casualties were fairly light. The stories told of the escapes of groups of horses from seeming annihilation were little short of miraculous.

It is worthy of note that the horses of the leading squadron (the 1st, under Major Hurst) were kept close up to the firing line, where they were sheltered from rifle and machine gun fire, and quite escaped shelling and had no casualties.

General Dobell, realising that the attack was everywhere held up and that his losses were very severe, decided to withdraw under cover of darkness. This was successfully accomplished, and the forces withdrew; those on the left, facing Gaza, holding what they had gained, including the Shiek Abbas position at Mansura. From there eastward the line fell back behind the Wadi.

Led horses under shell fire, Second Battle of Gaza.

Early on the 20th the Regiment moved to Weli Sheikh Nuran, being bombed from the air on the way. Outposts were put out, and all ranks had a little sleep—the first since leaving Belah. On April 22nd a position was taken up on the west side of the Wadi near Shellal, and an extensive line of trenches was dug. There was a plentiful supply of water at Shellal, gushing out of the ground from the eastern bank. There are remains of Roman cisterns of masonry, showing that in the old days the spring was used. But it was highly impregnated with salts, tasting not unlike commercial "table waters."

The Division now took over the right flank of the British position, and the Wadi became the base for ceaseless reconnaissances into the open country stretching away to Beersheba. This great stretch of country was explored in every detail, wells and cisterns were located, the enemy was continually harassed, and he was induced to prolong his line to Beersheba.

There are many "tels" or mounds of earth in Palestine. They all appear to have been made by man, and are usually the remains of ancient cities, such as Tel el Farama (Pelusium), Tel el Saba (Beersheba).

C.M.R. awaiting orders to attack, Second Battle of Gaza. Colonel Findlay in foreground watching bombs dropping among the Squadrons.

On the Wadi Ghuzze were two remarkable "tels," of which no history could be found, namely Tel el Jemmi where the Division crossed in its advance to the first attack on Gaza, and Tel el Fara, seven miles further south, where the Rafa–Beersheba road crosses. These two tels, flat topped and square sided, stand up above the plain and can be

Second Battle of Gaza

seen for miles on every side. Both drop sheer down into the Wadi. Tel el Fara has been built up in ages gone by with huge masonry buttresses and courses of cut stone.

The military railway which we had built from the Suez Canal across the desert had now reached Belah, and large reinforcements began to arrive.

General Sir Archibald Murray, who had so far borne the heat and burden of the day, was a wise far-seeing administrator, upon whose shoulders had fallen the difficult task of keeping Egypt quiet, of defending it from the Senussi on the west, and of organising the Egyptian Expeditionary Force and planning its advance into Palestine. In addition to these tasks—more than enough for one man—he had the control of the British forces at Salonika, and the handling of the difficult Hedjaz Arabs and the bringing of them into the war. His work not only made Egypt absolutely safe from invasion, but made easy the conquest of Palestine. Starting with a totally inadequate force, he cleared Sinai of the enemy, completely destroying the Turkish hopes of conquering Egypt. The magnitude of his work in the conquest of Sinai, can be gauged by the fact that by February, 1917, he had laid down 388 miles of railway reaching to Southern Palestine, with 300 miles of water piping and 203 miles of metalled roads. Truly and well had he laid the foundations for the overthrow of the Turkish armies. He was a man who placed implicit trust in his subordinates, and generously took upon his own shoulders their failures. His administration and organisation of the Egyptian Expeditionary Force had been masterly, but his many responsibilities kept him too far from the fighting in Palestine, and his trust in his subordinates led, upon their failure, to his recall by the War Office.

He was succeeded by General Sir Edmund Allenby, a cavalry officer of great reputation. He brought with him a fine spirit of optimism, which spread from him to the whole force as he speedily made himself known to every unit under his command. He was soon a familiar figure in every part of the line. He gave his whole time to the command of the Egyptian Expeditionary Force, being relieved of the administration of Egypt by Sir Reginald Wingate.

The increase in reinforcements made it possible to expand the two cavalry divisions by the formation of a third, called the Yeomanry Division, and the three Divisions with an extra Yeomanry Brigade became the Desert Mounted Corps.

The command of this cavalry corps was given to General Chauvel, General Chaytor took over command of the Anzac Mounted Division, and Colonel Meldrum (of the Wellington Regiment) was given command of the N.Z. Mounted Rifle Brigade.

The arduous patrolling of the Sharia–Beersheba area was now undertaken by one division at a time, with one in support about Abasan el Kebir and one on the sea beach at Marakeb, near Khan Yunus.

The patrol work was all to the east of the Wadi, towards Beersheba and Sharia. From the Wadi extends a flat plain for about five miles till one reached two low ridges called Goz el Basal and Karm; beyond these stretches ridge after ridge of rolling downs, each one slightly higher than the last, till the main range beyond Beersheba is reached. The whole of the land there, and also on our side of the Wadi, had been closely cultivated, and the constant passage of animals made the dust indescribable. It penetrated into everything, and when a force was on the move had to be seen to be believed; above all, it betrayed the movements of even a single horseman to the watching Turk.

Our patrols daily visited El Buggar, Im Siri and Hill 710, and the country towards the enemy lines at Sharia and Hareira, the watchful enemy posts always giving way in front of them. Very seldom could they be tempted into rifle range. They, on their part, endeavoured to lure us within range of their artillery, which would open fire on the least provocation. A "demolition squadron" was formed about this time from men from the various squadrons throughout the Brigades. The demand sent to each regiment for men "used to explosives" called forth the recommendation from one squadron commander on behalf of a corporal, "who was well used to explosives, having just been thrice blown up by shells!"

On May 22nd the Regiment took part in the raid on the Beersheba railway at Asluj, leaving camp during the night of the 21st and 22nd and marching south with the Division. Shortly before daylight the Regiment was detached to hold an outpost line near Umm Apir. Daylight showed new and strange hills. With the aid of maps and compass the position was found. Just then Divisional Headquarters signalled from some distance south-west, saying they were at Hill X, and asking for the Regiment's position. The reply was that Canterbury was also on Hill X and holding an outpost line according to instructions. This produced quite a local disturbance, but a topographer who had come out to correct maps, certified in favour of the Regiment.

The enemy made no attempt to interfere with either the covering or demolition parties. The demolition work was very thoroughly carried out. Some 15 miles of railway were destroyed, including many fine stone bridges. Each arch of every bridge was blown up with gun-cotton, and the rails destroyed by the blowing out of a piece in the centre of each alternate rail. The ride back to camp in the evening after the demolition party had completed their work was wearisome in the extreme. For some reason, known only to themselves, the head of the column led into many strange places, such as cactus hedges, wire entanglements and other camps, before the Colonel obtained permission for the Regiment to find its own way back.

With the heat, dust, flies and hostile planes, life did not bear a rosy outlook, and all were glad when, on May 28th, the Regiment handed over its job and returned to Abasan el Kebir for a spell. Here was experienced a fairly quiet time, except for the daily attentions of hostile planes. The Turks had absolute control of the air, and could do as they liked. Our Flying Corps did their best, but their machines were obsolescent, and they were only courting disaster every time they left the ground.

On June 8th camp was moved to the beach at Tel el Marakeb, where the clean sand and cool sea were beneficial to men and animals, the latter enjoying the bathing as much as the men. The weather was delightful, and there being very little work beyond ordinary camp routine, the general health of all rapidly improved.

On July 6th Tel el Fara and the old game of patrols was resumed. This work was only varied when a reconnaissance was made by the Brigade or Division. During the Regiment's absence infantry had dug trenches and put out wire entanglements, defending the main crossings of the Wadi.

Anti-Aircraft Protection.

A branch line, leaving the main railway line at Rafa, had been constructed to Shellal. This was now pushed forward towards Goz el Basal and was well beyond our entanglements.

On July 19th the Turks varied the monotony by a reconnaissance of our front. It is doubtful what their object was, but it appeared to be in the nature of a ruse to get our troops to move. No direct attack was made, but they had a lot of artillery which they evidently hoped to use on the mounted troops if they could be drawn within range. But the mounted man was not to be tempted. The Turks, losing patience, bombarded vigorously, but at too extreme a range to do much damage. Their aeroplane bombing was much more annoying, and the cause of heavier casualties and the loss of many horses. This bombing was the most severe and accurate yet experienced, and culminated at 1600 hours, when three enemy planes came over and took a line through the Brigade, dropping a bomb on Brigade Headquarters and then on the 1st and 8th Squadrons. Three officers, Major Bruce, Lieutenants Wilson and Livingstone were wounded, Wilson dying later through the effects of his wounds. Trooper Ferguson was killed and eight other ranks wounded.

Camel Convoy on the Beach.

The following extract from the Regimental War Diary will give a good idea of the work carried on by the Regiment at this time:—

Tel el Fara.
1917.
July 24th Camp routine carried out.
    25th Camp routine carried out. Inspection of Gas Helmets by Divisional Gas Officer.
    26th A reconnaissance carried out by the 1st Sqd. under Major Hurst on the night of the 25-26th July of Sana Redoubt.

A special party of 1 officer (Lt. D. B. Murchison) and 5 O.R. was told off to make a special reconnaissance. The Commander of the Sqd. supporting. Sqd. left camp at 1800 on the 25th inst., and cleared the wire east of Hiseia at 1915, arriving at Point 300 at 2025. Stayed there for 1¾ hours on account of moonlight, and at 2200, leaving the led horses under guard of 1 officer and 16 O.R., the Sqd. moved forward on foot, and by 2330 had made good the Wadi Sharia between 310 and 340. At 2335 the party making the special reconnaissance passed through the Supporting Sqd. At 0300 the reconnaissance was complete, and the Sqd. withdrew to Camp.

Report by Lt. D. B. Murchison on Special Reconnaissance: "At 2335 crossed Wadi Sharia at Point 400 yds. west of Khirbit Erk and moved round west side of Sana Redoubt (Ref. Map Sharia 1/40,000) at 0045 in a position 600 yds. north of Redoubt; then moved to N.E. corner and round the east side at an average distance of 200 yds. from it to a point midway between S of Sana and 5 of 365. Withdrew from here at 0200, and at 0300 arrived at Khirbit Erk Crossing. Fog made observations difficult. An enemy working party 100 strong was digging during reconnaissance in front of the N.W. trenches of the Redoubt, digging pits or new line trenches. This working party hindered the reconnaissance. Hostile patrols were numerous and strong, consisting of from 10 to 15 men, at least half of each being armed Bedouins. They moved quickly and silently but carelessly, but followed the well-defined tracks. At 0200 arrived a patrol from Redoubt moving towards El Magan. Working parties covered by two patrols each of 13 men, who patrolled the west front 600 yds. out from Redoubt; patrols also coming from direction of El Magan and direction of 310. Our party was challenged by hostile patrol on approaching Khirbit Erk, the challenge sounded like Ender). Our party got into Wadi and eluded the enemy patrol.

Redoubt: Evidently a detached post, not connected with any other work to the north or north-west. Very strong; Shape, oval; Wire, did not locate any; Pits did not locate any; Saw two machine gun emplacements. Two flares were put up. All patrols were armed with rifles and fixed bayonets."

A reconnaissance was also carried out by the Regt. (less 1st Sqd.) along the Abu Shawish Road from Contour 300 to Point 510, and of Wadi Imleih. Attached to Regt.: 2 guns R.H.A. and one Section of Machine Gun Sqd. Left Camp at 0530 and proceeded to Contour 400, N.E. Goz el Geleib. From this point patrols were sent out to following points:—

No. 1. From Point 510 Abu Shawish Road to Point 410 Wadi Imleih. This patrol got to within 800 yds. of Hut, when they were fired on by about 30 Turkish Infantry in trench at Hut between L and E in W-Imleih, while a Cavalry troop approached from Wadi, S.E. side of Hut. Our patrols then withdrew to Contour line 500 and opened fire with Hotchkiss Rifles at long range. The enemy cavalry then retired and took shelter in Wadi, our guns shelling trench and Wadi near Hut.

No. 2. to W in W-Imleih. Were fired on by enemy mounted patrol on north bank of Wadi and shelled from direction of Hareira-Tepe. (Ref. Map 1/40,000 Sharia.) Our patrols pushed on and took up position in Wadi, and remained unmolested all day.
No. 3. To Khirbit Erk. No opposition; remained in position all day. Enemy entrenched position in front of and north of Wadi Imleih. Enemy appears to have dug out in Wadi from this post. Cavalry patrols were seen at various places on north bank of Wadi. The Regt. withdrew at 1800 to camp.

On August 18th the Yeomanry Division arrived, and the Anzac Mounted Division moved to the beach at Marakeb, and a quiet fortnight followed. The sea bathing was a great boon to everybody. What a treat it was to get thoroughly clean and free from dust; even sand was pleasant—sand which had always been reviled in the Sinai deserts, but to which after months of dust everybody was glad to return. As the men grew stronger a rifle range was built, and instead of much of the dreary training all ranks went through a complete musketry course on the range, and quite a number of competitions were fired.

The Beach at Marakeb.

But this rest was too good to last, and on September 18th the Regiment moved over to Fukhari, near Abasan el Kebir, a dusty, dirty camp, with flies everywhere. Easy times were finished, and training started again with the necessary but tedious tactical schemes, in which the whole

Brigade took part, and though probably interesting and instructive to senior officers, were most uninteresting to the men.

At Fukhari an enemy aeroplane was seen brought down by our planes, in the first air fight on this front in which our planes had been successful. It had been very trying up to date to be reading the frequent communiques in the papers, which stated that our planes had control of the air, and at the same time to know that the enemy planes could go where they wished and do as they liked. Often there was a real doubt of the communiques from other fronts when there were such glaring examples of our own. But the new

Landing Stores on the Beach in Palestine.

machines were at least the equal of, if not better, than the Turks. On September 30th the strength of the Regiment was 23 officers, 492 other ranks. On October 16th there was a special parade of representatives from all units in the Division at Fukhari for the presentation of decorations and medals by the Commander-in-Chief, General Allenby. Colonel Findlay commanded the composite regiment representing the N.Z.M.R. Brigade, and Major Hurst the composite squadron representing the Regiment. Among the New Zealanders to be decorated was Captain R. P. Harper of the Canterbury Regiment, now in command of the machine gun squadron.

Second Battle of Gaza

October saw huge dumps being accumulated at Belah and Shellal. The Regiment prospected the country south, looking for the best route to Esani, and suitable camp sites there. Evidently another move was contemplated. The Turkish defences were strong from Gaza to Beersheba, and wherever the blow was struck it would require to be pushed home regardless of cost, to be at all successful. Leave, which had been granted much more freely since the arrival of the Commander-in-Chief, was cancelled. All baggage and surplus gear was sent to a main dump at Rafa in charge of a few unfit men.

During the late afternoon of October 24th the Regiment rode out to Esani, arriving there about midnight and the first move of the great attack began.

CHAPTER XIII.

Of the Breaking at Beersheba of the Turkish Line.

The Turkish forces in Southern Palestine in October consisted of nine divisions and one cavalry division, with an approximate strength of about 50,000 rifles, 1,500 sabres and 300 guns. This force was organised and controlled by a German staff, but owing to want of agreement in the Higher Command as to whether the Bagdad or the Palestine front should receive preference in reinforcements and material, the general state of efficiency was not high.

Our forces consisted of the Desert Mounted Corps (Australian Light Horse, Yeomanry and New Zealand Mounted Rifles), XX. and XXI. Infantry Corps and attached troops.

General Allenby's plan was to strike at Beersheba with his cavalry, seizing the town with its wells and the high ground surrounding it. The XX. Corps was then to deliver its attack against the Turk's open flank at the foot of the hills about Hareira and roll up the enemy line from east to west.

In order to deceive the enemy up to the last moment as to the real point of our main attack, to keep him in his main positions and to draw reinforcements away from his left flank, an attack by the XXI. Corps, preceded by several days' bombardment, was to be thrown against the Gaza defences, twenty-four hours previous to the commencement of the attack by the XX. Corps.

As the attack on Beersheba required a march of some 70 miles on the part of the cavalry, entirely in country where water was scarce, much preliminary work was necessary.

During the course of the many reconnaissances by the mounted troops all available sources of water had been carefully noted and their capacity measured. Among the best sources of supply were old wells at Khalasa, Abu Ghalyun and Esani, and measures were taken at once to develop these to their fullest extent. The Division's Field Squadron, under protection of a brigade, cleared the wells and installed pumps with oil-engine power. Frequent special reconnaissances of the high ground around Beersheba were made by the Commander-in-Chief, corps and divisional commanders, and a very thorough knowledge of the country over which the troops were to pass in the ensuing operations was gained by an innumerable number of officers. The work was heavy for the cavalry, as each reconnaissance entailed two nights and a day of ceaseless movement and wakefulness, without sleep or rest, during which time it was not uncommon for regiments to cover seventy miles or more. Apart from fatigue, the absence of water caused severe hardship to the horses and no little discomfort to the men. No water for horses was available from the afternoon of the day on which the Brigade moved out till the evening of the following day, when, as a rule, they got a drink at Esani, on the way back to Shellal. The men started with full waterbottles, and got one refill from the regimental water-cart.

The scattered squadrons were invariably bombed by the enemy, generally with effect, and the Turk's light guns brought out to concealed positions from which they had previously registered all high ground, wadi crossings, etc., added to the general discomfort.

It was now that the benefit of the constant patrolling and reconnoitring was felt. The Turk had become so accustomed to our mounted troops riding about the plains that our preliminary movements to the south to obtain a concentration point from which to descend upon Beersheba passed unnoticed. Every care was taken to conceal these movements, however, and no marches were made in daylight. A further protection came from the air service, now far ahead of the enemy's in speed, numbers and personnel; for our airmen kept the enemy planes away and forced them to fly so high that they apparently saw nothing.

The extension southwards began on October 22nd, when the 2nd Light Horse Brigade moved to Esani and the Camels to Abu Ghalyun.

From then onwards work on water development was carried on at high pressure night and day, tracks were improved and marked, and supply difficulties successfully contended with.

On October 24th the New Zealand Brigade moved to Esani, and on 29th to Asluj.

During these last days ceaseless preparation had been going on night and day. No fewer than 20,000 camels were employed in the preparations for the flank attack. In addition the resources of the military railway were strained to their fullest capacity, whilst the roads were thronged with every kind of transport. Still the movement was kept secret from the enemy. By day the area was comparatively calm, but as soon as night fell it became a buzzing line of industry as train followed train, and convoys rolled eastwards in the choking clouds of dust. The needs of the army, which had been sadly lacking hitherto, were now pouring into the country.

By the evening of October 30th, the day upon which the XXI. Corps, with the Navy, began the great bombardment of Gaza, the concentration of the Desert Mounted Corps was complete, consisting of the Anzac Mounted Division, the Australian Mounted Division and the Yeomanry Division, together with the I.C.C. Brigade and an extra Yeomanry Brigade (the 7th Mounted Brigade), in all eleven brigades, each with its horse artillery battery, a total of approximately twenty-eight thousand mounted men.

The mounted units were disposed as follows:—The Anzac Mounted Division at Asluj ready to encircle Beersheba; the Australian Mounted Division at Khalasa, with orders to follow the Anzac Division to the vicinity of Beersheba, where it was to come into action on its left; at Esani was the 7th Mounted Brigade, and at Shellal the Yeomanry Division, with the Camel Brigade close by.

At 6 o'clock in the evening of October 30th the Anzac Mounted Division moved off, and, following a track up the Wadi el Imshash, crossed the mountain range just east of Thaffa, which was reached at midnight, and the advanced guard halted for $2\frac{1}{2}$ hours to enable the column to close up and the track to G. el Shegeib to be reconnoitred.

The 2nd Light Horse Brigade then took the road down to the plains east of Beersheba through Bir Arara, and the remainder of the Division, with the Wellington Regiment as advanced guard, followed the track over G. el Shegeib. Some opposition was met with, but was brushed aside by the Wellingtons, and by 8 o'clock in the morning of October 31st the Division had reached the line Bir el Hamman (2nd Light Horse Brigade), Bir Salim Irgeig (N.Z.M.R.), with the 1st Light Horse Brigade in reserve behind the New Zealanders. The force was now within striking distance of the Beersheba defences, and the N.Z.M.R. began to attack Tel el Saba, the key to the Beersheba

Led Horses in Wadi.

defences on the east side. The Auckland Regiment advanced upon the hill, the Canterbury Regiment moving up on its right flank with the intention of enveloping the tel from the north.

The plain is much broken by the winding Wadi beds with steep banks. But though these obstacles slowed down the attack, they provided covered lines of approach, and the

Aucklanders, backed up by the Somerset battery, worked their way mounted to about eight hundred yards from the enemy main position, where excellent cover for horses was found. Good covering fire was also afforded, and the Canterburys slowly gained ground, against much machine gun and artillery fire, the latter coming from the high hills to the north.

The 3rd Light Horse Regiment of the 1st Light Horse Brigade was now sent forward to support the Aucklanders' left, with whom were now the Wellington Mounted Rifles, and the Canterburys made ground to the right until, passing over the Wadi Khalil, the Regiment brought fire to bear on the rear of the Tel, but owing to heavy fire from the large Turkish forces in the hills to the north, could go no farther.

At 3 o'clock the Auckland Regiment rushed the hill, and soon afterwards the whole Brigade concentrated in the Wadi under shelter of the Tel to escape the heavy Turkish artillery fire.

By dark the town of Beersheba was in our hands.

Early on November 1st the New Zealand Brigade was on the move into the hills on the north-east. The Canterbury Regiment in the lead, came under fire, but by a brilliant piece of work, in which the 10th Squadron and Lieutenant C. M. Milne's troop in particular made a frontal attack, and the 1st Squadron came in on the enemy flank, captured an officer and 12 men with a machine gun. For his excellent work this day Lieutenant Milne was awarded a Military Cross. In the evening, being relieved by the Aucklanders, the Regiment returned to the Wadi to water the horses at a few scanty pools.

The 2nd and 3rd were comparatively quiet days, apart from numerous fatigues and guards, but the latter gave the men little rest. On the afternoon of the 4th the Regiment was out again, this time to Ras el Nagb, where it relieved the 5th Mounted Brigade, and engaged in what might almost be called mountain warfare. The enemy shelled the Regiment riding in through the rough foothills, causing a few casualties. At 3 a.m. on the 5th a party of the enemy attacked, but were easily driven off. Later some of their cavalry massed in a low valley out of sight, but they were seen from the flanks, and gave good shooting as they galloped back to their own lines. At 11 a.m. they delivered a heavy attack, supported by artillery and machine guns. Their artillery fire was almost perfect, and in different circumstances would probably have evoked our sincere admiration, instead of the hearty curses that now greeted it. It was estimated that the Turks had fifteen guns firing from three different directions. Our 13 pounders could not find the hostile batteries; moreover, they could not have hit hard enough if they had done so. Our 18 pounder field guns had been withdrawn, and replaced by 13 pounder guns some time before. The new batteries were outranged and outweighted in every fight the Brigade was subsequently engaged in. The Turks got to within two hundred yards of our line, but could not get any closer, and the attack gradually died away.

Led Horses in the Gully behind Ras el Nagb.

It was during this attack that Trooper Greenslade gave his life in a very gallant effort to carry wounded men to cover. The bringing in of wounded men from the firing line was a very difficult matter. There were no regular trenches, and the communication from front to rear lay through a shrapnel-beaten zone. Greenslade was being helped by another man, and both men were hit, but Greenslade succeeded in placing his comrade out of danger, and then, in attempting to bring in the man they had been both going for, Greenslade lost his life. For this fine effort he was recommended for the Victoria Cross.

The artillery fire continued all day without intermission; the rapidity with which the enemy switched his fire from one target to another showed magnificent observation and co-operation on the part of his artillerymen. Our artillery was a direct contrast; they gave us little support and their observation was bad. The Brigade was expecting to be relieved in the afternoon, but for some reason or other the relieving brigade did not turn up. At dusk the artillery fire died down, and the night passed quietly. Our casualties had been serious, over 20 per cent. of the regiment being killed or wounded, besides thirty-two horses killed and many wounded.

No rations or fodder had been issued on the 5th, and in addition to being tired out everybody was hungry and suffering from the lack of water. The shortage of water was a serious matter for the horses, they having had none since early the day before. There still being no sign of the relieving brigade, it was finally decided to send the horses to Beersheba. After a long, weary ride, with tired men and exhausted animals, very little water was available there. Seemingly every animal in the desert Mounted Column was at Beersheba for water. Camels, donkeys, mules and horses were mixed up in hopeless confusion. The engineers, in an effort to cope with the rush, set a time limit for each unit. This being much too short, owing to sufficient pumps not being available to keep the troughs full, many animals got no water at all. At midday on the 6th the led horses arrived back at Kh el Ras, and there met the men from the line, who had been relieved by the Imperial Camel Corps. These men, tired, hungry and thirsty, had a strenuous five mile walk from Ras el Nagb, and were in a very exhausted state. Some of the horses, which it had been impossible to send to Beersheba, had been without water for forty-eight hours, and another fourteen hours were to elapse before they could be watered. The men fared very little better, many of them having had only one water bottle for the same time.

During the 7th, 8th and 9th, the Regiment remained at Kh el Ras, but with short rations and forage, and ten hours trip to Beersheba for water for the horses.

The object of this exceedingly difficult fighting in the mountainous country to the north-east of Beersheba was to hold off the enemy's counter attacks, made with the full strength of all his available reserves.

Eighth Squadron Officers.

It was evident that these attacks were made in the hope of driving the British right back on to Beersheba, and of attracting to this right flank General Allenby's reserves. But the British Commander refused to be drawn to the east, and, relying upon the Anzac Mounted Division and the 53rd Division to hold the enemy in check at Tel Khuweilfe, proceeded resolutely with his preparations for the assault on the left flank of the Turkish main position at the foot of the hills. Here the enemy's line was broken on the night of the 6/7th November, and at dawn on the 7th General Chaytor, with the 1st and 2nd Light Horse Brigades, rode through the gap made by the 74th and 60th Infantry Divisions, and by 11 o'clock was ten miles in rear of the Turkish front line.

CHAPTER XIV.

How the Brigade Rode Through the Plain of the Philistines.

Early on the morning of the 10th November the Brigade moved to Beersheba. Plenty of rations and water were now available, and men and horses were soon fit to move out again. At 4.30 p.m. on the 11th the three New Zealand Regiments rode out of Beersheba for the last time on what proved to be a very long and tiring march, made worse by bad leading and bad communication in the column. At one stage thirty-one miles took thirty hours to cover. The route lay past Tel esh Sharia and Tel el Hesy to Hamame, at which latter place, about fifteen miles north-west of Gaza, the Brigade rejoined the Division. The dust during this time was appalling, the route taken, being across the natural formation of the country, was intersected with deep wadis which could only be crossed in single file, while in some cases the transport and ambulance wagons had to travel many miles extra till they found crossing places. At Hamame the Brigade rejoined the Anzac Mounted Division and rested on the 12th, finding plenty of good fresh water for men and horses by digging in the sand on the sea shore. Adjoining the village of Hamame lay Medjel, a populous Arab city, which might almost be called the modern Ascalon, for a few miles away on the sea shore lie the extensive ruins of that once famous city*.

One of the five capital cities of the Philistines, Ascalon is mentioned many times in Biblical history. Here it was that Samson killed his thirty Philistines, and here Herod the Great was born, and in later times the city was captured and held by Richard 1st of England. No trace now exists of its once busy harbour, but judging by the massive ruins Ascalon must have been a strong place indeed.

*With reference to the great endurance shown by the horses, see an article written in the field by Major Stafford—the Regiment's veterinary officer—in Appendix A.

10th SQUADRON MAIN BODY JUST PRIOR TO THE ARMISTICE.

A few miles up the coast is Esdud, the Ashdod (or Azotus of the New Testament), one of the places where the giants, the mighty sons of Anak dwelt. Ashdod has the record of having stood a siege longer than any other city in history, for Psametik I. of Egypt besieged it for 29 years before it surrendered. On the beach still lie the great stone walls of the castle built by Richard I. in the year 1192 to defend his landing place.

On the ride through the plains from Beersheba we passed by Tel el Hesi, the ancient Lachish, one of the Canaanitish cities captured by Joshua. An illustrated account of its capture and sack by Sennacherib formed a bas-relief on the walls of the palace of Nineveh, and is now in the British Museum.

Eleven miles inland from Ascalon stands up on high Tel es Safi, once the famous crusading fortress of Blanche Garde, and whose native name means "shining hill." And white and shining it is to-day with its sheer cliffs of white limestone crowned with the ruins of the old castle. It was the ancient Gath, and must have been a very strong city, practically impregnable one would think in those days of slings and bows and arrows. And a little further north lies the modern Jewish village of Akir, once Ekron, which with Ascalon, Ashdod, Gaza and Gath formed the five capital cities of the Philistines.

On November 13th the advance was resumed, the Brigade crossing the Nahr Sukereir close to Ashdod by a fine old stone bridge with a roadway measuring 64 feet in width, and evidently dating from the time of the Crusaders.

The Regiment bivouaced that night close to Yebna, the Biblical Jamnia, and once the capital and seat of learning of the Maccabees. It lies on the banks of the Wadi es Surar, which takes its rise beside Jerusalem, and is called in the Book of Judges "the valley of Sorek," up which the Philistines sent the Ark of God when they returned it to the Israelites.

On the 14th the New Zealand Brigade crossed the Wadi Es Surar (known as the Nahr Rubin where it enters the sea) close to the sandhills, and with the 1st Light Horse Brigade on its right attacked the Turks in the orange groves of Wadi Hanein and the hills between these groves and the coast.

The Brigade advanced with the Canterbury Mounted Rifles on the right and the Wellingtons on the left, the Aucklanders being in reserve.

The Canterbury Regiment was soon well into the orange groves, and the Wellington Regiment was hotly engaged along the hills, which here, running parallel to the groves for about a mile, turned westward until merged in the sandhills. Along this ridge the Wellington Regiment slowly forced its way, and at noon General Meldrum sent in the Aucklanders on the left and the two regiments then advanced side by side against a very stubborn and determined enemy counter attack, which Kress von Kressenstein, our old friend of Sinai days, had launched.

The old stone quay, Jaffa.

These two regiments, after some very hard fighting, in which they suffered many casualties, and with their right well covered by the Canterbury Regiment, eventually broke the Turk's attack about dusk, and the whole Brigade bivouacked where it stood.

The next day the Regiment advanced to Beit Dejan, on the Jaffa-Jerusalem road, and on the 17th November entered Jaffa, taking over the government of the town from the Wellington Regiment. Colonel Findlay established his headquarters in the German Consulate.

Jaffa, the principal port of Palestine since the days of the old Philistines, is a picturesque city built upon a hill overlooking the sea. The word Jaffa means beautiful, and the city still deserves its name. A great sweep of green orange groves comes in from the plains melting into the gardens of the town.

At the foot of the old city (which covers the hill) is the solid stone quay of the Crusaders, and sheltering it a few hundred yards out, and protecting it from the prevailing winds, is the reef of Andromeda, and the rock to which she was tied is still shown. Here also is shown Simon the Tanner's house, and curiously enough the principal houses along the beach by the quay are still used as tanneries.

To the north of the old city spreads the Zionist Colony of Tel Aviv (the hill of Spring) with its modern buildings and great Jewish college.

The Regiment had been but a day or two in Jaffa when the inhabitants who had been expelled by Jemal Pasha, began to flock back to their homes. They came from the inland villages where they had taken refuge, on foot, on camels, and on mules and donkeys, one and all showing the signs of great privations. Food had been exceedingly scarce, and many Jewish families had literally been starved to death.

The New Zealand Brigade took up a protective line covering the town, along the river Auja, and the Regiment moved to Sarona, a German colony some two miles north of Jaffa. The inhabitants seemed a prosperous farming community and from them straw was obtained, which, with the aid of an old chaff-cutter, was soon turned into excellent chaff for the horses, who were suffering from the bare grain ration, which was all that the supply services had been able to bring up since the break through at Beersheba. Rations too were scarce, and a welcome addition to the 'bully beef' was made by taking over a number of bacon pigs from the German farms.

Patrols from the Brigade were actively reconnoitring to the front, and soon located the river Auja some four miles to the north of Jaffa. This is a deep and wide river, and the only

possible crossings that could be discovered were a bridge at
Khurbet Hadrah, over which ran the main north road; a ford
about two miles further east; another at Jerisheh (about half
way between Khurbet Hadrah and the sea); and a fourth
crossing at the mouth of the river on the sea beach. The
average width of the river was thirty-five yards, and the depth
five to seven feet, with steep banks and a soft muddy bottom.

While the occupation of Jaffa and the patrolling northward
to the Auja had been occupying the Anzac Mounted Division
since Nov. 16th, the Yeomanry Division, the Australian Mounted
Division and two infantry divisions (the 52nd and 75th) had

The Town Hall, Jaffa.

swung into the Judean hills in an attempt to seize Jerusalem.
The advance of these troops was stubbornly resisted by the
Turks, and the fighting was made doubly difficult by the sudden
change in the weather, a change from hot dusty days to bitterly
cold winds and much rain.

To prevent the withdrawal of troops of the Turkish VIII.
Army, who were holding the line of the Auja River in the
Plain of Sharon, to assist the VII. Army in its defence of
Jerusalem, an attack was ordered by General Allenby. The

Anzac Mounted Division received orders to cross the Auja and to establish bridge-heads north of the river covering the crossings.

The only troops available were the N.Z.M.R. Brigade, the remainder of the Division being engaged holding the enemy further east to the foothills.

Early on the morning of November 24th the Canterbury Regiment, with the 8th Squadron leading, crossed the Auja at the mouth, followed by the Wellingtons, and a brilliant little action followed. So rapid were the movements of the two regiments that the Turks were taken completely by surprise. The Canterbury Mounted Rifles, at a gallop, seized the hills on the far side of the ford and then rushed the village of Sheikh Muannis. The Wellington Regiment, moving through the Canterburys, galloped eastward and captured Khurbet Hadrah, which commanded the bridge on the main road. About 30 prisoners were taken with a machine gun and ammunition.

At dusk the 161st Brigade (54 Division) took over the line held by the N.Z.M.R., and asked that mounted men be left at the bridge and the village of Sheikh Muannis to patrol in front of the posts established by them.

So two squadrons of the Auckland Regiment and one squadron of the Wellington Regiment were placed in advance of the infantry posts. The 1st squadron of the Canterburys, under Major Hurst, took up a position in front of the ford at the mouth of the river.

The enemy was not long in accepting the challenge made by our crossing the river, for just before dawn on November 25th he heavily attacked the Auckland squadrons in front of the bridge-head at Khurbet Hadrah.

He was driven off, but, bringing up large reinforcements and many guns as the light grew, again came on. This attack rapidly grew in intensity and spread to Sheikh Muannis, where at about 8.30 a force of some two thousand Turks, covered by an accurate shell fire, made a very determined advance.

In order to save the horses of the three squadrons engaged, the horseholders, while the men on foot held off the Turks, took the horses down the river to the ford at its mouth, all other crossings being under hot fire.

The infantry were ordered to fall back across the river, and as soon as this became known General Chaytor ordered the New Zealand squadrons to fall back also as soon as the infantry were clear; in order to enable this to be done Colonel Findlay, with the remaining two squadrons of the Regiment, crossed over the ford on the beach and attacked the enemy's right, sending the 10th Squadron under Major Acton-Adams to the help of the 2nd Wellington Squadron at Sheikh Muannis.

Finding no cover for his horses, Major Acton-Adams sent them back to the ford at the beach, being prepared, as were the other Squadron Commanders, to get their men out on foot when the need came. Great use was made by our men of their machine guns in holding off the great masses of Turks, but they were given no help whatever by the artillery, who were caught on the move, changing positions with the incoming infantry division. But just as the Khurbet Hadrah position was being evacuated some guns of the 161st Brigade and of the Somerset battery (attached to the N.Z.M.R.) opened fire, but too late to influence the battle.

The evacuation of Sheikh Muannis was most skilfully carried out with the help of the Somerset battery firing from a position on the south side of the river at not more than 1,400 yards range. All the infantry were first sent across the river by means of a boat and the weir-head at a flour mill. Then followed the 2nd Wellington Squadron and two troops of the 10th Squadron. As soon as they were clear the remaining two troops of the 10th retired towards the mouth of the river, giving each other support from position to position.

The full force of the Turk attack now fell upon the 1st and 8th Squadrons of the Canterbury Regiment, who were covering the ford from positions on the hills immediately to the north of the river's mouth.

Colonel Findlay ordered the Regiment to fall back, and, handling his men in a masterly manner, soon had the troops from Muannis safely across. It was a very difficult movement, a withdrawal in broad daylight, when in close contact with a fresh enemy and under heavy fire.

Major Hurst's squadron formed the rear-guard, holding the hills to the last, with the help of Lieutenant Edridge and his machine guns, until all others were safely across. The Squadron then began its own retirement, troop by troop, falling back to fire positions, so covering each others movements until the ford was reached.

The last troop to reach the ford was commanded by Lieutenant Livingstone, who handled his men with the greatest skill and courage, held off the advancing Turks to the last possible moment, and then, sending his men across, he was killed as he followed them through the water.

The Regiment had many times broken off an action when in close contact with the enemy by moving rapidly at night, but to do so in daylight in open country, with the added difficulty of extricating men fighting on foot, and the care of the wounded, requires a very high standard of discipline, courage and skilful tactical handling.

The Turks were evidently content with their success, and made no attempt to cross the river, but the Regiment was kept ready to move at half an hour's notice. Guards, patrols and fatigues took up the time. A number of reinforcements marched in, which helped considerably. Even so the Regiment was sixty men below strength, but was expected to do, and did, the work of a full strength regiment, either in holding a line or in the matter of finding fatigues.

Under date December 3rd, 1917, the following entry occurs in the War Diary:—

"Stood ready to move at short notice. Two snipers detailed for duty to watch for signalling to Turks from Sarona. J.B.H." This entry recalls the story that rumours of lamp signalling at night were rife. It was said that the Germans in the farm colony of Sarona were in communication with the Turks. One very dark night an excited messenger rushed into New Zealand Brigade Headquarters on the outskirts of Jaffa saying that signallers out in front repairing lines had distinctly seen signalling from a house, and were prepared to guide a force to the place. The ——— Mounted Rifles, being in reserve that night, were immediately ordered to send off a troop on foot with the guide. The darkness was profound, and the troop after stumbling through orchards, scrambling through innumerable cactus hedges, and falling foul of a battery of 18 pounders, at last sighted a house very dimly lit on the rearward side. Elaborate precautions were taken by the troop leader, and after a triumph of intricate minor tactics the house was successfully surrounded, and there from a window in front were most unmistakable flashings. With his heart in his mouth and thoughts of a M.C. in his mind, the troop leader wormed his way to the window, stood cautiously up, and peering in saw Colonel Findlay and three others seated at a table, in the centre of which stood a lamp. It was the Colonel's deal, and as he dealt with his back to the window his moving arm——; but the troop leader did not wait for more. Hurriedly and very silently he gathered in his men and retired to camp.

On December 4th the Regiment went into the line and relieved a battalion of the Imperial Camel Corps, the change over being completed by midnight. The line consisted of a series of posts running from Hill 246 to Hill 265, between Jaffa and the foothills. The trenches were, in many cases, badly sited and afforded little cover. The horses remained behind, and a certain number of men were detailed to look after them. Sniping went on continuously, but caused few casualties, though the trenches were much damaged by shell fire. Owing to heavy shelling it was impossible to bring up rations and water to the trenches till after dark. The wet season had now arrived, and was to continue with very little intermission for the next two months. With shell fire, rain and shortage of rations the Regiment's stay in the trenches was not very pleasant. There was nothing to build up the trenches with, and they fell in or were blown in by the shells as fast as the men could dig them out, and to add to the general unpleasantness, everybody was wet through all the time.

It was found necessary to relieve some of the men in the trenches who were feeling the effects of the strain and continual exposure, so, on the 8th a change over was made with the men looking after the horses, these being the only ones available. The change over was a case of "out of the frying pan and into the fire."

These men, besides looking after four or five horses each, had to do fatigues and cart rations and water to the trenches, the latter at night.

Owing to the continual rain, the tracks and country generally became absolutely waterlogged. It was simply asking for trouble to go anywhere. The Australians talked about the "black soil plains" of their country, but even they were silent now. The trenches were simply gaps in the earth, half full of liquid mud, and fell in as fast as they were dug out. While this fighting was being carried on along the banks of the Auja to the north of Jaffa, the fighting in the mountains for Jerusalem was steadily continued. Bad weather, absence of roads, and want of transport (though some two thousand Egyptian donkeys did much to help), delayed and hampered the troops.

Jerusalem from the Mount of Olives.

Three infantry divisions, the 60th, 74th and 10th, were at this time within a few miles of Jerusalem on the western side, with their right resting on the railway in the Wadi Surar. On their right flank was the 10th Light Horse under command of Lieut.-Colonel Todd, and this regiment had the honour of being among the first British troops to enter the Holy City. The forces in the mountains had been helped by the Yeomanry and Australian Mounted Divisions, who fought on foot, leaving their horses on the plains.

On December 8th began the last great act in which the Holy City was to pass from the hand of the Moslem, who had held it since the days of the Crusades. At dawn, in the midst of rain and wind, the 60th Division (London Territorial), with the 74th Division (Dismounted Yeomanry) on its left, stormed the formidable hills to the east of the Wadi Surar; and by nightfall all the strong positions to the west of the city, so laboriously and so skilfully dug out of the solid rock, were in our hands.

During the night the 53rd Division pushed up the Hebron road and occupied Bethlehem.

General Allenby's report goes on to say:—"Towards dusk the British troops were reported to have passed Lifta, and to be within sight of the city. On this news being received, a sudden panic fell on the Turks west and southwest of the town, and at 5 o'clock civilians were surprised to see a Turkish transport column galloping furiously cityward along the Jaffa road. In passing they alarmed all units within sight or hearing, and the wearied infantry arose and fled, bootless and without rifles, never pausing to think or to fight.

"After four centuries of conquest the Turk was ridding the land of his presence in the bitterness of defeat, and a great enthusiasm arose among the Jews. There was a running to and fro; daughters called to their fathers and brothers concealed in outhouses, cellars and attics, from the police who sought them for arrest and deportation. 'The Turks are running', they called; 'the day of deliverance is come'. The nightmare was fast passing away, but the Turks still lingered. In the evening he fired his guns continuously, perhaps heartening himself with the loud noise that comforts the soul of a barbarian; perhaps to cover the sound of his own retreat. Whatever the intention was, the roar of the gun fire persuaded most citizens to remain indoors, and there were few to witness the last act of Osmanli authority.

"At 2 o'clock in the morning of Sunday, December 9th, tired troops began to troop through the Jaffa gate from the west and south-west, and anxious watchers, peering out through the windows to learn the meaning of the tramping, were cheered by the sullen remark of an officer, "Gitmaya mejburuz" (we've got to go); and from 2 to 7 that morning the Turks streamed through and out of the city, which echoed for the last time their shuffling tramp. On this same day, 2,082 years before, another race of conquerors, equally detested, were looking their

How the Brigade Rode through the Plain

last on the city which they could not hold; and inasmuch as the liberation of Jerusalem in 1917 will probably ameliorate the lot of the Jews more than that of any other community in Palestine, it was fitting that the flight of the Turks should have coincided with the national festival of the Hanukah, which commemorates the recapture of the Temple from the heathen Seleucids by Judas Maccabaeus in 165 B.C."

On December 11th the Commander-in-Chief, followed by representatives of the Allies, made his formal entry into Jerusalem. The historic Jaffa gate was opened after years of disuse for the purpose, and he was thus enabled to pass into the Holy City without making use of the gap in the wall made for the German Emperor William in 1898. The General entered the city on foot—and left it on foot.

For this occasion the Brigade sent a troop as a bodyguard to General Allenby. The troop was commanded by 2nd Lieutenant C. J. Harris, Canterbury Regiment, and was composed of one sergeant and ten men from the Auckland Regiment, nine men from the Canterbury Regiment, and nine from the Wellington Regiment, with three from the Machine Gun Squadron and one from the Signal Troop; a total of one officer and thirty-three other ranks.

On this day the Brigade was relieved in the front line by the 162nd Brigade (infantry), and marched to bivouacs in the vicinity of Ayun Kara; but the Auckland Regiment was sent into Jaffa, where it came under the orders of the 52nd Division; and on the 12th the Wellington Regiment was sent to the village of Beit Dejan, on the Jaffa-Ramleh road, where it came under orders of the 54th Division.

On the night of the 9th Colonel Findlay's headquarters were rudely disturbed by a Turkish officer, who had, in the darkness and rain, stumbled through our posts. He was discovered when he fell through the adjutant's bivvie. It was hard to say who was the more surprised, but the remarks of the Adjutant showed that he, at all events, was not pleased. The Turk sat and sobbed bitterly, while a man was being procured to escort him to Brigade Headquarters. Poor devil, he was evidently about the end of his tether, owing to fright and exposure.

On the evening of the 10th the London Battalion took over the trenches and the Regiment moved back to Ayun Kara, arriving about half past one on the morning of the 11th.

On the 13th the Regiment again moved, this time to the sandhills near Esdud. The ride over the plains and creeks,

Major D. S. Murchison.

the latter much swollen by the torrential rains, was a difficult one. Transport wagons got hopelessly bogged, and in one or two cases horses also. It was while endeavouring to get a horse out of a bog that the veterinary officer got a ducking. Some of the men had put a rope round the horse, but their efforts did not meet with the approval of the Vet. Getting another rope round the unfortunate animal, he called to one or two men standing near, "Here, pull this," at the same time pulling hard himself. The rope broke, and he had to be assisted out of the liquid sea of mud. Those who knew Veterinary officers will relish what he said.

It is worthy of note that in this same month of January, King Richard I. marched his forces from Ramleh to Ascalon over this self-same route, and that he too experienced to the full the discomforts of a winter's march on the plains of Palestine. His old chronicler says:—

"At dawn of day the men with the tents were sent forward, and the rest of the army followed; the sufferings of the day before were nothing to those which they now endured from fatigue, rain, hail and floods. The ground, too, was muddy and soft beneath them, and the horses and men had the greatest difficulty to maintain their footing; some of them sunk never to rise again. Who can tell the calamities of that day? The bravest of the soldiers shed tears like rain, and were wearied even of their very existence for the severity of their sufferings. When the beasts of burden fell, the provisions which they carried were either spoiled by the mud or dissolved in the water. This day was the 20th January, in the year 1192, and they encamped for the night, every man as well as he was able."

The new camp was a vast improvement on what had been experienced lately. The Regiment was bivouaced on the sandhills just clear of the black soil plain, on sand so hated in Sinai, but now welcomed as an old friend, for it was dry and clean, though the prevailing westerly winds did pile it up over the bivvies.

The higher authorities allowed no let-up in training, which was supposed to start at once, but the weather was more considerate, and till after Christmas the rain effectually precluded any systematic training being undertaken. Great endeavours were made to keep Christmas Day according to custom. Major Acton Adams had managed, by fair means or otherwise, to get to Cairo, and returned with everything needful. The weather excelled itself on Christmas Day, as the rain literally fell down. But the day was celebrated to the best of our ability. The carol-singers, led by Eric Harper, a well known Christchurch solicitor (who at a later date was killed in action down by Jericho, a loss much regretted by all who knew him both in the Regiment and at home), visited the different squadron lines in the evening and put a finish to the day.

The main work now was to build up the horses. Since leaving Esani two months before, except for a week at Sarona, they had

Major J. Stafford, Regimental Veterinary Officer.

been on a bare grain ration. Now the army ration is always a bare modicum, it does not profess to fatten, and at this time of the year, midwinter, no grazing or extras were available. The new single line railway which had been built from the Suez Canal across the Sinai and up the coast of Palestine, 150 miles in length, was having great difficulties, owing to washouts and flooding, in coping with supplies. The present railhead was at Esdud, and the plain round here, with the continual traffic of all descriptions, was a sea of mud, in the centre of which stood the fodder dump. So inaccessible was this that in places bales of compressed forage were used to build a road for the transport wagons. Second only to the cry for fodder, and more fodder, was the call for the horse covers, stored in far away Cairo. Our need of these did not escape the Corps Commander's notice, and in the second week of January, 1918, the covers were sent to us.

Fodder, good water and covers, combined with easy exercise and plenty of grooming, rapidly built the horses up again. The men also, considering what they had gone through, were in good health. They endured much. First there had been the long rides, with the dust so thick that only the outline of the troop in front could be seen, then the heavy fighting, followed by the long chase, which culminated in the trenches north of Jaffa. To weather so hot as to be almost unbearable, succeeded the last month of bitter cold and wet. All this time living on monotonous diet of bully beef and hard biscuits, and often without either, whilst the water question was always serious, these grand men laughed at it all and looked forward to the next advance.

The country around was interesting to us all. Esdud (Ashdod) was our present railhead, while a few miles north was Akir, the old Biblical Ekron. Like most of the towns on the plains of Palestine, Esdud is a city set on a low hill composed of the ruins of several previous cities which had been sacked and destroyed in the innumerable sieges which all these towns have experienced.

Considering the difficulties of bringing up supplies, the railway was being pushed forward in a wonderful manner. Bridges had to be built over the larger wadis, and many culverts put in. Wet weather or fine, still the work of construction went on, and a railhead was pushed forward to Surafend, near our old camp at Ayun Kara.

On January 12th, 1918, the Brigade moved back to this camp through pouring rain. The new camp was well situated on the slope of a hill of sand, now always looked for. Ayun Kara, or as it is more often called, Richon le Zion, is a Jewish settlement, one of the first founded in connection with the Zionist movement some years ago. It seemed a fairly prosperous place, despite Turkish misrule and three years of war. A noticeable feature are the wine vaults, which enjoy the reputation of being the third largest in the world. It has also extensive orange groves, and its mulberry trees are said to exceed twenty thousand in number.

A regiment from our Division had been holding a portion of the front line in the hills at Nalin, about ten miles east of Ludd, and it was now the Canterburys' turn for this duty. The Regiment relieved the 2nd Australian Light Horse here on the 20th. All the horses, except the Hotchkiss guns and ammunition packs, were sent back to Ayun Kara. Fourteen officers and two hundred and eleven other ranks remained at Nalin, and the balance of the regiment looked after the horses. Er Ramleh and Ludd, the two towns passed through on the road to Nalin, are situated about three miles apart in a huge olive grove, about eight miles east of Jaffa. At Ramleh, supposed to be the town of Arimathea of Biblical fame, the most noticeable feature is the "Tower of the Forty Martyrs," the only remaining portion of an early Christian church. Otherwise the place is uninteresting, consisting only of a narrow, crooked and dirty street. At Ludd is an old Crusaders' church, and in a crypt beneath the altar one sees the reputed tomb of St. George of England. Nalin is perched on the top of a high hill and looks picturesque enough from a distance, but loses all its beauty on closer acquaintance, and becomes a characteristic native village of the hills. The country round about consists of rocky hills, the foot-hills of the Judean range, and valleys running towards the plains. The view from the top of any of the hills is magnificent, showing the whole plain of Sharon to the blue sea beyond. It is a country of wonderful contrasts; within a few miles are hills and plains, orange groves and vineyards, fertile fields and barren sand dunes, inhabited by the most industrious yet poorest people in the world, with a history stretching back to the earliest ages.

The defences at Nalin consisted of a series of stone sangars, owing to the ground being too rocky to dig trenches, and much work was necessary to provide any protection in case of attack. The natural formation of the country, being steep and broken, was good from the Regiment's point of view, as it was here purely on the defensive. There were no roads, and the existing goat tracks had to be made into roads, so there was plenty of work for all to do. Regimental Headquarters established themselves in a cave, reported to have been, in happier days, the spot where Judas Maccabeus gloried and drank deep, no doubt on water, for there was no vestige of anything else about these rocks.

But water, though at present a superfluity, was likely to be the opposite the next summer if the Turkish line held, so the adjacent hills and valleys were explored, and numerous cisterns were found, probably a thousand years old, cut deep into the limestone rock, holding some millions of gallons of good water.

Once settled down there were generally fifty to eighty men working on the roads, whilst the remainder improved the defences. The infantry held positions on both sides, and much interest was taken in the shooting of the Hotchkiss and Lewis guns.

In several shooting matches held to try out the respective merits of these weapons, the Lewis proved the more reliable on the day.

On February 3rd the 6th Australian Light Horse took over the line, and the Regiment returned to Ayun Kara.

CHAPTER XV.

How the Regiment Went Up to Jerusalem and Through the Wilderness to Jericho.

The XX Corps, after much gallant fighting, had entered Jerusalem on 9th December; and by repeated attacks, culminating in heavy fighting on December 26th to December 31st, the 60th Division had forced the enemy northward along the Judean plateau for a distance of some eight miles from Jerusalem. But the Turks still occupied in strength the land of Moab, across the Dead Sea, and still held the Dead Sea and

Jaffa Gate.

Jordan Valley and the 'Wilderness' country up to within five miles eastwards of Bethlehem and Jerusalem. Along this eastern line the 53rd Division held him in check. For the further protection of Jerusalem and of our forces to the north, and to stop the large grain supplies that the enemy was receiving from Kerak and the country to the east of the Dead Sea by way of motor boat transport, landing near the mouth of the Jordan, the Commander in Chief decided to occupy Jericho. For this purpose the Anzac Mounted Division was ordered to the vicinity of Jerusalem.

On February 9th the Wellington Mounted Rifles left its bivouac at Richon and marched to Bethlehem, and engaged in close reconnaissance of the 'Wilderness' east of Bethlehem.

A few days later the rest of the N.Z. Brigade followed, taking a route away from the main Jaffa-Ramleh-Jerusalem road. The march took the Regiment across the plain past the garden colony of Deiran (Rechoboth), past Akir, the ancient Ekron of the Old Testament and one of the capital cities of the Philistines, and into the foot-hills, striking the old Roman road from Ascalon to Jerusalem, where it enters the Wadi es Sunt, the Valley of Elah. Close by is Tidnah (the ancient Timnath, the native place of Samson's wife), and the road passes by Tell Zakariya, the Azekah of Joshua's time, where he routed the Philistines in the midst of a hail storm. Beyond the narrow pass at Zakariya the wadi opens out into a level valley, cut in two by the steep bed of a stream. Here David slew Goliath.

The Regiment then followed the Roman road, which had been repaired by the Turks, and emerged on the Judean plateau a little south of Bethlehem on February 17th, camping close to the huge rock-cut reservoirs called King Solomon's Pools. Originally built by King Solomon for the supply of water to Jerusalem, they were rebuilt by Pontius Pilate, and the pools still show large areas of wall covered with Roman plaster.

The weather on the plains had been wet, but here on the bare Judean hills, 2,500 feet above sea level, the cold was severe.

Orders being received that no move would be made on the 18th, the opportunity was taken to send all available men to Jerusalem, and the padres proved invaluable as guides, for they one and all, enthusiastic students of the Holy Land, were well conversant with the city and its site from constant study.

Operations began on February 19th, and the troops available were the 60th Division, with one brigade of the 74th Division, together with two Brigades of the Anzac Mounted Division (the 1st Light Horse and N.Z.M.R.). The Infantry Brigades were in position covering Jerusalem, and were to attack eastward into the 'Wilderness,' following the road from Jerusalem to Jericho; while the two mounted Brigades were to concentrate in the vicinity of El Muntar, the hill of the 'Scape Goat,' upon which lay the enemy's left. The mounted

O

men were to push over El Muntar and, following native tracks, to assist the attack of the infantry by falling upon the enemy flank and threatening his retreat through Jericho.

Preceded by the Wellington Regiment as advanced guard the Brigade followed down the steep and narrow Wadi en Nar, marching all night; and daylight on the 20th found it strung out in single file over a rocky bridle track about a mile east of El Muntar. All night the men had been clambering over rocky tracks leading their horses, following

The Damascus Gate, Jerusalem.

what was marked on the map "Ancient Road." No wheels nor guns were taken, no supplies but such as could be carried on man and horse, and the reserve ammunition was conveyed by a small camel train of light active camels.

As day broke it was seen that the country east of El Muntar fell down in deep jagged ravines towards the Dead Sea some three thousand feet below; and the Turk soon made his presence felt by opening fire on the advanced guard. It appeared that he was holding a strong position on the far side of a broad level basin away down below, and it was 7 a.m. before the Regiment came into action.

The last 1,200 feet of descent was made in full view of the enemy, who must have been considerably shaken at seeing some eight miles of horses defiling down the hills right in his rear.

How the Regiment went to Jerusalem

Major Acton-Adams, who was temporarily in command of the Regiment, advanced against the enemy holding a strong hill (288), with the 8th and 10th Squadrons in front and the 1st in reserve, but seeing that the going was too rough for the 10th he brought it in and sent the 1st forward over better country. The Auckland and Wellington Regiments were on the right, and a vigorous attack was made against a strong position well supported by machine guns and a battery of artillery on the hills behind.

Modern Jericho.

The infantry attack down the Jerusalem-Jericho road was progressing well, and by mid-day the enemy gave way, retreating across a great gulch to the hills about Nebi Musa, the so-called tomb of Moses.

The bottom of the valley from which this attack was made is at about sea level, and the Dead Sea is 1,300 feet below sea level, so there still remained a further descent of over a thousand feet to reach the Jericho plain.

There were two narrow defiles down which it was possible to descend, but the Turks stubbornly defended these with machine guns and a battery of artillery until dark. During the night the 1st Light Horse managed to scramble down, and by dawn, when the Regiment sent the 10th Squadron across the gulch on foot, Nebi Musa was found to be abandoned.

At 5.30 a.m. on February 21st the Brigade began the last descent, with Canterbury leading, and the valley was reached at 9 a.m.

The sick and wounded men from the previous day's fighting, had a painful time following the column in the camel cacolets, and on several occasions they had to be removed from the camels and carried over the worst places. As always was the case, our ambulance men were magnificent; quietly, expeditiously and as gently as possible under the circumstances, their patients were brought down safely. Usually sick and wounded were evacuated at once, but this time the country was so rough that the Mounted Field Ambulance decided to bring them on with the hope of getting motor ambulances when Jericho was captured. Luckily this hope was fulfilled, though there was an unavoidable delay of a few hours till the road was repaired, it having been blown up in several places by the retreating enemy.

The 10th Squadron now rejoined from Neby Musa, and the Regiment immediately pushed on to Jericho. The 1st Light Horse who had clambered down during the night had ridden hard after the Turk, but he got away across the Jordan. The 8th Squadron were detached to repair the road, and rejoined in the afternoon. The regiment took up the line of the Jordan bank from the Dead Sea to the vicinity of the Ghoraniyeh crossing, where the enemy were holding the bridge over which passed the road to Es Salt and Amman. The 1st Squadron, who were in advance, took up their quarters in the monastery of Makhadet Hajla, commanding the Hajla and El Henu fords over the Jordan, and fraternised with the somewhat unwashed coterie of monks who lived there. The Turkish artillery near the Ghoraniyeh bridge was very active, and even shelled single riders crossing the plain.

So fell modern Jericho, a degenerate city full of loathsome disease.

Of all the cities of the east that our men had passed through, Jericho appeared to be the filthiest and most evil-smelling.

The inhabitants, numbering some five hundred, are of a very poor class said to be descended from slaves. It is an extremely unhealthy town, and no white man lives there in the summer time. There are three small hotels, a Russian hospice, a Greek church, a small block of Government buildings and a mass of mud huts. All the principal buildings were found to be filled with dead and dying Turks, victims of the dreaded typhus.

The climatic conditions down by the Jordan were very different from those experienced by the Regiment during the last three months. The sun was partially obscured by clouds, and there was not the extreme heat that was to be experienced

The Dead Sea.

here later. The whole plain was covered with a short grass, and the hills looked green in every direction. After the cold and rain the Jordan Valley was altogether delightful; later it was to be thoroughly hated. Now it was warm, restful and free of the heat, mosquitoes and dust which were to play such havoc with the forces in the summer. The Valley of the Jordan is simply a great crack severing the Judean mountains from the great Arabian plateau. It lies nearly 1,300 feet below sea-level, or nearly 4,000 feet below Jerusalem, and at its widest part is not more than twelve miles broad. On either side tower the mountains, on the western the mountains of Judea, and on the east the mighty wall of Moab.

Looking southwards down the length of the Dead Sea, with a stiff westerly gale blowing overhead and great masses of cloud and mist shrouding the mountain tops, reminded one of the New Zealand Sounds.

Close to modern Jericho could be seen some thirteen or fourteen "tels," obviously ruins of ancient cities or fortresses. The greatest of them is Tel Es Sultan, the Jericho of Joshua. Across the plain in many places lie the remains of Roman aqueducts and reservoirs, showing that the great fertility of the "City of the Palms," as it was called in Herod the Great's time, was no legend. But where once stood the mighty palm forest, 8 miles long and 3 miles broad, now struggle patches of brambles and wild thorn.

The Mosque of Omar.

Jericho is fed by a perennial spring, now called Ain es Sultan (the King's well), which comes from out the rock immediately by Joshua's Jericho. It is the spring of the prophet Elisha, who purified its waters by throwing in a handful of salt, as told in the Second Book of Kings. This procedure was easily understood by the men who had been daily witnesses of the medical orderly "chlorinating water" by throwing in a handful of bleaching powder. Apart from a small irrigated patch close to Jericho, the western side of the Jordan Valley is now a barren wilderness.

The 22nd was spent in patrolling. About 3 o'clock in the afternoon the western side of the river was reported clear of the enemy, and a Canterbury patrol succeeded in getting to the Jordan, though the Turk was strongly holding the bridge and all fords.

At 6 p.m. just as darkness was falling, began the long ride back to Jerusalem, this time by the road, leaving the Aucklanders to guard the Valley. Half way through the wilderness a halt was made, and men and horses absorbed much needed supplies, which had been brought to meet the column by camel transport. Bethlehem was reached at 5 o'clock on the morning of the 23rd, after passing through the village of Bethany and on round the shoulder of Olivet, where on the clear dawn of a winter's day there burst upon view, with her long battlemented walls and her towers and domes silhouetted against the sky, the city of Jerusalem, seated upon her hills. This view, above all seen of the Holy City, will our men ever remember.

Leaving the shoulder of the Mt. of Olives, the way dips down into the Valley of the Kedron, past the Garden of Gethsemane, and, rising, passes round the north-east corner of the city and brings one past St. Stephen's gate, the Damascus gate and the Jaffa gate to the main road to Bethlehem.

The following day as many of the men as could be spared from the multifarious duties of the camp were granted leave to visit the Holy City. A few went, but the majority had not recovered from their exhaustion of the previous four days' heavy work. Jerusalem appears to consist of two cities, ancient and modern, ancient Jerusalem being that portion which lies within the walls. Here the streets are impassable for vehicles, very narrow and in many places built right over, giving one the impression of walking through tunnels. In many places the streets consist of a series of steps, so steep is the hillside on which portions of the city are built. It is within the city walls that one finds the Mosque of Omar, Via Dolorosa, Church of the Holy Sepulchre and the Place of the Wailing. Modern Jerusalem, consisting of all the town outside the walls, dates back only about seventy years. There are many fine buildings, convents, churches, hospitals and schools, but little of interest to a sightseer. The dirt, poverty and begging gave a bad impression, though as time went on, the associations of the place grew on all.

The Jordan.

Bethlehem, where the Regiment was camped, has practically no modern quarter, and the place of most interest was the Church of the Nativity. This is said to be, of all Churches built at the Christian triumph, the only one that remains in any completeness.

Conquerors of Palestine in olden days destroyed all monuments of Christianity, but seem to have overlooked this building, and it remains to-day practically as first built.

On the 25th a return was made to the old camp at Ayun Kara, halting for one night at Zakariyeh. Here the old training continued; squadron and troop drill alternating with bayonet fighting and physical training. A fair amount of leave to Egypt was now being granted to all ranks, and there was no lack of candidates for the leave parties. On arrival in camp a message was received from General Allenby congratulating the Regiment on its work during the Jericho operations, and specially mentioning the manner in which the rough country had been traversed. In his despatches he states, with reference to the mounted men in these last operations "......The mounted troops had encountered considerable opposition, and had been much hampered by the difficulties of the ground. Two miles south of Neby Musa the enemy held the high ground at Jebel el Kalimum and Tubk el Kaneiterah. Compelled to move in single file over tracks which were exposed to machine gun fire from the enemy's position, and which had been registered accurately by the enemy's guns at Neby Musa, the progress of the mounted troops was necessarily slow. By 2 p.m., however, the enemy was driven from his position at Jebel el Kalimum and Tubk el Kaneiterah. The further advance of the New Zealand Brigade was hampered by the ground, and was finally checked at the Wadi Mukelik, the only possible crossing over which, was subjected to a heavy fire from Neby Musa........ On no previous occasions had such difficulties of ground been encountered. As an instance of this, a Field Artillery Battery took thirty-six hours to reach Neby Musa, the distance covered as the crow flies being only eight miles."

The departure of two officers and six men to join the Auckland Mounted rifles, who had remained at Jericho, pointed to something more doing in that direction. Preliminary orders for a move to Bethlehem were received, and on March 13th the Regiment was off again. A halt was made at Junction Station till the 16th, and the move was then continued to Zakariyeh. But it was now the season of the "latter" rains, and the journey was much hampered by the ceaseless downpour. The track from Junction Station was a quagmire.

The camel transport broke down hopelessly, and much baggage was lost. At Zakariyeh the whole countryside was a mass of mud and water. Camp lines were formed as well as possible, but bivvies were useless owing to the soaked condition of the ground, and the majority of the men sat by their horses all night with their waterproof sheets wrapped round them. Luckily it was warmer than it had been.

The march was resumed on the 18th, and Bethlehem was reached late in the afternoon. These may seem to be short marches, Ayun Kara to Junction Station ten miles, Junction Station to Zakariyeh eight miles, Zakariyeh to Bethlehem twenty miles, but until Zakariyeh was reached the route lay through the bottomless black mud of the plains.

At Bethlehem the Regiment's camp was in the bottom of a valley between the town and Beit Jala, a very wet and boggy place with a scarcity of firewood, and great difficulty was experienced in getting sufficient even to make tea, for though camped in a large grove of olive trees, none were allowed to be cut down. It was a great temptation but the rule was well kept.

CHAPTER XVI.

How the Regiment Crossed the Jordan For the First Time.

On the night of the 20th the Regiment rode down to Talaat ed Dumm, the halfway house to Jericho, called the House of the Good Samaritan. Here, the only water available was in the Wadi Kelt, a thousand feet below. This does not seem very far, but when it means taking horses down a barely discernible path winding round the face of a precipice, it is a long way, and the difficulties occurring through meeting camels going or coming caused endless delays. Many of the horses never got over the dread of these brutes, and even to the end of the campaign could not be got to face them.

It soon became known that the Jordan was to be crossed when the weather moderated, and the flood in the river subsided. A force consisting of the 60th Division, Anzac Mounted Division and the Imperial Camel Brigade was to make a rapid raid on Es Salt and Amman, the object being to destroy the Hadjaz railway at the latter place.

The 60th Division was to advance up the motor road to Es Salt and to occupy this town; the role of the mounted men being to protect the right flank of the infantry, to work up on to the plateau, and to make an opening for a raid to destroy the great viaduct on the Hedjaz railway at Amman.

Every available moment of time was used in studying the land across the Jordan, and from the heights at Talaat ed Dumm one saw the mountains of Moab and Gilead rising as a sheer wall some 4,000 feet above the Jericho plain. And up that wall there could not be seen a road; yet when the ascent was made it was found that the great plateau of Moab and Gilead was seamed by innumerable watercourses, many of them great gulches reaching far back from the Jordan.

Es Salt is to-day a city of some eighteen thousand souls, close to Jebel Osha, the ancient Mount Gilead, and is famous for its raisins.

Amman goes back into the dim ages of the Old Testament. It was the Rabbath Ammon captured by David's great soldier. Later as Philadelphia, it was one of the cities of the Decapolis, and is now the finest Roman ruin east of the Jordan, and is the centre of a grain growing district.

At this season of the year the Jordan is in flood and all fords impassable. The Turks had burned the Ghoraniyeh bridge, so it was decided to build at its site a pontoon bridge, and another at the Mahadet Hajla ford, where in all probability Joshua and his Israelites crossed to attack Jericho.

After much difficulty a party of the 2/19 London Regiment of the 60th Division got across at Mahadet Hajla and the Anzac Bridging Train soon commenced work and built a pontoon bridge. But at Ghoraniyeh the opposition put up by the Turks prevented anything being done. By noon on March 22nd two Battalions of the London Regiment crossed over the pontoon bridge, and at 4 a.m. on the 23rd the Auckland Mounted Rifles went over and immediately got to work to clear the enemy away. By a brilliant and gallant charge they drove a Turkish Squadron of Cavalry into the hills, rode down the Turkish infantry posts and cleared the plain right up to Ghoraniyeh.

The infantry were quickly across here and a pontoon bridge was built.

By daylight on the 24th the New Zealand Brigade was across and heading into the mountains by way of the Wadi Jeria.

At three o'clock in the afternoon the Regiment commenced the climb; the 1st Squadron, temporarily attached to the Auckland Mounted Rifles, forming the advanced guard. The lack of accurate maps and the entire absence of any tracks, made the task of finding a way passable for animals very difficult.

To make matters worse, it came on to rain again, and all view of the surrounding country was obscured by clouds. At 4.30 p.m. the Wadi Jeria was left, and ascending the steep hills the Regiment crossed over to the Wadi Sir. The country, so far as could be seen was magnificent. Wild flowers grew everywhere, and wherever one looked there was a blaze of colour, but in the wet, and riding in single file, one soon forgot how beautiful the country was. At dusk a halt was made at Sir Abbada, about halfway up the mountains. Here the column was joined by the first of the local Arabs, a poor collection of men of the Adwan tribe, armed with a variety of rifles, pistols, daggers and wooden clubs, whose declared object was to knock all wounded Turks on the head —in reality, it appeared they applied the practice impartially to both sides. In fact they knew no sides; the "sport" of knocking wounded men on the head, and loot, seemed the main object of their lives. Any petty thieving appealed to them, as the worthy Medical Officer found out to his cost; for lying down for a well earned rest with his boots beside him, he awoke to find them gone.

Some of the Hedjaz Arabs.

At daylight on the 25th the climb was continued, at first over small spurs, slipping off the flat shelving rocks into the mud, then into a rocky wadi in which the usually small creek was now a raging torrent of muddy water. The rain continued and the higher the force climbed the greater grew the cold, and the more difficult the rocky tracks. All wheels, including the guns, had been left behind owing to the simple impossibility of bringing them up tracks so steep and rough that for hours at a time the men had to lead their horses. All rations and forage also had to be left behind beyond what each man and horse could carry. Wet through and almost perished with cold, the advanced guard reached the plateau by midday, capturing about fifty prisoners in the village of Ain Es Sir as they passed through. Two hours later the remainder of the regiment had arrived and a halt was made while Brigade Headquarters tried to get in touch with Divisional Headquarters, who were struggling through the mountains somewhere south. The only means of communication was a small wireless set packed on horses and mules. Eventually an outpost line was taken up about two miles out on the plateau. At 11 p.m. a patrol of six German infantry marched right into our outposts and were captured showing that our arrival on the plateau was unknown to the enemy at Amman, and shortly after nine the following morning three mounted men came over the rising ground and were caught by the fire of two of our posts.

All day on the 26th the Regiment remained in the same position. Our patrols reconnoitred the country towards Amman, which lay about six miles east. The men suffered from the cold and wet, and were quite ready to vent their troubles on any stray Turks or Germans who attempted to approach our position.

The plan of operations provided for the concentration of the Division on the plateau, interception of the garrison of Es Salt (who were being attacked by the 60th Division) and finally for the capture of Amman and the cutting of the Hedjaz railway.

The concentration was successfully accomplished during the morning by the arrival of the 2nd Light Horse Brigade, the Camel Brigade and the Anzac Mounted Division Headquarters; and about noon news was received of the successful occupation of Es Salt by the Infantry with whom was the 6th Wellington Squadron.

But the Australian horses and the camels were too exhausted for an immediate advance.

At daylight on the 27th the attack on Amman began. The plateau was very boggy and progress was slow. Picking a way over the plain, the 8th Squadron, under Major Gorton, came in touch with the enemy east of Kusr. Finding it impossible to advance in the face of the machine gun and rifle

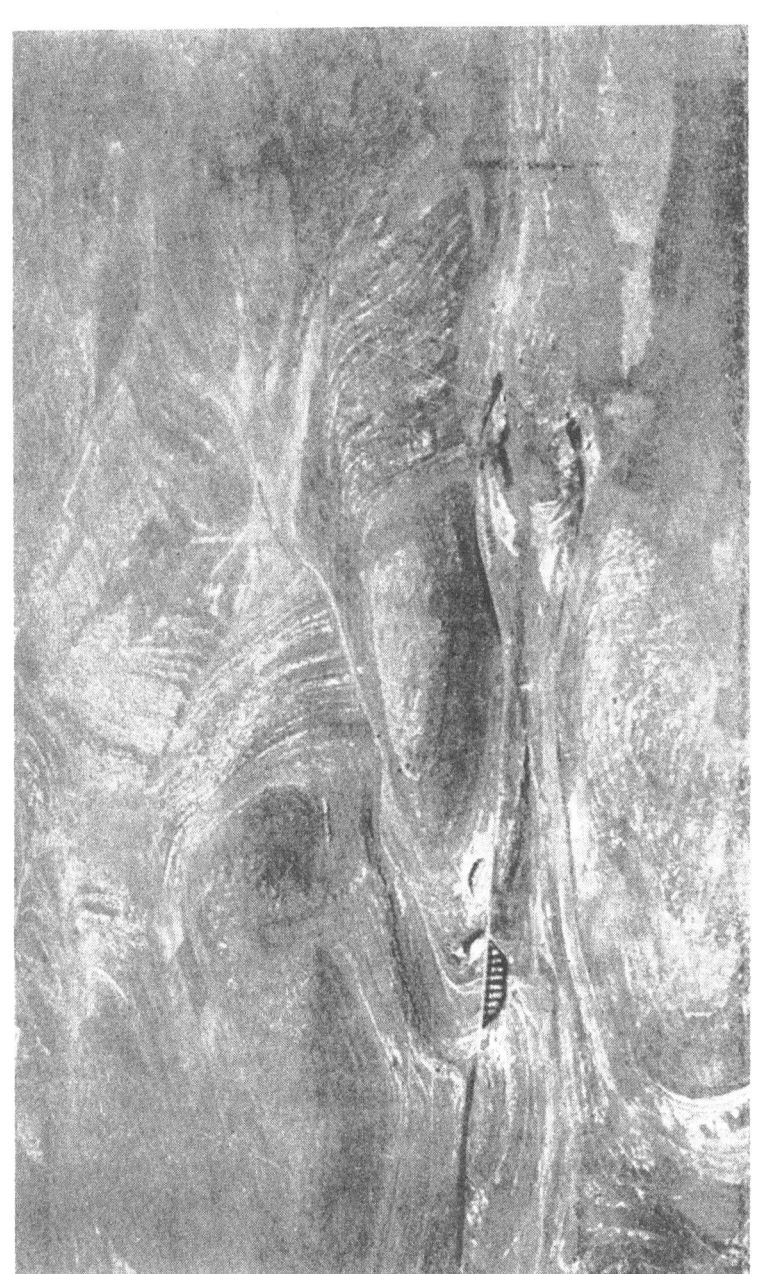

The Viaduct at Amman seen from the Air.

fire, this Squadron took up a line here, whilst the 1st Squadron, under Captain Macfarlane, went forward on their right and seized a small hill. Further on the right Wellington and Auckland crossing the Wadi were also held up. The Imperial Camel Brigade came up on the left of the 8th Squadron, with the 2nd Australian Light Horse Brigade on the left of the Camels.

A portion of the Canterbury line in the Wadi Amman.

At 4 p.m. the 8th Squadron endeavoured to advance in conjunction with the Imperial Camel Brigade, but beyond improving their position slightly, the advance failed. Enemy artillery and machine gun fire increased during the afternoon, but casualties were light owing to good cover.

At 7.25 p.m. the enemy advanced against the Regiment's right, but were easily driven off. During the night patrols investigated the enemy positions with a view to renewing the attack the following day, and a small party from the 2nd Light Horse Brigade penetrated to the railway north of Amman and blew up a two arch bridge.

At daylight on the 28th the whole force attacked again, but it was impossible to advance, for not only had the enemy numerous guns placed well back out of reach of our machine gun and rifle fire but he had a superiority in machine guns and, as it turned out, in men. There was also the added difficulty that the greater part of General Chaytor's force was attacking down a convex slope, so that the Turk always had our men on the skyline. The 1st Squadron took a small trench on their front but were then held up by machine gun fire. Wellington and Auckland Mounted Rifles on the right with the 4th Camel Battalion which was now attached to the New Zealand Brigade, were also held up for the same reason. The Brigade now held a good defensive line, but the bare country on to the front was dominated by the enemy on Hill 3039. This hill was strongly held by the Turks, and it became evident that as long as they remained there Amman could not be taken. The want of artillery was now felt acutely. General Meldrum had been asking for artillery all day, and during the afternoon two light camel guns of the Hong Kong Battery arrived but as they were short of ammunition they did not help matters much. The 181st Brigade (60th Division) from Es Salt, after a long tiring march, came up about mid-day and immediately attacked on the left of the Camel Corps. They suffered heavy casualties and were finally held up some distance from the enemy positions. All day and night the force hung on to its hard won positions, waiting for more infantry and artillery.

It rained without ceasing, and the troops were wet through and nearly perished with cold. Rations had been brought up by transport camels but great difficulty was experienced in getting them distributed to the men in the line. It was impossible to light fires, even if wood had been available.

Infantry and artillery were expected early on the 30th, so it was decided to make a dismounted attack on Hill 3039 early that morning. Here the enemy position was somewhat in the shape of a shamrock, the stem representing the ridge leading to the main and strongest position, which consisted of two trenches in tiers dominating the approach along the ridge, with a third trench on higher ground behind, and a fourth trench three hundred yards further back on the northern point of the hill. Officers and men in our present line

P

were reduced to a minimum, and finally 11 officers and 102 other ranks were withdrawn to the right flank to form part of the assaulting party. The Auckland Mounted Rifles and the 4th Battalion of the Imperial Camel Brigade, with a troop from Wellington Mounted Rifles, formed the balance of the party. At 2 a.m. on the morning of the 30th these men formed up and moved out to attack the hill. The attack was delivered in two lines, Auckland and the 4th Battalion forming the first under command of Lieut.-Colonel McCarroll, while the second consisted of Canterbury and Wellington men under Major Acton-Adams.

The plan adopted was to pass swifty and silently along the ridge betwen the two smaller positions and fall upon the main position "A" on the higher hill behind the two, the two flanking positions "B" and "C" being merely silently contained by small parties in case they became active. "A" having been captured it was considered that "B" and "C" would be compelled to surrender.

This plan was simple yet daring and required the most skilful leading in the dark and the utmost resolution on the part of every officer, N.C.O. and man. The position had been reconnoitred by the Auckland officers during the day and the plan was carefully considered and thoroughly talked over by General Meldrum with all the officers concerned.

At half past one on the morning of March 30th the small force concentrated dismounted at the line of deployment in the wadi at the foot of Hill 3039 in the midst of bitter rain and wind and in intense darkness. The advance of the two lines took place punctually at 2 o'clock over an open flat for a distance of 800 yards until the ascent of the ridge forming the stalk of the shamrock was reached.

Two subsections of machine guns went forward with the assaulting troops while the remainder of the machine gun Squadron took up a covering position in case a retirement became necessary.

The trenches at "A" were successfully reached without alarming the enemy in "B" and "C", and the garrison bayonetted with the exception of 23 Turks who surrendered with five machine guns.

The trenches and sangers were at once altered to face the other way while the 2nd line, Canterburys and Wellingtons, came through and went for the trenches behind "A".

There was about 300 yards to go and the thin line when about half-way across encountered a heavy fire from machine guns and rifles, momentarily checking its advance. But inspired by the coolness of Lieutenant Murray of the 10th Squadron the men, scrambling forward over the wet and slippery rocks, hurled themselves into the midst of the enemy, eventually capturing the position with fourteen live Turks and a machine gun.

As soon as this position had been consolidated and the 16th Company (New Zealanders) of the 4th Camel Battalion had come up, an attack was made on the final position on the front of the hill overlooking Amman. This was carried by the 8th Squadron (Canterburys) and the 16th Camel Company.

As soon as daylight came the enemy parties in "B" and "C" surrendered with one officer, forty other ranks, and five machine guns.

The line now ran across the hill from east to west as follows:—4th Battalion Camel Brigade, Wellington Regiment, Canterbury Regiment and Auckland Regiment, and all ranks were working for their lives to build some sort of defence but the ground was so hard and rocky that trenches could not be dug, sangers built up as high as possible taking their place.

Soon after daylight the enemy began to shell the top of Hill 3039. Stone sangers are effective enough against rifle and machine gun fire but against artillery fire they were veritable traps, shrapnel ricochetting in all directions and high explosive hurling the rocks and stones broadcast.

Counter-attack after counter-attack was flung back by this gallant little line throughout that dreadful day and between the attacks the enemy searched out every corner of that rocky area with shells from his guns.

At 9.30 the first attack came, pressed by the Turk with the greatest determination and preceded by a perfect tornado of shells. But the Brigade machine guns, aided by those of the Camels and five captured Turkish guns, had been well and carefully sited and brought a withering fire to bear upon the advancing enemy.

But his great numbers brought him right up to our line and on a misunderstanding the right of the line commenced to withdraw, allowing the enemy to reach the crest where they were checked by the machine gun fire from the Aucklanders on the left.

Seeing the gravity of the position and realising that nothing but the greatest determination could save the situation, Captain Hinson (Adjutant Canterbury Regiment), and Lieutenants Thorby and Crawford of the New Zealand Camel Company, by their inspiring example, each in his own part of the line, swept back their men in a magnificent charge. It was estimated by watchers at Divisional Headquarters across the valley to the west that from four hundred to five hundred Turks assembled on the northern slopes of the hill for this attack and that no more than fifty were seen to go back.

At 2 p.m. three enemy batteries opened a steady fire on 3,039 and continued for the rest of the day and at 4 p.m. another determined counter attack by the Turks was repulsed. The brunt of this fell upon the Camel Battalion and was beaten off by the help of a small troop of reserves sent in on their right from Brigade Headquarters.

At 5 p.m. just before dark, the last of the enemy attacks occurred and was successfully repelled.

During the whole of this exceedingly difficult day General Meldrum had been entirely without artillery support, with the exception of a few rounds from the section of Hong Kong and Singapore mountain guns.

But the machine gunners, as usual, were magnificent. Many of their own guns having been destroyed by shell fire, they used captured enemy guns. During the final Turkish attack they put a belt of fire across our front line that no living man could penetrate.

On the left of the New Zealand Brigade, the Camels, the infantry, and the 2nd Light Horse Brigade (on the extreme left of the line) had been desperately attacking all day and had made but little progress; in fact the 2nd Light Horse had been unable to go forward at all owing to the enemy's repeated endeavours to outflank them.

The principal objective given to the Division by the C. in C. had been a large railway viaduct at Amman. This had not been even seen and could not be destroyed, though the work of all ranks had been simply magnificent.

The brigades had been well handled; the regimental and battalion leadership thorough, daring and efficient; and with a complete confidence in the Divisional Commander every man fought unhesitatingly, carrying out devotedly everything that was asked of him through the most trying period experienced by the New Zealand and Australian mounted men during the Palestine campaign. Sir Philip Chetwode, who commanded the XX Corps, under whom this raid had taken place, stated in his report to the C. in C. "what the Anzac Mounted Division and the 60th Division could not do, no other troops could possibly undertake."

Amman—Hill 3039 seen in the background.

Though our first objective was unattained, the severe pressure put upon the Turkish forces east of the Jordan compelled them to evacuate Kerak, the grain centre of the Moabite uplands, thus allowing the forces of the King of the Hedjaz to advance northward and to join hands with our troops on the Jordan. This and the ultimate object in the C. in C.'s mind, to attract to the east of the Jordan as many of the enemy reserves as posible, caused him to speak with unqualified satisfaction of the result of the raid and, bearing in mind the extreme difficulties in further providing for the troops on the plateau, he ordered the withdrawal to the Jordan.

Then began the most difficult of military operations, a withdrawal when in contact with the enemy.

The first thing to be done was to move back the New Zealand Brigade and the 4th Camel Battalion from the right. General Meldrum received his orders at 6 p.m. to withdraw to the edge of the plateau just above the village of Ain Es Sir. The greatest difficulty was the evacuation of the wounded. These unfortunate men had to be carried down the hill in blankets to the dressing station. From there to the nearest clearing station on the Es Salt road was a distance of 10 miles over country so boggy and slippery that the cacolet camels, the only means of ambulance transport, could not be used. So each sufferer was strapped on to his horse and so taken over 10 miles of agony to the dressing station. As a trooper remarked as he was being strapped on a horse "a man was lucky to be killed."

By 11 p.m. all wounded were got away and the Brigade retired to Ain Es Sir, throwing out an outpost line some two miles forward on the plateau to cover the withdrawal of the remainder of the force down the Es Sir defile.

The 1st Squadron took up the line it had held on arrival on the plateau and the remainder of the Regiment tried to get some much needed rest. But this was not to be, for the Turks showing up in front of the 1st Squadron, the whole Regiment moved into the line and the Aucklanders came up in support.

A certain amount of sniping took place all the afternoon and evening but no attack was made.

This night (March 31st) was the most bitter yet experienced. The wind blew the cold drenching rain through all clothing. The men, exhausted with eight days' ceaseless marching and fighting, disappointed with apparent failure, and sorrowing for their lost comrades, suffered torture from the icy blasts.

All that night a ceaseless line of infantry, camels and mounted men climbed and slipped and fell down the greasy rocks and muddy water channels of the Wadi Es Sir. At 4 a.m. on April 1st the Wellington Regiment took over the outposts and Canterbury Regiment moved off after the rest of the Brigade. As the last of the Wellington Regiment, following as a rearguard, passed through the village of Ain Es Sir, the Circassian inhabitants, our supposed friends, suddenly opened fire from some houses at point blank range and several of the Wellington officers and men fell. The Wellingtons promptly turned and cleaned up the houses from which the treacherous fire had come.

Recrossing the Jordan after the Amman Raid.

By dusk the Jordan plain was reached and the wearied men, marching for the last few hours through wild flowers of gorgeous colouring reaching up to the stirrups, in a delightfully calm, peaceful evening with the light of the western sun in their faces, could scarcely believe that only a few short hours before they were fighting for their lives in wind and cold and wet. Here by the Jordan was peace and a sweet balmy air so warm after the wild uplands that many lay down as they were in their torn and muddy clothing and slept the sleep of exhausted men.

Prisoners taken by the force were twenty officers and five hundred and ninety-five other ranks. The enemy abandoned on the Amman road two field cookers, twenty-six motor lorries and five motor cars, besides much horse transport. On the Hedjaz railway an enemy airplane was taken. All were destroyed on our retirement.

The quality of the Turkish troops was exceptionally good. They were Anatolians, fresh troops and of fine physique and particularly well clothed to stand the winter weather.

The one bright spot in the operations was the magnificent effort put up by the supply services. Rations and forage arrived throughout the nine days across the Jordan with unfailing regularity. The force when investing Amman was eighty-six miles from the railhead on the Philistine plain, for the Turkish railway from Ludd station to Jerusalem was undergoing relaying as a broad gauge railway. Supplies were brought up the winding road to Jerusalem by lorry, then down through the wilderness by other lorry trains, across the Jordan plain by horse transport and then up the 4,000 feet on to the plateau of Moab and Gilead by camels. The slippery mountain tracks and the bitterly cold winds and rains caused heavy casualties among the camels and their Egyptian drivers.

At Amman fell Captain H. B. Hinson of the New Zealand Staff Corps who had so ably performed the arduous duties of Adjutant for some time. A graduate of Duntroon Military College he had joined the Regiment as Signalling Officer. He met his death leading a most gallant charge on Hill 3039. Here also fell Lieutenant S. Berryman and 2nd Lieutenant H. Benson and many of the best and bravest in the Regiment.

This raid into the land of Moab and Gilead had shown us a lofty plateau bounded on the west by the great Jordan cleft and on the east by the desert sands of Arabia. It is a country crying out to the agriculturalist for development and to the archaeologist for exploration, a country that once was one of the granaries of the world and could well be so again, a country which has seen the rise and fall of many religions and civilisations, the ebb and flow of many great world forces, whose stories are written all over the face of this land for those who have eyes to see and patience to decipher.

As we were to find out later when the heights of Moab were again invaded, the town of Amman lies in a deep valley through which runs a sparkling stream. The citadel is high above it on a narrow tongue of land almost impregnable except at the narrow neck where it joins the plain. Across this neck is the ancient wall of great strength, making the whole position a hard nut to crack before the days of artillery. Here we have the scene of the tragedy of Uriah the Hittite, and the part that so long defied the armies of Joab would be the citadel which may possibly contain some of the

Pontoon Bridge over the Jordan.

ancient stone work of the time of David. Years later, after the Ammonites and all the kindred tribes had been swept away, when the great nations surged over these parts, Amman rose phoenix-like from its ashes, and under the title of Philadelphia became the most southerly of the remarkable federation known as Decapolis, which was a league of Greek cities founded by Alexander the Great, who tried to Hellenize the East; and in the Roman period the city was allowed rights of coinage and other privileges. As you go through Amman you see signs of these Greek civilizations everywhere, fragments of columns built in to existing walls, but the glory of Amman is its theatre, which remains in wonderful condition.

Part of the colonnade in front is still standing, while alongside is the Odeon, or concert hall. Behind the city is an old tower and curiously high arched bridge.

 It was in many ways a disappointment that we did not remain in occupation of the country to the east of the Jordan, so that we could have a sight of the wonderful ruins of Jerash, and the extraordinary underground cities, of which Edrei is the most famous, a testimony to the continuous insecurity of this region which, with a single exception, has for thousands of years frustrated all attempts to develop a land blessed more than most with health and fertility. Ruins and traces of other peoples meet the eye everywhere throughout this land. What is its future? If history has any coherent meaning at all, if upon it lessons and deductions can be based, surely it is this: that under enlightened and just government, free from any danger of invasion, as well as from internal oppression, then Jordan will recover its former prosperity and again there shall be found "balm in Gilead."

CHAPTER XVII.

Down by Jericho.

For a few days after the return from the heights of Moab, the warmth of the valley 'down by Jericho' was pleasant and comforting. But on April 17th the first Khamsin of the season began to blow and lasted for 48 hours. The temperature henceforth rose to an unbearable degree and the dust and flies by day and mosquitoes by night made life particularly unpleasant. There were no tents or sun shelters and shorts were prohibited to all mounted men owing to the danger of septic sores where the knee rubbed the saddle.

With the lessons of Salonica before them our medical officers began an anti-malarial campaign. Swamps were drained, all running water canalised and water that could not be drained off or made to run was treated with crude oil to prevent the malaria-carrying mosquito from breeding. This work entailed a great deal of labour and the Regiment daily found its quota.

A bridge-head formed by the 1st Light Horse Brigade guarded the Ghoraniyeh bridges and outpost positions were formed to cover the various fords. Working parties consisting of all available officers and men were continually digging and wiring at these posts. Each garrison comprised one officer and twenty to twenty-five men on duty for twenty-four hours, and the Regiment took its turn in finding them.

On April 2nd the Brigade re-crossed the Jordan. The Canterbury Regiment camped about two miles southeast of Jericho, close to the site of Joshua's Gilgal, and reinforcements soon made good the wastage caused by the raid upon Amman. Lieutenant G. J. H. Reid now became Adjutant.

On the 11th the Turks attacked the bridge head but were easily beaten off by the 1st Light Horse Brigade and suffered heavy casualties. Beyond the fact of causing the Regiment to stand-to, ready to move, this attack did not affect the New Zealanders. On the evening of the 18th the Regiment moved down to the bridge head and there camped for a few hours, moving out through the defences next morning on a reconnaissance of Shunet Nimrin. Crossing over the plain under shell fire our patrols managed to get within a thousand yards

Jebel Kuruntul (the Mount of Temptation).

of the enemy's positions in the foothills. The Regiment remained here all day, and withdrew in the evening, suffering light casualties.

On the 30th what appeared at first to be a strong reconnaissance developed into a big fight. The object was to envelop the right of the enemy forces at Shunet Nimrin and capture Es Salt. The troops engaged were the 60th Division, the Australian Mounted Division and the Anzac Division. The infantry were to attack Shunet Nimrin, while the Australian Mounted Division ascending the hills to Es Salt attacked the strong force of Turks holding the foot hills at Shunet Nimrin. The advance over the plain was made under heavy shellfire from Shunet Nimrin and both the infantry and the Canterbury Regiment were held up by strong posts of the enemy in the foothills. Casualties were heavy and the Regiment lost forty-five horses, besides a number slightly wounded.

May 1st saw the New Zealand Brigade in Corps Reserve for the attack on Es Salt. Being in reserve is not always an easy job. It usually means being pushed into the nastiest place of the fight in an endeavour to help some other unit in difficulties. Or it means being rushed about from flank to flank. It proved to be the latter this time. At mid-day the Regiment was ordered out to co-operate with the 179th Infantry Brigade in the attack on El Haud. The Regiment was to attack from the north via the Wadi Abu Tarra. The advance was made in column of troops from the shelter of the bridge head, on to the open plain at walking pace.

For three miles ahead stretched the plain sprinkled with a little grass, a few small patches of scrub, rocks and stones, broken here and there by small stony watercourses. Beyond, the line of hills rose abruptly; those to the right front strongly held by the Turks, while slightly to the left front a deep dark gully showed up. This was our objective. Before long a black puff ball shell burst in the air, followed half a minute later by another. The Turk was ranging. Colonel Findlay extended the line and increased the pace, first to a slow trot, then to a steady canter. The Turks for their part, were not slow, and soon had sixteen guns firing, varying high explosive and shrapnel with his old favourite, universal. The horses liked it no better than their riders, but the latter had much to look out for. While the horse fought to increase the pace, the rider had to maintain his place in the ranks with an open ear for orders, keeping his excited mount under him on his feet, and an eye on his troop leader for change of direction. Once in the gully, sheltered from the final disappointed roar of shells, men and horses were quite happy, but surprisingly short of breath. Meanwhile the tail-end of the column, the pack and led horses, had prudently halted, taking the role of spectators and allowing the squadrons the whole stage to themslevs. Then when things quietened, they came on unobtrusively and rejoined the Regiment.

A Bedouin and Horse.

But no sooner had the comparative shelter of the gully been reached than orders were received to return over the plain to Umm Es Shert. So the shelling had to be faced all the way again.

At Umm Es Shert the Regiment remained till late in the afternoon of the 2nd, digging trenches and generally improving the position. Then orders came to move out at short notice to support the 4th Australian Light Horse Brigade who were in difficulties holding the road from the Ed Damieh ford to Es Salt. This Brigade had been holding the valley of the Jordan and protecting the communications of the troops attacking Es Salt, but were being slowly forced back. For the next twenty-four hours the Regiment held a small portion of the line here, and then sending the horses back to Umm Es Shert on the Jordan plain, proceeded dismounted up the mountains to Es Salt, to help the withdrawal of the Australian Mounted Division.

The mountain track was climbed on foot during the night of the 3rd, and the Light Horse Regiments successfully withdrawing, the Regiment walked down again the following morning, bringing some prisoners the Australians had captured and suffering a considerable shelling from the Turks. Neither prisoners nor escort thought it was quite fair. On arrival on the flat the Regiment connected up with the infantry in the foothills, and held this line till all the Australians had passed through. Then the horses were brought up to the foothills, and acting as rearguard the Regiment withdrew across the plain to Ghoraniyeh, arriving at 4 a.m. on the 5th. During these four days the Canterbury Regiment had been under constant shellfire, and was occasionally bombed by aeroplanes but had escaped with light casualties.

These operations were, as was later heard, made at the instance of our so-called Allies, the Arabs. These followed their usual tactics and did not show up with their promised support, though probably they would have appeared in thousands, looking for loot, it the attack had been successful. General Allenby in his despatches says "As the assistance of the Beni Sakhr had not materialised, the Ain es Sir track was still open to the garrison of Shunet Nimrin. Further Turkish reinforcements were known to be on the way. It was evident that the Shunet Nimrin position could not be captured without losses, which I was not in a position to afford ...... The raid has undoubtedly rendered the enemy apprehensive of further operations east of the Jordan, and has compelled him to maintain considerable forces in the Amman-Shunet Nimrin area."

In camp, working parties and outposts took up the time of officers and men, and frequent bombing by enemy aeroplanes kept life from becoming monotonous. Our own planes were seldom seen, owing to the difficulty experienced by them in rising out of the valley. The anti-aircraft guns expended a lot of ammunition and were cursed nearly as much as the aeroplanes were, owing to their habit of landing spent shrapnel and shellcases among the camps.

On the 16th the New Zealand Mounted Rifle Brigade left the valley and went into reserve at Talaat ed Dumm, under the command of Colonel Findlay as General Meldrum had gone to hospital. Major Acton-Adams assumed the tempor-

Marching out of the Plain of Jericho by way of the Roman Road.

ary command of the Regiment. First impressions of this place, whilst camped here before the first Amman raid, had not been at all favourable and the longer the men stayed here the more they hated it. There was barely enough ground for a troop to camp on, not to speak of a regiment. Water for man and animals was now pumped out of the Wadi Kelt to large reservoirs near the road, but as often as not the engines refused duty. Being in the midst of the "Wilderness," what little vegetation there had been on the hills had now withered off, and dust was everywhere. Instead of digging trenches the Regiment became roadmakers and road menders. The constant traffic had cut up the roads badly, and as yet there were insufficient Egyptian Labour Corps to do the work.

An arrangement had been come to by which a limited number of officers and men, who were unfit but yet not hospital cases, were to be sent to the Rest Camp at Port Said, and would be replaced by available reinforcements from Ismailia. This wise provision commenced about this time and thenceforward regular drafts were sent away. It proved a great boon and undoubtedly saved many men from hospital who, though not ill enough to be evacuated, required a spell from the continuous strain and work. Many of the cases of sickness at this time were nothing more nor less than exhaustion, both physical and mental.

On May 27th the 8th Squadron left for a tour of duty at the School of Instruction, Richon; and the following day the time in reserve being up, the Brigade moved to a camp about five miles south of Bethlehem. Here was comfort. A limited number of tents were available; a canteen was handy and the men were able to supplement their food supply considerably, for in the colder climate of the hills the scale of rations, though ample in the valley, required additions.

On June 3rd, the King's Birthday, an official ceremony was held at Bethlehem, at which the Regiment was represented by a troop. But the stay here was all too short and on the afternoon of the 13th the Brigade again rode out to the Valley, halting en route at Talaat ed Dumm for twenty-four hours. The temperature this day at Jericho, just below, registered 125 degrees, and to the men, coming in the night from the cool hilltops, was a trying change. Several men suffered from heatstroke, including Major Wain, who had just re-joined from New Zealand.

On arrival in the Valley the camp of the 9th Australian Light Horse Regiment at Ain Ed Duk was taken over.

The actual duties in the line were easy, one outpost only being found, but the odd jobs that came along were legion. The medical people, for example, were endeavouring to stamp out or reduce to a minimum, malaria which rages in the Valley during the summer months. Every day fifty or more men were supplied from the Regiment to work under their directions. All units out of the line found their quota towards this necessary work. The three or four streams that entered the plain from the hills were gradually straightened and cleaned. Small marshes were drained, and as far as possible it was ensured that there was no stagnant or non-flowing water to become a breeding ground for mosquitoes. In addition to this work roads and camps were improved. It was now very hot. The official return of temperatures taken at Jericho showed that the daily average for June was 119 degrees and July 112 degrees in the shade. Flies were few, killed by the heat, in fact for this reason June and July are much freer from many insects than May or September, but mosquitoes revel in the hot nights. Work of any sort, even at night was very trying in this climate. Though traffic was kept to well defined tracks away from camp areas, dust was everywhere. For no known reason, and without a breath of wind, the dust would gradually rise. Looking down on to the plain from the hills, nothing could be seen but dust, which hung like a fog over the valley. It was impossible to sleep at night with any degree of comfort owing to the heat. As many men as could be spared were sent to rest camps, but this only made it harder for those remaining. Insects of all descriptions haunted the bivvies and snakes were numerous. One cheerful optimist informed us that there were eighty-seven different varieties of snakes in the Valley, but he did not think they were all of a poisonous nature.

From the camp at the foot of Jebel Kuruntal the whole plain of the Jordan Valley could be seen, a sunscorched piece of the earth, notable because it was 1,200 feet below sea level and to the historian one of the most interesting places of ancient history. In the plain, midway between the hills and the river, lies the dirty modern city of Jericho. Between it and the hills is a small patch of irrigated land, practically the only cultivation on the plain, the water being drawn from Ain Sultan.

Near the spring is a large mound, covering several acres, being all that remains to mark the site of the ancient Jericho of the day of Joshua. Two miles south of this the Wadi Kelt cuts its way through the plain. Just where the wadi emerges from the hills, another group of mounds marks the Jericho of Herod, guarding the old Roman road to Jerusalem, which rises steeply up the gorge of the Wadi Kelt. Four or five miles east of Jericho the River Jordan cuts the plain in two. For a mile on each side of the river the ground is much broken by wadis and ravines descending steeply to the river-bed. The Jordan itself is a muddy looking river, thirty to fifty yards wide, between dense belts of tamarisk and other trees. The distance from its source to the Dead Sea is about sixty miles, but so winding is its course that the actual length of the river is one hundred and thirty miles. At the back of the camp rose steeply the hill called Kuruntal, the Hill of The Forty Days, the reputed site of the temptation of Our Lord. Halfway up the hill a monastery clings to the face of the almost perpendicular cliff.

On June 26th the Turks enlivened matters considerably by using a long range gun, impartially shelling camps, dumps and roadways. On one occasion this great gun, from far across the Jordan, threw a shell on to the top of Jebel Kuruntal. The Turk, being some thousand or more feet above our camp, had a good view of all the Jordan Valley from the hills on both sides and from now till the final operations this gun caused a lot of trouble. It was sometimes said to have been put out of action by being bombed, but the next day usually gave the lie direct to this. On the last night of the month the Regiment formed a chain of posts, connecting with the 53rd Division on the tops of the Judean hills, in an endeavour to catch a supposed spy, who was reported to be trying to get through to the Turks. No spy was caught but all hands had some strenuous hill climbing.

On July 10th the 8th Squadron rejoined from Richon. They had had an easy time, and were much refreshed by the spell.

The Turks attacked the 1st Australian Light Horse Brigade holding the line on the west side of the Jordan at the Auja river during the early hours of the 14th, pushing well in behind the advanced posts before being checked. The New Zealand Brigade stood to, ready to move, but were not required till one o'clock in the afternoon, the 1st Squadron of the Canterbury Regiment then being sent to the Wadi Auja, near where it entered the plain, to deal with any Turks who attempted to get water there. Just before dusk the 8th and 10th Squadrons cleared the ground between the posts held by the 1st Light Horse Brigade, being shelled heavily whilst doing so. After dark the Regiment withdrew to camp, leaving the 10th Squadron to watch the Auja Gorge during the night. During this action a great capture of German infantry was made.

On July 19th the spell in the Valley was finished and the New Zealand Brigade went to Talaat Ed Dumm for its turn there. It must be explained that all units did a certain tour of duty in the Valley, then returneed to Talaat Ed Dumm for ten days or a fortnight in Corps Reserve, after which a

A Halt on the Road to Jerusalem.

fortnight was spent in the hills near Jerusalem before returning to the Valley. At Talaat Ed Dumm, owing to the limited area available, the camping grounds were in a filthy condition, and the ground was rocky and stony. Everyone was glad when the move came to Jerusalem on the 27th and a clean and healthy camp was chosen close to Solomon's Pools.

The change from the Jordan to the colder climate here was greatly felt and many men who had discarded blankets while down below had a chilly night or two till new ones were issued.

Guards and picquets were numerous but the stay on the Judean highlands was enjoyable. The Christ College Old Boys in the Regiment held a dinner in Jerusalem at the Grand Hotel, a happy function, and Colonel Findlay resumed command of the Regiment. Cricket matches were played and sports meetings held. The Canterbury Regimental cricket team won the Brigade tournament, though suffering badly from nerves in the final match. Success was achieved also at the Brigade sports and horse show, the Regiment winning eight events out of the sixteen on the card. The sports and show were quite the biggest thing in this line that we had attempted since leaving New Zealand and the Colonel forgave the Regiment a lot of its sins for the success achieved.

CHAPTER XVIII.

How the Regiment Crossed the Jordan for the Last Time.

But the pleasant time was ended, and on August 16th the Valley was entered again. The Regiment did not return to its old camp, but took over that of the 9th Hodson's Horse near the Auja bridge head. Here all the old work recommenced. In addition to the numerous fatigues, officers and N.C.O.'s had to make themselves acquainted with the line, and by the time this was fitted in with patrols, etc., their day and most of the night was used. Time passed quickly and early in September rumours were floating round about a "big push." Lectures were given to all hands. The choice of subjects and the order in which they were given indicated something doing in the near future. Everybody was quite sure of this when the doctor gave the final lecture and chose "First Aid" as his subject. Little things like this, and the sudden interest shown by troop leaders in everybody having their "field dressings" in possession could point only to one thing.

The situation in Palestine at this time, early September, may briefly be described as follows:—

The Turkish armies were occupying a line from the sea to the Jordan of some forty-five miles with a depth of about fourteen miles. This line was held by the VIIIth Turkish Army with headquarters at Tul Keram on the plain of Sharon, and by the VIIth army stretching across the Judean Plateau to the edge of the mountains where they descended abruptly into the Jordan, with headquarters at Nablus.

Across the Jordan Valley and along the foothills of Gilead and Moab the line was held by the IVth Turkish Army under Djemal Pasha with his headquarters at Es Salt. His troops were estimated to number six thousand rifles, two thousand cavalry and seventy-four guns. Further to the south another Turkish force of six thousand rifles and thirty guns was operating against the Arabs about Maan.

The Commander in Chief resolved to attack this long line on the plains north of Jaffa with the XXIst Corps supplemented by the 60th Division of the XXth Corps and a number of heavy guns.

The line across the Judean hills was to stand fast until the XXIst Corps had broken through and the mounted attack was well under way. The latter was to be made by the whole strength of the Desert Mounted Corps less the Anzac Mounted Division and was to follow through the gap on the plain of Sharon made by the XXIst Corps. In the meantime General Chaytor, in command of the Anzac Mounted Division with certain other troops added, was to hold fast the Turkish IVth Army, prevent it from sending any troops to reinforce other parts of the line, and to use every endeavour to protect the right of the XXth Corps holding the Judean hills; when it advanced he was to seize the bridge over the Jordan at Ed Damieh, move across the river and, capturing Es Salt and Amman, was to co-operate with the Arabs in smashing the Maan force.

Realising that his hopes of success lay in surprise, General Allenby proceeded to mislead the enemy as he had done at Gaza. The Mounted troops, Australian Mounted Division, Yeomanry Division and 5th Cavalry Division, were marched over the hills from the Jordan to concealment in olive groves in the vicinity of Jaffa, during many nights.

The camps they left remained standing with fires kept alight by parties of the Egyptian Labour Corps. On the horse lines were dummy horses and the illusion of activity in the Valley was kept up by squadrons of mounted men quietly riding up to Jerusalem during the night and then coming down again by day amidst clouds of dust in full view of the Turkish troops across the Jordan. When Fast's Hotel at Jerusalem, which had been taken over by the Canteens Board for a hostel for officers, was suddenly emptied of its lodgers and sentry-boxes placed at the doors, on which G.H.Q. notices were posted, all Jerusalem soon buzzed with the news, and its leakage to the enemy was a matter of days only, and he became more convinced than ever that the next attack of the British would be again across the Jordan or along the Nablus road. Such were the preparations that occupied the early days of September leading up to the great moves which were to fulfill the aims of the Commander-in-Chief with a completeness rare in military history.

By the middle of September the troops in the Jordan Valley consisted of:—
> The Anzac Mounted Division, less one Squadron
> 20th Infantry (Imperial Service) Brigade
> 1st and 2nd Battalions British West India Regiment
> 38th and 39th Battalions Royal Fusiliers (Jewish Battalions)
> 18th Brigade Royal Horse Artillery
> A/263 Battery Royal Field Artillery
> 198th Battery Royal Garrison Artillery
> 29th and 32nd Indian Mountain Batteries
> 2/75 m.m. Turkish Guns
> 2/5.9 Howitzers
> No. 6 Trench Mortar Battery
> 96th, 102nd and 103rd Anti-Aircraft Sections
> Detachment A. T. Company

the whole being known as "Chaytor's Force," General Chaytor now commanding all troops in the Jordan Valley.

All the troops leaving the Valley went by night, and those entering it came by day. Everything had been done so quietly that it seemed impossible that the Division formed the major part of the troops here. The day patrols were increased both in number and size, and night patrols seemed to be everywhere. What was lacked in numbers was more than balanced by activity.

On the morning of September 19th the attack commenced in the coastal sector. Our patrols kept in touch with the enemy in case they showed any inclination to retire, but they had evidently learnt little of what was happening on the other portions of the front. On the 20th the enemy fell back from some of their advanced positions west of the Jordan but their retirement was orderly and covered by a strong rearguard. On the river and to the east they still presented a bold front.

During the evening of the 21st the Regiment moved out via the Wadi Obeidah to join up with the Brigade at Kh

Fusail on the west bank of the Jordan. From here the New Zealand Mounted Rifle Brigade rode on towards Jisr Ed Damieh to seize the bridge. Auckland Mounted Rifles were in advance following the old Roman road up the river and brushing aside all opposition arrived in the vicinity of the crossing at daybreak, seizing the Nablus—Es Salt road.

The Jisr ed Damieh. Crossing the Jordan for the last dash upon Amman.

The Wellington Mounted Rifles were acting on the Canterburys' left towards El Makhruk, which they seized at daybreak, capturing the headquarters of the 53rd Turkish Division. Shortly after daylight the enemy attempted to advance on Wellington's left, and the 10th Squadron was sent to support them. The attack did not develop and the Turks' fleeing from the attacks of the XX Corps, eventually retired into the hills. Everything was quiet for a time, and then, at 10.30 a.m. the 1st Squadron co-operated with Auckland and one company of the British West India Regiment in an attack on the bridge at Jisr ed Damieh. After a spirited attack culminating in a fine bayonet charge the Turkish resistance broke and heavy casualties were inflicted on them as they retired. The bridge was captured intact, and the 10th Squadron having now rejoined, chased the remaining Turks into the foothills below Es Salt. In the evening the Regiment withdrew across the bridge, leaving the 1st Squadron to hold the crossing against a possible counter-attack.

Only a miracle of good fortune could now save the IV Army from destruction. To offer further resistance to "Chaytor's Force" was to reduce the already slender chances of escape, and the withdrawal in the night became a flight, as they marched hurriedly for Amman. Here they might hope for a time to resist, as they had done so successfully during the Amman raid, and so give the six thousand Turks at Maan time to join the IV Army.

Shortly after mid-night General Chaytor received information of the general withdrawal of the enemy and ordered his whole force to be in readiness to advance early in the morning. He directed General Meldrum to leave some troops to hold the Damieh bridge, and climbing up the mountains as rapidly as possible, to ride for Es Salt, while the 1st and 2nd Light Horse Brigades and all available artillery clambered up the Shunet Nimrin-Es Salt track.

The New Zealand patrols were out before daybreak and collected a few stragglers lurking in the foothills. At mid-day the ascent of the mountains commenced, the Canterbury Regiment forming the advanced guard. Wire entanglements were met with, stretched across the road and backed by a machine gun but the enemy were quickly outflanked and rushed. Spiritedly led by Major Hurst, who now commanded the Regiment, the advanced guard stopped at nothing, overcoming without pause the scattered opposition put up by the beaten enemy. An attempt was made to hold Es Salt but by half-past three in the afternoon the Regiment passed through the town and occupied a line on the hills to the east, having captured this day two hundred and fifty men, three field guns, and many machine guns.

On the 24th the Regiment moved on to Suweile and was ready for the attack on Amman, so filled with bitter memories in the minds of all the Anzac Mounted Division and all ranks and all ranks eagerly looked forward to adjusting the score with the Turk. At Suweile the New Zealand Mounted Rifle Brigade was joined by the 1st and 2nd Light Horse Brigades, a battalion of British West Indians and a battalion of Jews.

During the night a party of Aucklanders, by a fine ride in the dark, reached the railway line to the north of Amman and blew up the railway line at Kalaat Ed Zerka and so temporarily blocked the escape of the enemy.

Major Hurst, who commanded the Regiment on its last dash upon Amman.

Early on the 25th the Brigade moved towards Amman and got in touch with the enemy about two miles northwest of the town, where they held two strong posts guarding the approaches. The Wellington and Auckland Mounted Rifles were in the line, their right flank joining up with the 2nd Australian Light Horse Brigade who were attacking from the west and there was much friendly competition between the two Brigades as to who should be the first into Amman.

The Canterbury Regiment with one section of the Machine Gun Squadron was ordered to move forward to a position of

readiness from which to break through and take the enemy
in rear. At noon the Regiment was off but the advance was
temporarily held up by the fire of about two hundred Turks
on a ridge supported by machine guns; but nothing could stop
the men now and though shelled by a battery of light guns they
soon took the position. The 1st Squadron was then brought
up on the left and the whole Regiment again went forward.
The Citadel, which during the raid upon Amman had put up
such a stubborn resistance to the attack of the Camel Brigade

Canterbury Mounted Rifles riding through Es Salt.

and Infantry Battalions, now gave some trouble, but was gallantly rushed by the 10th Squadron and some of the 8th at the
point of the bayonet. Its garrison of nineteen officers and one
hundred other ranks (mostly Germans including the commanding officer and staff of the 146 Battalion) with six machine guns
surrendered. The commanding officer, a German, caused some
amusement. He was wounded and apparently could not speak
English—but being asked by Major Hurst if he would like some
brandy he said "yes" and after the drink spoke English
fluently.

Immediately the stone tower was captured, the whole regiment rushed the town and by 4.30 p.m. were through and out to the railway station. The enemy troops were fresh and stiffened by Germans, but nothing could stand up against such an irresistible attack. Not even in the days of Gallipoli had the Regiment displayed more dash, and much of its success in these last days was due to the fine leadership of Major Hurst.

This officer, the beau-ideal of a cavalry leader had been offered a command with promotion in March, 1916, in the Infantry Division—but his duty to his commanding officer and to the Regiment weighed so greatly with him that he refused to transfer. On foot or on horseback he was a dashing, resourceful and yet careful leader, for added to his vigorous body and active mind was a sound practical judgment.

The Regiment's captures consisted of over one thousand two hundred prisoners, fourteen machine guns, and a large amount of war material.

Owing to sickness and casualties the strength had been much reduced and the Regiment was only three hundred and fifty strong, yet had taken prisoners over three times its own strength.

The change to the cooler climate of the hills was telling its tale in the sick parades. Malaria was rampant, and now that the excitement of the fighting was over the men simply collapsed. Remaining near the town till the 29th, collecting prisoners and war material, advantage was taken of the proximity of Hill 3039 to do up the graves of those who had been killed in the first attack on Amman. A cairn was built on the top of the hill as a memorial to those of the regiment who had fallen in the different fights for the town.

General Chaytor immediately prepared for the destruction of the Turkish force at Maan. This force, alarmed at the news of the fate which was overtaking the IV. Army, was endeavouring to march north along the Hedjaz railway, and numbering some five thousand to six thousand was in no danger from the Arabs, but with Amman in our hands its supplies were cut off.

The airmen reported this force as having reached Ziza some 16 miles to the south of Amman and close to the Kastal railway station, and the 2nd Light Horse Brigade was sent to reconnoitre. The Turks were found almost surrounded by a great host of the Beni Sakr tribe, and soon surrendered to General Chaytor. During the night of the 29th-30th the Regiment moved south to Kastal, taking over an outpost line from the Auckland Mounted Rifles. At Kastal were a large number of prisoners, the remains of the 2nd Turkish Army Corps. They were in a deplorable condition through lack of food and water, and had even drunk the water from the boilers of the engines lying at the railway. Dead and dying lay about everywhere. In addition to other duties, our men had the job of looking after these prisoners, a comparatively light task. The hardest work was to keep the Arabs, who were swarming over the countryside, from robbing and murdering the unfortunate Turks.

On October 2nd the 8th Squadron went south to occupy Madeba, but found the Arabs already there, so returned to Kastal. Late in the afternoon of the 3rd, the Regiment was relieved by the 3rd Australian Light Horse Regiment and moved to Kissir, the first stage of the return journey to the Valley. Leaving here again early next morning, Jericho was reached via Ain Es Sir, halting for one night at Shunet Nimrin. At the latter place was seen the long range gun that had been so annoying during the long months of the summer. Now "Nimrin Nelly," as it was known, was lying upside down in a small wadi, where the Turks had thrown her when their retreat was cut off.

Malaria was now raging through all the troops. Shunet Nimrin, where the Regiment had camped, had been a large bivouac of the Turks and the one night there seemed to have infected the whole Brigade. Since September 20th, eighteen officers and one hundred and fifty other ranks suffering from the disease had been evacuated to hospital, and the figures for the whole force must have been enormous. There had been for the last nine months a certain amount of malaria in a comparatively mild form, but the disease now was of a most malignant type with a high percentage of deaths. On the ride down to Jericho it was no uncommon sight to see one man riding, leading four or five horses.

Major C. Hercus, of the New Zealand Field Ambulance and later D.A.D.M.S. Anzac Mounted Division, says:—

"The arrival of the warmer weather in April found the Division in the Jordan Valley, that unique scorching valley some 1,200 feet below the level of the Mediterranean, notorious for subtertian or malignant malaria, and in which with brief respite we were to spend the summer. The portion of the valley within our lines was crossed by several streams issuing from the hills and making their way down to the Jordan (the Auja, the Mellahah, the Nueiameh, the Kelt) and also contained the Jordan with several extensive marshes in the jungle which fringed its banks. The problem was a difficult one, the area involved was large, and the climatic conditions were trying. The Wadi el Mellahah was a particularly dangerous stream commencing in marshes in No Man's Land and running in a swampy valley choked with reeds across our line down to the Wadi Auja just before the latter entered the Jordan. Its whole valley was swarming with anopheles larvae. A working party of one thousand men was put on to work and within a week the marshes in No Man's Land were drained as far as the enemy would permit; and the stream within our lines was canalised and cleared and the reeds cut or burnt out. No breeding could be demonstrated three days after the work was completed. The work in the other wadis consisted of canalising, cutting down jungle, filling in holes and oiling stagnant pools.

The work when once carried out required constant attention and maintenance and the Sanitary Section with the unit malarial squads, were continually employed on the maintenance work, special working parties being provided for the initial work. Two large swamps on the east bank of the Jordan, one at El Ghoraniyeh bridgehead, the other at El Henu ford, were found to be prolific breeding places and were drained and oiled. A large amount of this extensive work was carried out by the Indian Infantry Brigade. Breeding was also found to be rife at Ain es Sultan the source of Jericho's water supply, situated about one-and-a-half miles north of Jericho. Here there was an area of several acres in extent consisting of banana plantations and other cultivated land copiously irrigated by the over-flow from the Ain es

Sultan spring. With the aid of a company of E.L.C. six hundred strong working for two months, breeding was suppressed in this area.

"This in brief was the extent of the problem with which we were confronted. The measure of the success of the work carried out can be best estimated by the rise in the malarial incidence when we advanced into unprotected country. During the six months prior to the advance on September 21st the percentage of incidence of malaria in the Desert Mounted Corps was just over five and the majority of these cases were contracted in the front line where the evening breeze brought down hordes of mosquitoes from the Turkish positions and No Man's Land. In the reserve areas where the protective measures were fully operated the incidence of malaria was very low.

"On September 21st the New Zealand Mounted Rifle Brigade, the 1st Light Horse Brigade, and the 1st and 2nd B.W.I.'s moved forward into the Jisr ed Damieh area, swampy ground in which no attempt had been made to cope with the mosquito menace. The air was full of hordes of peculiarly aggressive and blood-thirsty mosquitoes, laden with, as subsequent events proved, the parasites of malignant malaria. It was here that a great deal of infection was incurred, for the 2nd B.W.I. Battalion which remained in this area when the rest of Chaytor's Force moved eastward into Moab, suffered severely. By October the 18th, seven officers, seven hundred and nineteen other ranks of this unit (practically the whole strength) were evacuated with malignant malaria. Malaria began to appear in the mobile force in Moab on September 28th. The 1st Light Horse Brigade were the first to experience the epidemic, evacuating one hundred and twenty-six cases during the week. The New Zealand Mounted Rifle Brigade almost simultaneously commenced to evacuate large numbers of men acutely ill with the disease. The incidence reached a climax on October 4th when the 3rd Light Horse Regiment evacuated sixty-two, 1st Light Horse Regiment fifty-eight, and the New Zealand Mounted Brigade one hundred and forty-five. Many dramatic incidents occurred on the march back into Judea. There were cases of one man leading as many as eight horses, all his mates having been stricken down, and many men fell from their saddles in high fever. This exceptionally high rate of malignant malarial cases was experienced until October 9th when the numbers fell abruptly. Additional proof that the Jisr ed Damieh area was responsible for the majority of the infections is supplied by the 2nd Light Horse Brigade which moved directly from the protected area into the hills. Their evacuations from malaria during the period September 21st to October 10th were fifty-seven as compared with two hundred and thirty-nine cases in the 1st Light Horse Brigade and three hundred and sixteen in the New Zealand Mounted Rifle Brigade for the same period. It has been truly said that the last phase of the Palestine campaign was fought and won in the incubation period of malignant malaria (10 to 14 days).

"To people accustomed to ordinary benign tertian malaria the serious and dramatic nature of the malignant type was most alarming. The men attacked were suddenly prostrated in high fever, 105° and 106°F. being frequently reported, and they were often delirious and occasionally maniacal. Unless treated immediately and efficiently with quinine the mortality was high. Once again it was amply proved that prevention is better than cure."

October 8th saw the Regiment riding out of the Valley for the last time, bound for Jerusalem, which was reached on the 9th. A halt was made here till the 13th, and many took this opportunity to pay a last visit to Jerusalem and Bethlehem. It was expected that the Brigade would be sent to join the Desert Mounted Corps, at this time working north of Damascus, but there was evidently no need of more troops there. From Jerusalem the Regiment returned, via Latron, to its old camp at Ayun Kara. Here it was joined by a large draft of reinforcements. Nobody was sorry to see them, for during the last week or two every man had been looking after three or four horses. Then, besides doing camp duties, they were on horse picquet four nights out of five.

So ended the last operations of the Anzac Mounted Division across the Jordan, and in these the Canterbury Regiment had borne its full share. In nine days Chaytor's Force had captured ten thousand three hundred prisoners and fifty-seven guns, one hundred and thirty-two machine guns, eleven railway engines, and one hundred and six trucks, and a great quantity of material, including wireless sets, motor lorries and other vehicles, and much ammunition. Owing to the dash and skill of all ranks, the casualties were light, though the wastage by malaria was daily becoming alarming.

CHAPTER XIX.

Of the Return to the Battlefields of Gallipoli.

At Ayun Kara matters went on quietly, all units being engaged in replacing old and worn-out horses, and in receiving and organising drafts of reinforcements. On October 31st news of the armistice with Turkey arrived and was received with quiet relief and a satisfaction that the job was at length finished. Training went on uninterruptedly, but more time was allowed for sports. Football was soon in full swing, and preparations were completed for a Divisional sports meeting and horse show. Every unit had a small sports meeting and horse show of its own, at which every horse that could jump, and many that could not, were trained and tried out.

The armistice was followed by the Allied occupation of the Dardanelles and Constantinople, and sentiment prompted a decision that the Australians and New Zealanders should be represented in the force to be landed on the Gallipoli peninsular. The choice fell upon the 7th Light Horse Regiment of the 2nd Light Horse Brigade and the Canterbury Regiment of the New Zealand Mounted Rifle Brigade.

Early in November the Regiment received word of a probable move to an unknown destination. A good deal of secrecy was maintained about it, but finally the news came through that the 7th Australian Light Horse Regiment and the Canterburys were to go to the Dardanelles as part of the Army of occupation. As the Regiment was to go as infantry, the best of the horses were distributed amongst the other units of the Brigade, and the remainder handed in to the Remount Department, leaving for embarkation a few riding horses and transport animals only.

Entraining at Ludd on November 13th en route to Kantara, the Regiment experienced a disagreeable trip on the train, for heavy rain came through the roofs of the trucks, wetting everybody to the skin, but the hot sunshine of Kantara in the early morning of the 14th made things right again.

A Party from the Regiment sitting on a 14-inch Gun at Kalid Bahr.

The camp was about four miles east of Kantara on the open desert, alongside the railway. Not knowing what the duties were to be at Gallipoli, nothing was left to chance, and ordinary training continued, varied by rifle exercises and route marches, while ceremonial drill was also brushed up. The strength of the Regiment for embarkation was limited to twenty-five officers and four hundred and sixty-four other ranks, while eighty-one animals were allowed for riding horses and transport purposes. Any officers or men over this number were to return to the training unit at Ismailia. Preference was given to old hands, if they passed the doctor, to go with the Regiment, as against those who had recently joined. After several false alarms a boat at last arrived on the 27th, and the Regiment immediately embarked. The Australians also embarked at the same time. The transport, H.M.T. "Huntscastle," a captured German, had probably been quite a decent boat originally, but after being burned out and then re-conditioned as a horse boat at Athens, with accommodation for one hundred men and a thousand animals, later mined, and then for the last twelve months tied up in Alexandria Harbour, she was not, to say the least of it, quite a suitable boat for one thousand men and one hundred and sixty animals. Her decks leaked everywhere during wet weather, and there was no hospital for sick men.

Sailing from Kantara early on the morning of the 28th, the "Huntscastle" reached The Narrows on December 2nd, and the Regiment disembarked on the 5th and went into billets in a very dirty and verminous Turkish hospital between Maidos and Kilid Bahr, but the 10th Squadron was detached from the Regiment and established a comfortable camp in a ruined mosque and surrounding buildings at Maidos.

The weather was extremely cold, and there was much influenza and some malaria among the men, but the six weeks spent on Gallipoli was a season of deep interest to all ranks.

All or nearly all of the officers and most of the men had fought at Anzac, and they explored the old positions with feelings of emotion stronger and deeper than could be awakened in their hearts by any other battle-ground of the war.

For the purpose of finding out if the Turks were complying with the terms of the armistice, the Regiment was ordered by the 28th Division, under whom it was serving, to make a detailed reconnaissance of an area bounded by a line Gaba Tepe—Kilia in the south to a line Karakova Burnu—Kara Acaj Limon on the north. This reconnaissance took place between the 11th and 15th, and three officers and forty-five other ranks took part in it.

A view of Walker's Ridge after the Armistice.

Many visits were made to the old battlefields at Anzac, and special parties searched for graves and missing comrades of the Canterbury and other regiments; all graves were tended with loving care and great pains taken to have them properly marked and recorded.

E. R. Peacock, writing on the spot, says:—"The spirit of true comradeship towards the dead shows itself in a wonderful and beautiful manner. Going over each remnant, buttons and scraps of cloth and other details they found sufficient to be convinced that the remains were those of a comrade. It is impossible to describe or to do justice to the tender, reverent, care with which each particle was gathered together, a grave dug, and the whole buried in quiet impressive solemnity.

There was no funeral service but no dignitary ever received a more truly loving Christian burial than did these remains. Those, big strong rough looking troopers with their shovels hunting for their comrades on the old battlefields is a picture no artist could paint nor any poet do justice to. They represent the true spirit of the Anzac. We grant them brave as lions, facing dangers without a sense of fear, enduring hardships and privations that would kill most mortals and we talk of their self-reliance, confidence, resourcefulness and bluff, but when it comes to this kind of work what seems to be a new characteristic appears. They displayed a tenderness, care and love which could not be excelled by mother or wife or child."

The men of both the mounted regiments were treated with the greatest consideration by the British Command, and nearly all the officers and some of the men visited Constantinople.

C.M.R. Cemetery on the beach at Anzac (after the Armistice).

On January 17th four officers and forty-five other ranks went across to the Asiatic shore and visited ancient Troy.

Less four officers and ninety other ranks, with the horses and transport vehicles, the Regiment embarked on board H.M.T. *Norman* on January 19th, and arrived at Port Said on the 22nd, going through by train to Kantara. Next morning the journey to Rafa was continued by train, and the Regiment went into camp with the rest of the Brigade.

At Rafa the time was taken up by a certain amount of training and the inception of an "Educational Scheme;" on February 15th there was held a Divisional Gymkana; and on a never-to-be-forgotten occasion the men of the Regiment presented the 'old Colonel' with a walking stick—still cherished by him as the greatest gift he has ever received.

In the early days of March rumours of disturbances in Egypt had been current, but little attention was paid to them. But on the 17th at noon orders were received for the whole Brigade to move immediately to Kantara, which was reached by the Regiment at 6.30 on the morning of the 18th. Horses and saddlery were drawn from the Remount Depot and Ordnance Stores respectively, and Regimental Headquarters with the 1st Squadron marched to Benha, in the Delta, on March 21st, and on the 23rd the whole Regiment moved by rail to Tanta. The next day a small column was formed, consisting of the Canterbury Regiment, four armoured cars and a small armoured train, which proceeded to march through the Delta.

This duty imposed an enormous amount of patrolling upon all ranks, and the force was received at first with feelings of great fear in the multitude of small villages with which the Delta is filled. Our men were tired by many years of campaigning and exasperated at being retained in Egypt long after the war was over and all other troops had returned to their homes, and so went about their work with a determination and thoroughness that soon brought peace and quietness to a turbulent community.

Though received with fear, their departure was the signal for much regret and lamentation on the part of the head men and peaceable villagers, who found that, though strict and stern to evildoers, our men were generous and just to a degree.

Kafr el Sheikh was a typical disaffected area. By a night march it was surrounded at daylight, and much amusement was given the men by the desperate efforts of the disaffected portion of the inhabitants to escape. Among these was the Omda (or head-man of the village) who tried to escape in a motor car. Later on, when peace and order was established, he became a firm friend of the Regiment, and gave a dinner at which he made a speech. "I was in much fear of the men in the big hats," he said, "and when a man came up to me after my arrest and told me to put my arms to my sides and to stand up and hold my head erect, at the same time placing his hands on his belt, I felt my last moment had come, and began trembling and to say my prayers and to consign myself to God, when he pulled out a camera and took my photograph I could have kissed him."

All rioters arrested were tried immediately by a Court set up by Colonel Findlay, and, if guilty, sentenced to fines, imprisonment and the lash.

In a few weeks the whole district was patrolled and all disaffected people dealt with, and the usual quiet village life resumed.

As soon as the first excitement of patrolling and bringing in offenders wore off, sports of all kinds were instituted to keep up the spirits of the tired and home-sick men. Inter-squadron and inter-regimental tournaments were held, and a team went to Cairo to play cricket.

But the greatest pleasure was derived from the horse races, and in these the natives took an immense amount of interest, and helped in the arrangements and provision of the various racecourses required. A totalisator run on New Zealand lines was established. There was no charge for admission, and the inhabitants were invited to come and bring their horses. They came in large numbers, and, being great gamblers, a large amount of native money used to pass through the "tote."

This participation in a sport they understood undoubtedly largely helped in the pacification of the inhabitants of the district patrolled by the New Zealand Brigade.

Race meetings were held in Alexandria and in Cairo, and many races were won by New Zealand horses, among them the Allenby Cup by a Wellington Regiment horse, and a great race at Cairo by a Canterbury horse—Trooper Quigley's "Sunday," magnificently ridden by Trooper A. E. Wormald, who is well known in New Zealand racing circles.

On June 17th orders were received to return all horses to the Remount Depot at Belbeis, and the whole Regiment moved to a camp at Chevalier Island, Ismailia.

After the great disappointment at Rafa when the Brigade, instead of embarking for home, was re-equipped and went to its trying duties in the Delta, the move to the Canal was welcomed with quiet thankfulness.

On June 30th, 1919, over seven months after the close of the war, the New Zealand Mounted Rifle Brigade was disbanded, and 75 officers and 1,014 other ranks embarked under the command of Colonel Findlay on the transport *Ulimaroa* for New Zealand, and on the last transport to leave Egypt, the *Ellenga*, on July 23rd, 1919, there were a few officers and men of the Canterbury Mounted Rifles, mostly "main body" completing that "band of brothers"—the old Canterbury Mountd Rifles, the "C.M.R's."

Mainly drawn from the country districts of Canterbury, Marlborough, Nelson and the West Coast, the officers, non-commissioned officers and men proved to be a body of men in whom initiative, tenacity of purpose and a high sense of duty were the predominating characteristics. And it was a most encouraging fact that the latest reinforcements were of the same fine character as were the veterans of the Main Body. Though an essential qualification was that of a horse-lover, other qualities were necessary to the successful life of a mounted rifleman, and were provided in abundance because of the varied professions hitherto followed in civil life by members of the Regiment. There was the sheep-farmer, the dairyman, the musterer from the hills, the ploughman of the plains, the surveyor, the engineer, the city man who rode to hounds. No matter what work was on hand—the building or demolition of a bridge, the crossing of a deep river, the finding and development of water, the running of a steam or petrol engine, the formation of a road, the administration of a city—all came easily to such a body of men, and through it all ran a steady purpose—the War had to be won. No sick or holiday leave was allowed to interfere, nor did implacable climate daunt when operations began.

To these qualities, so essential for the work in hand, was added a fine sense of the conduct necessary in dealing with lower races. Of such a nature was this instinctive quality, that the district taken over by the N.Z.M.R. Brigade during the riots in Egypt after the Armistice was at once quieted and a perfect discipline preserved with the goodwill of the inhabitants. The big men on the big horses were met in fear and trembling, and yet when the time came for them to go the people openly expressed their regret.

One outstanding feature was the fine loyalty shown throughout the Regiment to its commanding officer, a loyalty which also bound officers and men to each other. In Colonel Findlay all officers and men placed implicit trust, and he was ably seconded by Major Overton in the early days. From 1916 onwards to the return to New Zealand, Major Acton-Adams carried on the duties of second-in-command. Untiring in his zeal, he left no

Aotea Home from the Air.

stone unturned in his constant endeavours for the good and well-being of the Regiment. To a cheerful and courageous personality he added a marked skill in the judgment of country and the use of maps, and he commanded the Regiment with ability and success on many occasions. He was a great judge of horseflesh and to this valuable understanding he added, as the campaign went on, a wonderful knowledge of horsemanship under active service conditions. To him and his wise care the Regiment largely owes the reputation of "second to none" so often bestowed upon its horses.

No member of the Regiment would forgive anyone attempting to record their doings in the Great War if he did not mention the Regiment's undying gratitude to the Aotea Home. Opened modestly in Heliopolis on the 25th November 1915, as a small convalescent home of 25 beds for New Zealanders, by 1918 it had increased to 250 beds and was firmly established as the Home of the New Zealand Mounted Rifle Brigade. Truly was it a "home away from home," and always with grateful memories will that devoted band of women be remembered. They were Matron M. A. Early, Sisters K. Booth, N. L. Hughes and Misses E. Macdonald, M. Macdonald, R. Cameron, L. McLaren and M. McDonnell. They were ably supported by Sergeant G. H. Sleight and Gunner Stewart who had charge of the cooking. Aotea was a piece of New Zealand and every man felt in duty bound to treat the staff as his hostesses and to his everlasting honour be it said the Mounted Riflemen throughout the whole of the life of the Home "played the game."

Also it will be remembered that the large amount of Regimental and Squadron funds with which the Regiment was able to supplement the Army rations, will always bring to mind the strenuous work of friends in New Zealand. To Mr. Snodgrass and the Patriotic Society of Nelson and to Sir Heaton Rhodes and Colonels Deans and Milton, and their many helpers, we will ever owe much. Their enthusiasm in organising public meetings and bazaars, and making speeches whereby the funds were collected throughout the towns and country is gratefully remembered, and every man who went away feels that the soldier alone could not have won the war without the assistance of those at home, nor without the sympathy courage and endurance of our women.

APPENDIX A.

THE THOROUGHBRED, RACING, AND REMOUNTS.

By Major J. Stafford, D.S.O., N.Z. Veterinary Corps.

Palestine, 1918.

The suppression of racing in England and the British Colonies has focussed no little attention on the breeding of remounts for army purposes. Many of the leading studmasters strenuously advocate racing on this account.

Unfortunately most of the writers are racing men pure and simple. They have had little or no experience in the field or on active service. The greater number entirely miss the crux of the question they attempt to discuss.

The writer of this article has been on active service since the outbreak of the War, and has under his charge over 2,000 horses. The greatest number of these have withstood a desert campaign that will assuredly live in equestrian history as the most trying on horseflesh in the annals of warfare. The three and a half years of service has been with a force from the Antipodes, where the horse still holds his own in spite of motor cars and other mechanical contrivances which have endeavoured to relegate the most beautiful animal in the service of man to a day that is dead.

It is not because New Zealand was the adopted home of the writer for a few years prior to War breaking out, but solely as a result of observation, he being in a position to note the good and bad features of horses gathered from various quarters of the globe, that leads him to the conviction that New Zealand and Australian bred horses stand out pre-eminently in a class by themselves.

New Zealanders and Australians are not the only men who appreciate the steed bred in the countries under the Southern Cross. Every British officer who appreciates good horseflesh is satisfied if he can obtain one, for it is known throughout the Army the odds are with the horse standing up to his work.

Now, why should the horses from New Zealand and Australia stand the rigors of a campaign so well?

(a) Is it because they are bred in an ideal climate, where the climatic conditions and environment are such as to produce an ideal constitution?

(b) Is it the care given to selection and breeding?

(c) Is it the preponderance of the Thoroughbred?

The questions may be answered seriatim.

(a) Is it because these horses are bred in an ideal climate where the climatic conditions and environment are such as to produce an ideal constitution?

The horse is bred and reared in an ideal climate. During his early days he lives a natural outdoor life; the climate is such that there is an abundance of feed for both dam and offspring. The environment is such that the true characteristics of the equine race are developed. The different types of animals of the same species are more often developed by the climatic conditions and environment than by the interference or influence of man.

Even in the human, the part played by climatic conditions and environment can be easily seen. To illustrate this point, take the population of the Delta of the Nile in Egypt. Although the original race which populated this region has been conquered many times by other nations, the influx of the Arab race was preponderant, yet the type to-day tends to revert to the same as the original type of the Early Egyptians. This reversion is best seen amongst the agricultural workers away from the larger towns, although in the streets of the cities the Early Egyptian type is frequently seen.

To prove the above assertion it is only necessary to visit the Egyptian Museum in Cairo and study the facial features and physique of the mummies which have been deprived of their wrappings. Take the mummy of Remeses; compare it with the men of the Delta at the present time. You find the same facial features, stature, and physique in hundreds of them.

This tendency to revert to the early Egyptian type is nothing more or less than the influence of climatic conditions and environment. As it is with the people of the Delta so it is with horses. Climatic conditions produce races of men and also of horses.

The racehorse was originally produced from the Arab. It was not the interference or influence of man that produced the type, but the climatic conditions and environment. Without these, man's work would have been of little or no avail, and the thoroughbred horse as known to-day would not have existed.

Take again the Argentine. This country imports yearly hundreds of thousands of pounds worth of Shorthorn bulls. Now why should this country import pure-bred bulls to this extent? The question is not difficult to answer. The climatic conditions in the Argentine are such that Shorthorn cattle tend to revert to the original type, and in the course of time would revert to it or produce a breed of cattle distinct in characteristics from the fixed type of Shorthorn bred in England to-day. Therefore, the Argentine must import pure-bred stock yearly to keep the breed fixed to type. Breeds are not made in entirety by man's selection; the influence of climatic conditions and environment are the potent factors.

(b) Is it that the best foundation stock only has been imported?

This can be dismissed in a very few words. The horses imported into Australasia were by no means the best. Other countries imported more valuable and better bred horses; the foundation stock in Australia and New Zealand could very easily be classed as only of medium quality. It must be clearly understood that the very best sires are not used for breeding the commercial horse. The best bred sires in New Zealand and Australia are used for the breeding of racing stock. The sires used on the stations are horses that have been sold as unsuitable for racing; their breeding may be good or indifferent. Therefore, it is the racing which keeps the standard high. Every year there are numbers of yearlings and two-year-olds that have met with injuries or accidents which render them useless as racehorses; these are the class which find their way into the stations and are used as sires on good class mares. This is where the New Zealand and Australian remount comes from.

(c) Is it the care given to selection and breeding?

No more care in selection is used in New Zealand or Australia than in other countries.

(d) Is it the preponderence of the Thoroughbred?

Making due allowance for the climatic conditions and environment as the most potent factors, experience and observation show that the preponderence of thoroughbred blood is the remaining factor. A fixed breed has been imported into countries which have a climate and environment where the horse does not deteriorate, but improves. It is a well recognised axiom with breeds of stock that the value of any family is mainly in proportion to the "purity of its origin."

The Arab and Barb breeds are undoubtedly the purest known form of what are to-day called thoroughbred horses. The Arab and Barb are practically identical in race and surroundings and may be classed under the same heading. There is not the slightest doubt that these two—the Arab and the Barb—represent the great fountain heads or sources from which sprang our present Racing Stock. These horses of the desert were originally war horses. The Arab training was systematically directed to produce a war horse. Arab horsemen are recognised as the only race who surpass the British as horsemasters. The Arab horsemen expended the youngster's energy not to attain speed but to produce the essential qualities of a war horse, viz: Strength, hardiness, endurance, stamina, and courage. These to-day are the essential qualities a remount should possess. Now, although this Eastern blood plays such an important part in making the Thoroughbred what he is to-day, it has only asserted itself in the male line in three instances in the offspring of these three great Eastern sires—Darley Arabian, Byerley Turk, and Godolphin Barb.

The origin of the present day racehorse in the female line was from a number of mares. Some of these were called Royal Mares; others Barb Mares and Natural Barb Mares. In vol. I. of the English Thoroughbred Stud Book some one hundred original mares are entered; in the volumes of recent years only the offspring of some fifty remain. Although there are no records to prove that the so-called "royal mares" were of Eastern descent, it is possible that some of these mares were of pure Eastern descent. In Vol. I. of the English Stud Book it is stated that Charles I. had three Morocco mares at Tatsbury in 1643.

It will be seen from the above that the English Racehorse of to-day is the original Arab Warhorse, improved where climatic conditions and environment, assisted by man's selection, have played the important parts.

New Zealanders are a horse-loving people; they are sportsmen to the core. Whether in athletics or equine contests, their enthusiasm is great. The pioneers who left Britain to people this Britain of the South included sportsmen who imported, bred, and raced horses for sport and not pecuniary gain. What is the result? The production of a warhorse that stands out from all others. His thoroughbred origin has stood to him. He has stamina and endurance; the true qualities of a racehorse are in him though he may have an admixture of some other blood. In his veins he has the blood of the Arab, the original war horse whose cardinal points were stamina, courage, strength, hardiness, and endurance.

The horses that have stood the campaign the best are low-set, well balanced horses. Remounts should show breeding. I do not mean to convey that they should show distinct thoroughbred characters, but true characteristics of the equine race.

Well-built ponies from 14.1 to 14.3 hands, with good, straight, clean action, have withstood the rigours of the campaign much better than taller horses. Most of these ponies are simply miniature thoroughbreds. Seldom have these ponies become debilitated through the effects of short rations and bad water; these little horses have carried their men and equipment day in and day out, never losing a day and always looking well and keeping their condition.

The big horse is not wanted, neither is the trotter. Big horses seldom have the true make, shape, and constitution of the equine race, and they are quite unsuitable for regular and continuous saddle work. Trotters are generally badly ribbed up, slack in the loins, badly coupled, and the hindquarters do not move in sympathy with the fore. The horse has what the enthusiasts for trotters call "a gait." This class of horse is useless for campaigning; he finds his way into veterinary hospital after every hard day.

I make no remark about legs and feet or fancy points, but good flat bone, big joints, well muscled fore-arms and thighs, are what is wanted, irrespective of weight of bone. If buyers would be impressed with one simple axiom, and they would not allow their own whims to persuade them to buy certain types, the remounts would come forward and stand the rigours of the campaign. The axiom is simply well balanced, clean actioned, medium-sized horses and the more breeding they show the better. How often has it been said, "Look at his shoulder?" and the horse bought for one point only, a big raking shoulder. What is the good of a shoulder if the horse is not balanced? And again, it is said, "Look at his rein," yet he is no horse behind the withers. Every batch of remounts brings them forward, horses with one good point and a hundred bad ones. It is the greatest pity in the world that some of the remount buyers are not sent for six months to ride some of the angular brutes they buy; they would be more careful in buying after their experience. They should remember that the horses they are buying will one day be carrying men of the best material that the world has ever seen. Therefore, to carry them, buy horses the best that can be found. The reputation of our great Empire depends upon our men, and the men depend on their horses. Therefore, let the watchwords of our remount buyers be, "good, clean action, balance, and symmetry." If every buyer threw his leg over the horse he bought and asked himself whether he would like to ride him from twenty to twenty-five miles during the night, fight all day, and ride him back next night, he cannot get far wrong.

APPENDIX B.

Killed in Action, etc.

*7/296	Abbott, L/Cpl. A. C., Egypt, 8/5/15, D. of S.
7/810	Abbott, Tpr. G. D., Gallipoli, 28/8/15, K. in A.
7/152	Abraham, Sgt. W. P., Gallipoli, 6/7/8/15, K. in A.
7/1328	Armstrong, Tpr. R. V., Malta ex Gallipoli, 15/12/15, D. of S
7/509	Archer, L/Cpl. S. R., Gallipoli, 22/6/15, K. in A.
7/299	Anderson, Tpr. D., Gallipoli, 25/8/15, K. in A.
7/157	Arnold, L/Cpl. R., Gallipoli, 17/7/15, D. of W.
7/600	Bain, Tpr. M. S., Gallipoli, 28/8/15, K. in A.
7/693	Ballantyne, Tpr. R., Gallipoli, 28/8/15, K. in A.
7/9	Bassett, Tpr. S. E., at sea ex Gallipoli, 23/6/15, D. of W.
7/164	Bate, Tpr. H. S., Gallipoli, 17/7/15, D. of W.
7/11	Bell, Sgt. N. M., at sea ex Gallipoli, 20/7/15, D. of S.
7/815	Belworthy, Tpr. W. A., Gallipoli, 28/8/15, K. in A.
7/697	Berry, Tpr. C. F., Gallipoli, 6/7/8/15, K. in A.
7/816	Bindon, Tpr. J., Gallipoli, 28/8/15, K. in A.
7/308	Birdling, Tpr. R. F., Gallipoli, 6/7/8/15, K. in A.
7/15	Black, Tpr. J., Gallipoli, 28/8/15, K. in A.
7/171	Boden, Sgt. R. A., Gallipoli, 22/5/15, K. in A.
7/17	Booker, Tpr. G. E., Gallipoli, 21/8/15, K. in A.
*7/920	Bowie, Major R. R., Egypt, 10/7/15, D. of S.
7/18	Bowker, Sgt. S. J., Gallipoli, 21/8/15, K. in A.
7/312	Brent, Tpr, T., Gallipoli, 21/8/15, K. in A.
7/939	Brewer, Tpr. O., Gallipoli, 28/8/15, K. in A.
7/748	Brighton, L/Cpl. George, at sea ex Gallipoli, 27/11/15, D. of W.
7/533	Brislane, Tpr. M. E., Malta ex Gallipoli, 20/8/15, D. of W.
7/495	Brittan, Tpr. E. G., Gallipoli, 28/8/15, K. in A.
7/942	Brittan, L/Cpl. Henry Bertram, Gallipoli. 28/8/15, K. in A.
7/542	Bull, Tpr. A. J., Gallipoli, 6/7/8/15, K. in A.
7/315	Burn, Tpr. R. B., Gallipoli, 6/7/8/15, K. in A.
7/821	Byrch, Tpr. F. V., at sea ex Gallipoli, 9/8/15, D. of W.
7/24	Calvert, L/Cpl. R. S. L., Gallipoli, 28/8/15, K. in A.
7/27	Campbell, Tpr. J. R., at sea ex Gallipoli, 30/6/15, D. of W.
7/826	Carlyle, Tpr, J. F., Gallipoli, 28/8/15, K in A
7/827	Carter, L/Cpl. D. R., Gallipoli, 27/8/15, K. in A.
7/31	Cochrane, Tpr. J. A., Gallipoli, 13/8/15, D. of W.
7/799	Collins, L/Cpl. H., Gallipoli, 28/8/15, K. in A.
7/1211	Collinson, Tpr. A. G. V., Egypt, 6/11/15, D. of S.
7/830	Comer, Tpr. G. I., Gallipoli, 28/8/15, K. in A.
7/319	Conway, Tpr. F. J., at sea ex Gallipoli, 31/8/15, D. of W.
7/831	Copestake, Tpr. W., Gallipoli, 27/8/15, K. in A.
7/183	Crook, Tpr. C. T., at sea ex Gallipoli, 4/7/15, D. of W.
7/321	Currie, Tpr. T. E., at sea ex Gallipoli, 22/7/15, D. of W.
7/185	Dalton, Tpr. W. H., Gallipoli, 19/5/15, K. in A.
7/37	Daniel, Tpr. E. F., Gallipoli, 22/8/15, K. in A.
7/835	Davidson, Tpr. G., Gallipoli, 28/8/15, K. in A.
7/38	Davis, Tpr. W. J., Mudros, 1/9/15, D. of S.
7/639	Davison, Lieut. F., Gallipoli. 7/8/15, K. in A.
5/322a.	Dawson, Tpr. J. R., Gallipoli, 28/8/15, K. in A.
7/187	De Castro, Tpr. A. H., Gallipoli, 6/7/8/15, K. in A.
7/797	Deck, 2nd Lieut. R. H., Gallipoli, 29/8/15, K. in A.

S

4/147a.	Dick, Tpr. H. J. at sea ex Gallipoli, 13/7/15, D. of S.
7/1350	Dorman, Tpr. C. P., Gallipoli, 18/12/15, K. in A.
3/171a	Downing, Cpl. W. G., Egypt ex Gallipoli, 14/12/15, D. of W.
7/838	Duncan, Tpr. J., Gallipoli, 28/8/15, K. in A.
7/804	Duncan, Tpr. J. M., Gallipoli, 28/8/15, K. in A.
7/800	Edwards, L/Cpl. J., Gallipoli, 28/8/15, K. in A.
7/634	Evans, Sgt. J. M. W., Gallipoli, 28/8/15, K. in A.
7/193	Everett, Tpr. Edmund, U.K. ex Gallipoli, 11/9/15, D. of S.
7/194	Everett, Sgt. S. C., Malta ex Gallipoli, 31/7/15, D. of S.
7/329	Fairweather, Sgt. F., at sea ex Gallipoli, 24/8/15, D. of W.
7/841	Ferguson, L/Sgt. G. W., Gallipoli, 21/8/15, K. in A.
7/198	Fleming, Tpr. J., Gallipoli, 25/8/15, K. in A.
7/441	Fleming, Sgt. R. A., Gallipoli, 6/7/8/15, K. in A.
7/640	Fox, Sgt. C. F. D., Gallipoli, 12/6/15, K. in A.
7/333	Gallagher, Tpr. W. J., Gallipoli, 21/8/15, K. in A.
7/478	Gardiner, Tpr. Herman, Gallipoli, 6/7/8/15, K. in A.
7/720	Gibson, Tpr. S. J., Gallipoli, 28/8/15, K. in A.
7/721	Glover, Tpr. A. H., Gallipoli, 21/8/15, K. in A.
7/334	Godfrey, Tpr. D., at sea ex Gallipoli, 9/5/15, D. of W.
7/340	Greenwood, L/Sgt. A. R., Gallipoli, 6/7/8/15, K. in A.
7/921	Guinness, 2nd Lieut. F. B. H., at sea ex Gallipoli, 25/8/15. D. of W.
7/724	Gynes, Tpr. J., at sea ex Gallipoli, 31/8/15, D. of W.
7/64	Hagerty, Tpr. Jas. Michael, Gallipoli, 27/8/15, K. in A.
7/498	Hall, Tpr. S., Malta ex Gallipoli, 11/9/15, D. of W.
7/592	Hamilton, 2nd Lieut. H. A., Gallipoli, 22/8/15, K. in A.
7/515	Hanmer, L/Cpl. A. H., Gallipoli, 10/8/15, K. in A.
7/206	Hannen, Tpr. J., Gallipoli, 6/7/8/15, K. in A.
7/726	Happer, Tpr. J., Gallipoli, 19/5/15, D. of W.
7/207	Harding, Tpr. W. F., Gallipoli, 31/5/15, D. of W.
7/344	Hassall, Cpl. W. R., Gallipoli, 21/8/15, K. in A.
7/62	Hay, Tpr. W. H., Gallipoli, 14/5/15, K. in A.
7/63	Hayter, Lieut. C., Gallipoli, 28/8/15, K. in A.
7/850	Hedley, Tpr. W., Gallipoli, 21/8/15, K. in A.
7/727	Hobson, Tpr. F. E., Gallipoli, 31/5/15, K. in A.
7/428	Holmes, L/Cpl. J. A. H., Egypt ex Gallipoli, 30/9/15, D. of S.
7/730	Hopkins, Tpr. H. W., Egypt, 3/8/15, D. of S.
7/523	Horgan, Tpr. T., Egypt, 18/11/15, D. of S.
7/562	Hunter, Tpr. P., Gallipoli, 26/5/15, K. in A.
7/69	Huxford, Tpr. W. T., Gallipoli, 30/5/15, K. in A.
7/479	Ilsley, L/Cpl. G. L., Gallipoli, 6/7/8/15, K. in A.
7/352	Jackson, Cpl. G. W., Egypt, 16/7/15, D. of S.
7/353	Jarman, Tpr. F. E., Gallipoli, 6/7/8/15, K. in A.
7/218	Jenkins, Tpr. D., at sea ex Gallipoli, 24/7/15, D. of W.
7/735	Jenkins, L/Cpl. P. J., Gallipoli, 27/8/15, K. in A.
7/501	Jones, L/Cpl. E. J., Gallipoli, 25/8/15, K. in A.
7/219	Johnson, L/Sgt. W. J. P., Gallipoli, 23/5/15, K. in A.
7/72	Johnstone, Tpr. A. McC., Gallipoli, 28/8/15, K. in A.
7/73	Johnston, Tpr. J., Gallipoli, 30/5/15, K. in A.
7/336	Jordan, Tpr. Edgar Percy, at sea ex Gallipoli, 9/7/15, D. of W.
7/74	Joyce, Tpr. H. B., Gallipoli, 22/8/15, D. of W.
7/857	Keefe, Tpr. E. J., Gallipoli, 28/8/15, K. in A.
7/577	Kerr, Tpr. F. W., at sea ex Gallipoli, 13/6/15, D. of W.
7/220	Kidson, Tpr. F. G., Egypt ex Gallipoli, 18/6/15, D. of W.
7/1373	Kirkness, Tpr. J. G. B., Gallipoli, 10/12/15, D. of S.
7/861	Knox, Tpr. E. H., Gallipoli, 28/8/15, K. in A.
7/222	Lafrentz, Tpr. H., Gallipoli, 21/8/15, K. in A.
7/359	Leaman, Tpr. Lewis Maurice, Gallipoli, 14/7/15, K. in A.

CANTERBURY MOUNTED RIFLES 259

7/610	Low, Tpr. G., Gallipoli, 28/5/15, K. in A.	
7/445	Luisetti, Tpr. Pictro Max, U.K. ex Gallipoli, 26/10/15, D. of S.	
7/364	Lusk, Tpr. R., Gallipoli, 6/7/8/15, K. in A.	
7/460	McDonald, Sgt. D. McL., Gallipoli, 22/8/15, K. in A.	
7/228	McDonald, Tpr. J., at sea ex Gallipoli, 7/7/15, D. of W.	
7/79	McDonald, Tpr. T. A., Gallipoli, 28/8/15, K. in A.	
7/1010	McFerran, Tpr. J. A., Gallipoli, 28/8/15, K. in A.	
7/367	McInnes, Tpr. M., Gallipoli, 7/8/15, K. in A.	
7/1497	McKay, Tpr. R. H., at sea ex Gallipoli, 15/10/15, D. of S.	
7/481	McLean, Tpr. L. A., Gallipoli, 6/7/8/15, K. in A.	
7/546	McMahon, Tpr. C. P., Gallipoli, 6/7/8/15, K. in A.	
7/758	McMenamin, Tpr. J., Gallipoli, 21/8/15, K. in A.	
7/86	McVey, Tpr. D. M., Egypt, 28/8/15, D. of S.	
7/744	Martin, Tpr. F. B., Gallipoli, 27/8/15, K. in A.	
7/179	Mayne, Lieut. G. C., Gallipoli, 8/8/15, K. in A.	
7/232	Mead, Tpr. R. S., Mudros ex Gallipoli, 27/9/15, D. of S.	
7/875	Middlemiss, Tpr. D., Gallipoli, 28/8/15, K. in A.	
7/876	Miles, Tpr. H. J., at sea ex Gallipoli, 20/12/15, D. of W.	
7/1637	Mitchell, Tpr. James H., at sea ex Egypt, 24/4/17, D. of W. en route to N.Z.	
7/750	Moore, Tpr. G., Gallipoli, 30/5/15, K. in A.	
7/377	Moore, L/Cpl. M. O., Gallipoli, 6/7/8/15, K. in A.	
7/238	Morrison, Tpr. F. J., at sea ex Gallipoli, 13/8/15, D. of W.	
7/881	Mortimer, Tpr. A. F., Gallipoli, 28/8/15, K. in A.	
7/379	Mounsey, Tpr. J., Gallipoli, 6/7/8/15, K. in A.	
7/539	Nalder, Cpl. G., at sea ex Gallipoli, 2/9/15, D. of W.	
7/243	Nalder, Cpl. L. W., Gallipoli, 6/7/8/15, K. in A.	
7/688	Nancarrow, Lieut. V. F., Malta ex Gallipoli, 4/8/15, D. of S.	
7/465	Napier, Tpr. P. N., Gallipoli, 28/8/15, K. in A.	
7/246	Neal, Tpr. W. J., Gallipoli, 6/7/8/15, K. in A.	
7/96	Nicholas, Tpr. R. H., Gallipoli, 31/5/15, K. in A.	
7/557	Norrie, Tpr. A. E., Gallipoli, 28/8/15, K. in A.	
7/505	Norris, R.S.M. (W.O.1.) F. H., Gallipoli, 22/8/15, K. in A.	
7/763	O'Brian, Tpr. Harry, Gallipoli, 25/8/15, K. in A.	
7/766	O'Keeffe, Tpr. V. A., at sea ex Gallipoli, 23/8/15, D. of W.	
7/994	Okell, Tpr. Norman, Gallipoli, 28/8/15, K. in A.	
7/555	Orr, Tpr. J. J., Gallipoli, 16/8/15, K. in A.	
7/384	Overton, L/Cpl. G. S., at sea ex Gallipoli, 10/8/15, D. of W.	
7/503	Overton, Major P. J., Gallipoli, 7/8/15, K. in A.	
*7/483	Paget, Tpr. G. C., United Kingdom, 5/1/16, D. of S.	
7/98	Parker, Tpr. A., Gallipoli, 28/8/15, K. in A.	
7/386	Parkinson, 2nd Lieut. L., M.C.	
7/550	Patmore, Tpr. H. R., Egypt ex Gallipoli, 5/8/15, D. of W.	
7/99	Patrick, Tpr. J. H. H., Gallipoli, 28/8/15, K. in A.	
7/255	Patterson, Tpr. T. C. C., Gallipoli, 30/5/15, D. of W. z
7/389	Petrie, L/Sgt. W. H., Gallipoli, 28/8/15, K. in A.	
7/583	Pidgeon, Tpr. H., at sea ex Gallipoli, 25/8/15, D. of W.	
7/888	Pinch, Tpr. G. F., Gallipoli, 28/8/15, K. in A.	
7/262	Primrose, Tpr. J. T., at sea ex Gallipoli, 13/7/15, D. of W.	
7/776	Prince, Tpr. L. V., at sea ex Gallipoli, 29/8/15, D. of W.	
7/999	Pugh, Tpr. G., Gallipoli, 27/8/15, K. in A.	
7/891	Rae, Tpr. D. A., at sea ex Gallipoli, 28/8/15, D. of W.	
7/112	Rickman, Tpr. E. A., Gallipoli, 20/8/15, K. in A.	
7/1280	Robinson, L/Cpl. C. K., Malta ex Gallipoli, 8/12/15, D. of S.	
7/1137	Rudman, Tpr. H. S., Gallipoli, 17/11/15, K. in A.	
7/115	Rutherford, Sgt. W., at sea ex Gallipoli, 13/7/15, D. of W.	
7/895	Sanders, Tpr. E., Gallipoli, 21/8/15, K. in A.	
7/780	Saunders, Cpl. C. W., Egypt ex Gallipoli, 2/9/15, D. of S.	

7/394   Senior, Tpr. E. H., at sea ex Gallipoli, 30/8/15, D. of W.
7/268   Shain, Tpr. H. A., Gallipoli, 6/7/8/15, K. in A.
7/121   Sloan, S.S.M. R., (W.O.I.), Gallipoli, 21/8/15, K. in A.
7/560   Smith, Tpr. G. W., Gallipoli, 6/7/8/15, K. in A.
7/123   Smith, Tpr. H. R., Gallipoli, 22/8/15, K. in A.
7/124   Smith, Tpr. W. A., at sea ex Gallipoli, 26/8/15, D. of W.
7/125   Snushall, Tpr. H. E., Gallipoli, 21/8/15, K. in A.
7/786   Stemner, Tpr. A., Gallipoli, 19/8/15, K. in A.
9/999   Stewart, Lt./Col. G. H., Mudros ex Gallipoli, 20/11/15, D. of S.
7/900   Sullivan, Tpr. P., Gallipoli, 28/8/15, K. in A.
7/467   Sustins, Tpr. L., Gallipoli, 21/8/15, K. in A.
7/484   Sustins, L/Cpl. N., Gallipoli, 21/8/15, K. in A.
7/790   Sutherland, Tpr. G., Gallipoli, 17/8/15, K. in A.
7/132   Tavendale, Tpr. W., Gallipoli, 27/6/15, D. of W.
7/791   Taylor, Tpr. G., Gallipoli, 12/6/15, K. in A.
7/1009 Tickell, Tpr. R. M. G., Gallipoli, 28/8/15, K. in A.
7/904   Urquhart, Tpr. A. M., Gallipoli, 6/7/8/15, K. in A.
7/284   Walker, L/Cpl. J. H., Gallipoli, 21/8/15, K. in A.
7/906   Wallace, Tpr. A. G., Gallipoli, 28/8/15, K. in A.
7/692   Waters, Tpr. C. J., Egypt ex Gallipoli, 31/8/15, D. of W.
7/1019 Watson, Tpr. D., Gallipoli, 27/8/15, K. in A.
7/288   Watson, Tpr. H. P., Gibraltar ex Gallipoli, 9/8/15, D. of S.
7/722   Way, Tpr. F. M., Gallipoli, 8/8/15, D. of W.
7/143   Weight, Cpl. E. G., Gallipoli, 28/8/15, K. in A.
7/414   Winkler, Tpr. H., Gallipoli, 28/8/15, K. in A.
7/487   Young, Cpl. R. McG., Gallipoli, 19/8/15, D. of W

7/163   Batchelor, Cpl. A. L., Palestine, 27/11/17, D. of W.
7/814   Bedelph, Cpl. T., Palestine, 5/12/17, K. in A.
7/1545 Benson, 2/Lieut. H., Palestine, 31/3/18, D. of W.
7/166   Berryman, Lieut. S., Palestine, 30/3/18, K. in A.
49866   Bews, Tpr. Wm., Gallipoli after Armistice, 18/12/18, D. of S.
7/1568 Blakeney, Lieut. C., Egypt, 9/8/16, K. in A.
16373   Boag, Tpr J. W., Palestine, 2/5/18, D. of W.
7/1196 Bowron, Lieut. H. A., Egypt, 23/12/16, K. in A.
9/2152 Brewer, Tpr. H. C., Egypt ex Palestine, 1/11/18, D. of S.
16067   Bruce, Tpr. J. McQ., Palestine, 31/3/18, D. of W.
50628   Burrow, Tpr. E. B., Palestine, 1/11/18, D. of S.
7/1705 Cameron, Tpr. J., Egypt, 2/12/16, D. of S.
16070   Campbell, L/Cpl. C. A., Palestine, 25/9/18, K. in A.
7/28   Carr, Sgt. J. J., Palestine, 30/3/18, K. in A.
17384   Carr, Tpr. O., Palestine, 30/3/18, K. in A.
7/318   Caskey, Tpr. T. J., Palestine, 24/12/16, D. of W.
7/1209 Clayton, Tpr. M., Palestine, 5/11/17, K. in A.
60904   Clear, Tpr. W. T., Palestine, 15/10/18, D. of S.
7/703   Cooke, Sgt. R. G., Egypt, 23/12/16, K. in A.
7/633   Cotton, Tpr. A. E., Palestine, 20/2/18, K. in A.
7/1215 Crowe, L/Sgt. C. H., Egypt, 9/8/16, K. in A.
7/707   Davis, L/Cpl. G., Egypt, 9/8/16, K. in A.
7/433   Devon, Farr/Sgt. D., Palestine, 27/11/17, D. of W.
7/326   Douglas, Cpl. H., Palestine, 10/11/17, D. of W.
17393   Downie, Tpr. J., Palestine, 1/5/18, D. of W.
7/1351 Drain, Tpr. H., Palestine, 16/10/18, D. of S.
7/1614 Ferguson. Tpr. D. J., Palestine, 19/7/17, K. in A.
7/1464 Ferris, Tpr. O. E. O., Egypt, 9/8/16, K. in A.
7/1228 Fifield, L/Cpl. J., Gallipoli after Armistice, 20/12/18, D. of S.
50698   Fincham, Tpr. T. D., Egypt ex Palestine, 7/11/18, D. of S.

CANTERBURY MOUNTED RIFLES 261

16393	Fletcher, Tpr. A. W., Palestine, 9/12/17, K. in A.	
58345	Fowler, Tpr. G., Palestine, 16/10/18, D. of S.	
7/1321	Garland, Tpr. E., Egypt, 24/12/16, D. of W.	
7/1021	Gibb, Tpr. R. J., Palestine, 30/3/18, K. in A.	
7/514	Gibbs, Tpr. L. W., Palestine, 9/1/17, K. in A.	
7/335	Gold, L/Cpl. W. D., Palestine, 14/8/17, D. of W.	
7/1732	Good, Tpr. A. H., Egypt, 7/8/16, D. of W.	
7/959	Goodrik, Tpr. F., Egypt, 9/8/16, K. in A.	
12597	Graham, L/Cpl. H. W., Palestine, 30/3/18, K. in A.	
7/602	Gray, Sgt. W. M., Egypt, 9/8/16, K. in A.	
7/1473	Greenslade, L/Cpl. L. J., Palestine, 5/11/17, K. in A.	
58408	Grooby, Tpr. L. R., Palestine, 27/10/18, D. of S.	
36226	Haines, Tpr. E. E., Palestine, 10/12/17, D. of S.	
7/590	Hammond, Major H. H., Egypt, 9/8/16, K. in A.	
57509	Hampton, Tpr. B. L., Palestine, 20/5/18, D. of S.	
62986	Hampton, Tpr. F. S., Gallipoli after Armistice, 28/12/18, D. of S.	
7/1244	Handisides, Tpr. D., Egypt, 20/1/17, D. of W.	
35694	Harper, Tpr. E. T., Palestine, 30/4/18, K. in A.	
7/516	Harper, 2/Lieut. G. G., Egypt, 12/8/16, D. of W.	
7/1475	Haslett, Tpr. D., Palestine, 5/11/17, D. of W.	
7/1625	Henson, L/Cpl. F. W., Palestine, 30/3/18. K. in A.	
18221	Hinson, Capt. H. B., Palestine, 30/3/18, D. of W.	
35416	Hole, Tpr. A., Palestine, 28/4/18, D. of S.	
43152	Holyoake, Tpr. W., Palestine, 30/3/18, K. in A.	
18384	Humphreys, Tpr. J. S., Palestine, 12/10/18, D. of S.	
16410	Jackson, Tpr. F. H., Palestine, 19/4/17, K. in A.	
58329	Jennings, Tpr. A. H., Palestine, 25/9/18, K. in A.	
35419	Johnston, Tpr. W., Gallipoli after Armistice, 15/12/18, D. of S.	
35888	Jones, Tpr. J. W., Palestine, 14/11/17, K. in A.	
7/1096	Kennedy, Tpr. H. J., Egypt after Armistice, 25/1/19, D. of S.	
16412	Kennedy, Tpr. J. J., Palestine, 30/3/18, K. in A.	
7/1253	Kennedy, Tpr. T. R., Palestine, 6/11/17, D. of W.	
17420	Kerr, L/Cpl. L. P., Gallipoli after Armistice, 14/12/18, D. of S.	
43735	Kingsbury, Tpr. A. H., Egypt ex Palestine, 25/10/18, D. of S.	
17422	Knowles, Tpr. F., Palestine, 30/3/18, K. in A.	
7/1255	Lambie, Tpr. R. H., Egypt, 9/8/16, K. in A.	
16417	Lawson, Tpr. B., Gallipoli after Armistice, 18/12/18, D. of S.	
16041	Ledingham, Sgt. A., Egypt, 9/1/17, K. in A.	
7/1258	LeLievre, Tpr. M. J., Egpyt, 9/1/17, K. in A.	
7/1182	Levett, Sgt. F. J., Palestine, 30/3/18, K. in A.	
12553	Livingstone, Lieut. A. R., Palestine, 25/11/17, K. in A.	
68578	Luxton, Tpr. A. D., Egypt ex Palestine, 29/10/18, D. of S.	
13352	McConachie, Tpr. C. G., Palestine, 30/3/18, K. in A.	
7/1766	McGuckin, L/Cpl. H., Gallipoli after Armistice, 9/12/18, D. of S.	
7/1113	McIntosh, Cpl. C. F., Egypt, 10/1/17, D. of W.	
16429	McIntyre, Tpr. C. C., Palestine, 30/3/18, K. in A.	
7/1264	McKay, L/Cpl. J., Egypt, 9/8/16, K. in A.	
63389	McKibbon, Tpr. W., Palestine, 5/10/18, D. of S.	
7/1101	Mackie, L/Cpl. F. G., Palestine, 31/3/18, D. of W.	
7/1499	McNeill, Tpr. J., Egypt, 9/8/16, K. in A.	
46770	McNeill, Tpr. W., Palestine, 30/3/18, K. in A.	
50101	McPeak, Tpr. J. R., Palestine, 13/10/18, D. of S.	
69029	McTainsh, Tpr. A. E., Palestine, 19/10/18, D. of S.	
16420	Manship, Tpr. H., Gallipoli after Armistice, 19/12/18, D. of S.	
7/2283	Manson, Tpr. L., Egypt, 5/8/16, K. in A.	
7/89	Marchant, Capt. Frederick N., Egypt, 31/12/16, D. of injuries.	
7/1635	Mardon, Tpr. W., Egypt, 26/1/17, D. of S.	

7/1319	Mathias, Sgt. O., Palestine, 30/3/18, K. in A.
52095	Mee, Tpr. A. R., Palestine, 26/10/18, D. of S.
7/92	Menzies, 2/Lieut. W. B., Egypt, 9/8/16, K. in A.
18351	Milliken, Tpr. W. T., Palestine, 28/3/18, K. in A.
16107	Mitchell, Tpr. G. A., Palestine, 9/1/17, K. in A.
7/234	Moore, Tpr. A., Egypt, 9/8/16, K. in A.
7/1870	Morrison, L/Cpl. J., Palestine, 30/3/18, K. in A.
7/1394	Morton, Tpr. E. C., Egypt, 7/8/16, D. of W.
7/988	Mulholland, Sgt, A., Palestine, 26/3/17, K. in A.
7/1501	O'Brien, Tpr. E., Egypt, 10/3/19, D. of S.
61372	O'Fee, Tpr. D. D., Gallipoli after Armistice, 16/12/18, D. of S.
7/1126	Penwell, T/Cpl. F. P., Palestine, 5/11/17.
7/1649	Pickens, Tpr. J. G. A., Egypt, 4/8/16, K. in A.
7/260	Pigou, Lieut. A. C., Galipoli after Armistice, 12/12/18, D. of S.
50038	Pike, Tpr. E. N., Palestine, 30/4/18, K. in A.
7/1403	Pugh, Tpr. N., Palestine, 30/4/18, K. in A.
7/1276	Raine, Tpr. J. H., Egypt, 9/8/16, K. in A.
7/1651	Rees, Tpr. F. O., Egypt, 5/8/16, K. in A.
78933	Robertson, Tpr. A. C., Egypt, 16/4/19, D. of S.
17363	Robertson, Tpr. D., Palestine, 26/10/18, D. of S.
35407	Rodger, Tpr. A., Palestine, 29/9/18, D. of S.
35925	Rogers, Tpr. G., Palestine, 30/3/18, K. in A.
17575	Rolph, Tpr. L. E., Egypt ex Palestine, 15/11/17, D. of W.
7/1511	Ross, L/Cpl. T., Palestine, 8/11/17, D. of W.
7/1653	Ross, Tpr. W. W., Gallipoli after Armistice, 21/12/18, D. of S.
36019	Rudd, Tpr. F. W., Palestine, 22/10/18, D. of S.
43782	Samuel, Tpr. W., Palestine, 30/3/18, K. in A.
7/1410	Sanderson, Tpr. W., Egypt, 9/8/16, K. in A.
13475	Scott, Tpr. W. T., Palestine, 18/1/17, D. of W.
7/1783	Sharland, L/Cpl. T. J., Palestine, 1/4/18, D. of W.
11/2238	Sheehan, Tpr. P., Palestine, 12/8/17, D. of W.
7/1004	Shields, L/Cpl. J., Palestine, 22/4/17, D. of W.
16127	Smith, Tpr. A., Palestine, 28/10/18, D. of S.
50071	Smith, Tpr. G. W. H., Palestine, 24/5/18, Killed (accidentally).
7/1899	Steele, Tpr. T., Palestine, 4/5/17, K. in A.
7/1420	Sutton, Tpr. R., Egypt, 5/8/16, D. of W.
7/1663	Thomson, Tpr. A. J. C., Palestine, 19/4/17, K. in A.
17569	Thornton, Tpr. W. C., Palestine, 25/11/17, K. in A.
49208	Throp, Tpr. G. W., Palestine, 28/3/18, K. in A.
43243	Townsend, Tpr. G. A., Palestine, 30/3/18, K. in A.
24942	Twomey, Tpr. F. H., Palestine, 5/11/17, K. in A.
7/1300	Vincent, Tpr. R. S., Palestine, 5/11/17, K. in A.
24944	Waghorn, Tpr. S. D., Palestine, 19/4/17, D. of W.
7/1165	Walker, Tpr. J., Egypt, 6/8/16, D. of W.
17545	Walker, Tpr. R. L., Egypt ex Palestine, 23/7/18, D. of S.
7/566	Wanden, 2/Licut, E. W., Palestine, 25/9/18, K. in A.
7/1304	Watson, L/Cpl. N. A., Palestine, 28/3/18, K. in A.
57775	Watt, Tpr. A., Palestine, 14/7/18, K. in A.
34995	Watts, Tpr. W. E., Palestine, 21/10/18, D. of S.
12662	Wilkinson, L/Cpl. G., Palestine, 7/10/18, D. of S.
50340	Williams, Tpr. H., Palestine, 30/3/18, K. in A.
7/1930	Williams, Tpr. S. W. V., Egypt ex Palestine, 22/5/17, D. of W.
12663	Willocks, Tpr. J. C., Palestine, 30/3/18, K. in A.
7/1307	Wilson, L/Cpl. C., Palestine, 30/3/18, K. in A.
7/149	Wilson, Licut. J. L., Palestine, 23/7/17, D. of W.
50050	Withers Tpr. T. W., Palestine, 9/10/18, D. of S.
7/295	Yaxley, Sgt. H. W., Egypt, 11/3/19, D. of S.

APPENDIX C.

Awards of Decorations and Medals.

7/297	Acton-Adams, Major P. M., D.S.O., Order of the Nile (4th class) conferred by H.H. the Sultan, m.i.d.
7/689	Alexander, Tpr. F. J., St. George (4th Class), Russian Decoration
7/4	Bain, Sgt. L., m.i.d.
7/659	Barr, Sgt. J. A., D.C.M., m.i.d. (2).
7/1590	Barrett, Cpl. (T/Sgt.) W., M.M.
7/1031	Bilton, Tpr. (T/Sgt.) F. J., m.i.d.
7/170	Blackett, Lt. G. R., M.C., m.i.d.
7/309	Blair, Capt. D. B., M.C., D.S.O., m.i.d. (3).
7/311	Boocock, Tpr. J. M., Serbian Decoration (Silver Medal) awarded by King of Serbia, m.i.d.
7/1030	Bremner, Sgt. O. H., D.C.M., m.i.d.
7/290	Burrows, Sgt. L., D.C.M.
7/1826	Butterworth, Tpr. S., M.M.
7/1051	Campbell, Sgt. D., D.C.M., m.i.d.
15/29	Chaytor, Lt.-Col. D'A., C.M.G., C.B.E., Egyptian Order of the Nile (3rd Class), m.i.d. (3).
7/528	Clarkson, S.S.M. E., D.C.M., m.i.d.
7/643	Creed, Cpl. (L/Sgt.) W. H. P., D.C.M., m.i.d.
7/707	Davis, L/Cpl. G., m.i.d.
7/1348	Davis, Cpl. P. C., m.i.d. (2).
7/188	Denton, 2nd Lt. T. J., m.i.d.
17391	Diamanti, Tpr. R. J., M.M.
7/437	Doherty, 2nd Lt. P. G., M.C.
7/1352	Duggan, L/Cpl. L., M.M.
7/800	Edwards, L/Cpl. J., m.i.d.
16088	Ferguson, Tpr. H., M.M.
7/598	Findlay, Lt.-Col. J., C.B., D.S.O., Egyptian Order of the Nile (3rd Class), m.i.d. (3).
7/441	Fleming, Sgt. R. A., m.i.d.
7/351	Foster, Sgt. J., M.M.
7/457	Gibbs, Capt. T. L., m.i.d.
12597	Graham, L/Cpl. H. W., m.i.d.
7/1734	Grant, L/Cpl. T. B., M.M.
7/340	Greenwood, L/Sgt. A. R., m.i.d.
7/535	Griffith, Sgt. W. D., m.i.d.
7/516	Harper, 2nd Lt. G. G., D.C.M., m.i.d.
7/517	Harper, 2nd Lt. R. P., D.C.M., D.S.O., M.C., m.i.d. (3).
7/63	Hayter, Lt. C., m.i.d.
7/489	Hindley, Capt. T/Maj. F. L., O.B.E., M.H.S., m.i.d. (4).
7/349	Hurst, Major H C., D.S.O., Order of the Nile (4th Class), conferred by H.H. the Sultan, m.i.d. (5).
7/530	Hutton, Major G. F., D.S.O., m.i.d.
7/218	Jenkins, Tpr. D., m.i.d.
12552	Johnston, 2nd Lt. A. B., M.C., m.i.d.
7/1251	Juggins, L/Cpl. J. F., M.M.
7/1377	Lewis, T/Cpl. T., M.M.
3/1054	Lineham, Cpl. C. A., M.M.
7/366	McClatchie, L/Sgt. P. J., M.M.

7/1166	MacFarlane, Capt. L. R. C., M.C.
7/1261	McGahan, Sgt. J., M.M.
7/1766	McGuckin, Tpr. H., M.M.
7/84	McKibbin, Sq.-S.M. V. J., m.s.m.
7/90	Martin, Sgt. T/Sq.-S.M. A., D.C.M., m.i.d.
7/1317	Mathias, Lt. G., M.C., m.i.d.
7/376	Mills, A/C. Q.M.S. M. F., M.M.
7/2218	Milne, Lt. M. C., M.C.
7/753	Murchison, Lieut. D. B., M.C.
7/380	Murchison, Major D.S., D.S.O., m.i.d.
17553	Murray, Lieut. F. L., M.C., m.i.d.
7/250	O'Brien, Sgt. M. J., D.C.M., m.i.d.
7/764	O'Connor, Tpr. D. J., D.C.M.
7/506	Overton, Major P. J., m.i.d.
7/636	Pavelka, Sgt. M., M.M.
7/583	Pidgeon, Tpr. H., D.C.M.
7/108	Rees, Sgt. F. L., m.i.d.
7/109	Rhodes, Capt. A. E. T., M.C., m.i.d.
7/264	Robertson, Sgt. F., D.C.M
7/1411	Scrimgeour, Tpr., A. R., M.M., Serbian Decoration (Gold Medal), m.i.d.
7/270	Sheridan, Lieut. N. C., M.B.E., M.H.S.
7/1004	Shields, L/Cpl. J., m.i.d.
7/1293	Studholme, Major T/Lt-Col. J., C.B.E., D.S.O., m.i.d.
18128	Sutherland, Cpl. A. J., M.M.
7/277	Taylor, Lt. G. N., m.i.d.
7/1907	Taylor, Cpl. W. J., M.M.
7/1320	Tennent, T/Sq.-S.M. K. B., M.M.
7/134	Thompson, Sgt. W. J., m.i.d.
7/1792	Thomson, Tpr. D. W., M.M.
7/1532	Trotter, Tpr. J. R., M.M.
7/426	White, Tpr. W. C., Medaille Militaire (French), M.M., Serbian Medal awarded by King of Serbia.
7/1307	Wilson, T/Cpl. C., M.M.
7/486	Young, 2nd Lieut. R. A., M.C.

Note :

C.B.	Companion of the Order of the Bath.
C.M.G.	Companion of the Order of St. Michael and St. George.
C.B.E.	Commander of the Order of the British Empire.
M.B.E.	Member of the Order of the British Empire.
O.B.E.	Officer of the Order of the British Empire.
D.S.O.	Distinguished Service Order.
M.C.	Military Cross.
M.M.	Military Medal.
m.i.d.	Mentioned in Despatches.
m.s.m.	Meritorious Service Medal.
m.h.m.	Meritorious Service at Home.

A REGIMENTAL DIARY.

1914.

Aug.	12	The first man reported to the Mobilisation Camp, Addington.
Sept.	23	The Regiment embarked on the "Tahiti" and "Athenic" at Lyttelton.
	25	Went into camp at Lyall Bay and Trentham.
Oct.	14	Embarked on transports "Tahiti" and "Athenic."
	15	Sailed.
	21	Called at Hobart.
	28	Joined the Australian transport fleet at Albany.
Nov.	9	H.M.A.S. "Sydney," one of the convoy's protecting ships, defeated and destroyed the German cruiser "Emdem."
	16	Arrival at Colombo.
	24	Called at Aden.
Dec.	1	Arrival at Suez.
	3	Began disembarkation at Alexandria.
	4	Arrived at Zeitoun, a suburb of Cairo.
	23	March through the streets of Cairo.
	30	Inspection by General Birdwood.

1915.

Jan.	9	Parade held for Sir T. Mackenzie, High Commissioner for N.Z.
	28	First tactical exercise held in desert, vicinity of signal towers.
Feb.	3	First Turkish attack on Suez Canal.
	26	Trek to Bilbeis.
March	12	First Khamsim experienced.
	22	Review by Sir H. McMahon, High Commissioner for Egypt.
	29	Review by Sir Ian Hamilton.
April	25	N.Z. Infantry landed at Anzac.
May	5	Orders received to go to Gallipoli as infantry.
	9	Embarked at Alexandria on "Grantully Castle."
	12	Landed at Anzac Cove.
	15	Major Overton's first reconnaisance. Raid on Lala Baba.
	18-19	Great Turkish attack driven off.
	24	Armistice for burying the dead.
	25	H.M.S. "Triumph" torpedoed.
	28	Capture of "Old No. 3" by 1st Squadron C.M.R.
June	29-30	Second great Turkish attack driven off.
July	1	C.M.R. takes over trenches, Russell Top.
Aug.	5	Regiment moves to No. 2 Outpost.
	6	At 9 p.m. moved out to attack Walden Point and Bauchop Hill.
	7-8-9-10	The desperate fighting on Chunuk Bair.
	21	Attack on Hill 60 (Kaiajik Aghala).
	22-23	Holding on to Hill 60.
	27	Second and final attack on Hill 60.
Sept.	2	Moved to Cheshire Ridge.
	13	N.Z.M.R. Brigade goes to Mudros for rest and reorganisation.
Nov.	10	Returned to Anzac and camped in Waterfall Gully.
	27	Relieved Suffolk Yeomanry and a portion of the 162nd Brigade on the Aghyl Dere.
	28	A cold blizzard swept the lines.

T

Dec.	12	Definite steps began to be taken for the evacuation.
	18	First portion of Regiment left Anzac.
	19-20	Evacuation takes place.
	21	At Mudros.
	22	Embarked on "Hororata" for Egypt.
	26	Arrived at Zeitoun and horses again taken over.

1916.

Jan.	18	N.Z.M.R. Brigade inspected by Colonel R. H. Rhodes.
	23	Trek to the Canal begun.
	29	Regiment arrived Serapeum.
March	6	C.M.R. takes over lines at Ferry Post.
	21	H.R.H. The Prince of Wales visited the Regiment.
April	7	Arrived at Salhia.
	24	Crossed Suez Canal into Sinai.
	25	Moved to head of Military Railway at "Canterbury Post."
May	7-8	Cutting canal from sea to Sabkhet el Bardawil.
	11	Moved to Et Maler.
	15-16	Reconnaissance—heavy Khamsin.
June	23	Moved to Hill 70.
Aug.	4-5	Battle of Romani.
	6-12	Actions of Katia, Ogratina, Bir el Abd.
Sept.		
Oct.		Advance through the desert.
Nov.		
Dec.	20	Night march to surround El Arish.
	22-23-24	Advance on and action of Magdhaba.
Dec.	27	Camped at beach Masaiol.

1917.

Jan.	8	Night march on Rafa.
	9	Battle of Rafa.
	10	Return to El Arish.
Feb.	23	Reconnaissance of Khan Yunus.
		Camped on beach at Rafa.
March	11	First reconnaissance of Gaza.
	25	Final reconnaissance of Gaza and the crossings of the Wadi Ghuzze.
	26	First Battle of Gaza.
April 17-18-19		Regiment crosses Wadi Ghuzze at Shellal. Second Battle of Gaza.
April 20-May 22		Reconnaissances east of Wadi Ghuzze.
May 22-23		Raid upon Beersheba-Asluj railway.
June	8	On beach at Marakeb.
Oct.	16	Special parade for presentation of honours and awards by General Allenby.
	24	Moved to Esani.
	29	Moved to Asluj.
	30	Advance on Beersheba by all-night march.
	31	Action of Beersheba and capture of Tel el Saba.
Nov.	1-6	Actions of Ras el Nagh and Tel Khuweilfeh.
	7-8-9	Occupying position Kh el Ras.
	10-11-12	Rode north through Plain of Philistines and reached Hamame (near Ascalon).
	13	Advanced to Yebna.
	14	Action of Ayun Kara.
	17	Took over the City of Jaffa.
	24	Advanced across River Auja and seized enemy covering positions.
	25	Action of Khirbet Hadrah and withdrawal across river.

CANTERBURY MOUNTED RIFLES 267

Dec.	4-10	Holding lines between Jaffa and foothills.
	11	Allenby's entry into Jerusalem.
	13	Moved to sandhills at Esdud.

1918.

Jan.	20	Moved to Nalin.
Feb.	3	Moved to Ayun Kara (Rishon le Zion).
	17	Arrived at Bethlehem.
	19-20-21	Advance on Jericho.
	22	Reconnaissance of Jordan.
	22-23	Marched up to Jerusalem.
	26	Returned to Rishon le Zion.
Mar.	13-18	March to Bethlehem.
	20	Arrived at Talaat ed Dumm (in the Wilderness).
	24	Crossed the Jordan.
	25-26	Climbing Mountains of Moab.
	27-30	Attack upon Amman and capture of Hill 3039.
	31	Retirement to edge of plateau.
April	1	Descent to the Jordan.
	2	Camped near Jericho.
	30	Action on east side of the Jordan.
May	1-6	Raid on Es Salt.
	16	Moved to Talaat ed Dumm.
	27	8th Squadron goes to Richon.
	28	Regiment camped near King Solomon's Pools.
June	3	Special King's Birthday Parade at Bethlehem.
	14	Back in Jordan Valley—camping at Ain ed Duk.
	26	The Turks began long range shelling with "Jericho Jane."
July	14	Combined German-Turk attack driven off.
	19	Camped at Talaat ed Dumm.
	27	Camped near King Solomon's Pools.
Aug.	16	Returned to the Valley of the Auja River.
Sept.	21	Advanced up west bank of Jordan.
	22	Captured Damieh Bridge.
	23	Capture of Es Salt.
	24	Regiment moved to Suweile.
	25	Capture of Amman.
Oct.	2	8th Squadron goes to Madeba.
	3	Regiment moved to Kissir.
	4	Return to the Jordan.
	8	The Regiment rode out of the Valley for the last time.
	14	Reached Ayun Kara.
Nov.	13	The Regiment, without horses, entrained at Ludd.
	14	Arrived at Kantara.
	27	Embarked on "Huntscastle."
Dec.	5	Disembarked at Maidos, at the Dardanelles.
		Visits to the old battlefields.

1919.

Jan.	17	A party of officers and other ranks visited ancient Troy.
	19	Embarked on "Norman."
	22	Arrived Port Said and went to Rafa.
March	23	Regiment mounted moved to Tanta.
April, May, June		Patrolling in the Delta.
June	17	Camped at Chevalier Island.
	30	First portion of Regiment embarked on "Ulimaroa."
July	23	Remainder of Regiment embarked for N.Z. on "Ellenga."

www.ingramcontent.com/pod-product-compliance
Lightning Source LLC
Chambersburg PA
CBHW021836220426
43663CB00005B/272